Being and Relating in P

Being and Relating in Psychotherapy

Ontology and Therapeutic Practice

Edited by
Christine Driver,
Stephen Crawford
and
John Stewart

palgrave
macmillan

First published 2013 by
PALGRAVE MACMILLAN

Palgrave Macmillan in the UK is an imprint of Macmillan Publishers Limited,
registered in England, company number 785998, of Houndmills, Basingstoke,
Hampshire RG21 6XS.

Palgrave Macmillan in the US is a division of St Martin's Press LLC,
175 Fifth Avenue, New York, NY 10010.

Palgrave Macmillan is the global academic imprint of the above companies
and has companies and representatives throughout the world.

Palgrave® and Macmillan® are registered trademarks in the United States,
the United Kingdom, Europe and other countries

ISBN: 978-0-230-28246-9

This book is printed on paper suitable for recycling and made from fully
managed and sustained forest sources. Logging, pulping and manufacturing
processes are expected to conform to the environmental regulations of the
country of origin.

A catalogue record for this book is available from the British Library.

A catalog record for this book is available from the Library of Congress.

Table of Contents

Acknowledgements

The authors and publisher would like to thank John Wiley & Sons Ltd for their permission to publish Chapter 14 'Religions in Relation to Values'. An earlier version was originally published as : Black, D.M., 'What sort of a thing is a religion? A view from object-relations theory', *The International Journal of Psychoanalysis*, 74(3), 1993.

With thanks to all who assisted in the creation of this book.

Notes on Contributors

Editors

Christine Driver is a Psychoanalytic Psychotherapist and Jungian Analyst. She is Director of Training at WPF Therapy and teaches, supervises and works in private practice. She has written and co-edited, *Supervising Psychotherapy*, (Sage, 2002); *Supervision and the Analytic Attitude*, (Whurr, 2005) and a number of papers.

Stephen Crawford is a Psychoanalytic Psychotherapist and a Senior Programme Manager at WPF Therapy and teaches and supervises there while also working in private practice. He taught Ontology at WPF for several years and has written several papers on psychotherapy and supervision.

John Stewart is a Psychoanalytic Psychotherapist and a Jungian Analyst. He was formerly an Assistant Head of Training at WPF Therapy and co-ordinator of counselling services in a medical practice. At present, he teaches, supervises and is in private practice. He has written a number of papers and articles.

Authors

David M. Black is a Psychoanalyst. He taught Human Development for many years at WPF Therapy and was later on its Board of Trustees. He is the author of *Why Things Matter: the place of values in science, psychoanalysis and religion* (Routledge, 2011) and the editor of *Psychoanalysis and Religion in the 21st Century: competitors or collaborators?* (Routledge, 2006).

Gabrielle Brown is a Psychodynamic Psychotherapist. She is a seminar leader at WPF Therapy and an Honorary Consultant Psychotherapist in Reflective Practice and Team Development for South London and Maudsley NHS Trust. She has a long-term interest in the role of psychotherapy in addressing chronic social exclusion and works as a Psychotherapist, Organisational Consultant and Supervisor in St Mungo's Homelessness Charity. Her private practice is in South London.

Michael Elfred is an Anglican Priest and a Psychodynamic Psychotherapist. He ran an Ontology Seminar at WPF Therapy and also undertook client assessments. He supervises trainee counsellors at Nescot College, Epsom. He has a small private practice and is the Bishop's Advisor on the Paranormal and Pastoral Advisor for the Croydon Episcopal area of Southwark Diocese.

Meg Errington is a Psychoanalytic Psychotherapist, works with adults and adolescents and is also a university counsellor. She has worked as a seminar leader and supervisor at WPF Therapy and taught a Diploma in Working with Adolescents. She has jointly written a book, *Setting Out* (Routledge, 2005) with Lesley Murdin and a number of papers.

Brid Greally is a Psychoanalytic Psychotherapist. She worked as the clinical director of the Maya Centre for 10 years and later as clinical director of the Red Admiral. At present, she is a member of the training staff at WPF Therapy, provides workshops to other training institutes and works in private practice.

Stephen Gross is a Psychotherapist in private practice. He supervises at WPF Therapy where he has taught Ontology for nine years. He works for other training organisations and has published widely particularly on psychotherapy and Shakespeare. His first play: 'Freud's Night Visitors' has recently been performed at the Freud Museum

Lynsey Hotchkies is a Group Analytic Psychotherapist and Counsellor. She is a Senior Programme Manager at WPF Therapy for the introductory courses, the group analytic psychotherapy training and the continuing professional development programme. She teaches on a number of courses and workshops and has worked with clients in a variety of settings including working with patients with terminal illness.

Neil Hudson is a Psychodynamic Psychotherapist and works in private practice in central London. He has written and presented workshops on Loss and Bereavement, Living with Mortality, Working Through Betrayal and Facilitating Support Groups. He has a specialist interest in working with patients who are living with chronic illness.

Lesley Murdin is a Psychoanalytic Psychotherapist. She was Chief Executive of WPF Therapy and teaches, supervises and is in private practice. She has written a number of books including *How Much is Enough*, (Taylor and Francis, 2000); *Setting Out*, (Routledge, 2005) and *How Money Talks* (Karnac, 2012).

Juliet Newbigin is a Psychoanalytic Psychotherapist. She works in private practice, and has specialist interests in diversity and in working with young adults. She was, for many years, a member of staff at WPF Therapy, both as a supervisor and a member of the training department. She has taught, among other things, a course entitled 'Issues of Diversity'.

John Rignell is a Psychoanalytic Psychotherapist. He has taught at a number of training institutions, including WPF Therapy, and worked as a therapist in a variety of settings. He is now engaged in researching the contribution psychoanalytic theory can offer to the understanding of film.

Mary Thomas is a Psychoanalytic Psychotherapist. Originally trained in Fine Art, she supervises, teaches and has a private psychotherapy practice in central London. She has previously published 'Through the Looking Glass: Creativity in Supervision' in *Supervision and the Analytic Attitude*, Driver C. & Martin E. (eds), (Whurr, 2005), and 'Absence and Absent-mindedness,' in *Aggression and Destructiveness: Psychoanalytic Perspectives*, Harding, C. (ed.). (Routledge, 2006).

Editors' Note

The authors have mostly used the generic terms of psychotherapist and client in their chapters. However, some use theory and ideas which have emerged from psychoanalytic discourse and so the terms psychoanalytic, psychoanalyst and patient are also used where relevant.

The theories used by the authors reflect their own particular interests and represent the different ways in which we all come to understand ourselves and others.

Christine Driver
Stephen Crawford
John Stewart
(Editors)

Part I

The Therapeutic Relationship

The centrality of relationship in therapeutic work is one that is firmly accepted within all therapeutic endeavours in spite of the different theoretical perspectives that have developed over the past hundred years or more. Whatever theories we use, it is the encounter with the other and the emotional states that they present us with and evoke in us which are both the challenge and resource of our therapeutic encounters. This book has emerged from thinking and discussion about these issues, the importance of ontology, 'being' in its broadest sense, and the need to consider this in our therapeutic work.

The first chapter by Christine Driver sets the scene and introduces the reader to the importance of the question of 'being' and consideration of the other in the therapeutic relationship. In Chapter 2, Michael Elfred goes on to provide an overview of theories and ideas about the therapeutic relationship and gives his own thoughts and views as to its healing nature. In Chapter 3, Meg Errington explores the dynamics of 'speaking' and 'not speaking' in what has been called the 'talking cure', and in Chapter 4, Stephen Gross engages with Buber's (1937) exploration of the I-Thou and the I-It to consider the therapeutic relationship further.

The book is aimed at practising psychotherapists and clinicians, and we hope it will provide a thought provoking and challenging perspective that broadens and enriches thinking, reflection and understanding in our work with our clients.

Reference

Buber, M. (1937) *I and Thou*. (Edinburgh: T & T Clark). 1970.

Part I

The Therapeutic Relationship

1

Ontology and the Therapeutic Relationship

Christine Driver

Introduction

In the Musée de Cluny (Museum of the Medieval Age) in Paris there is a set of six beautiful medieval tapestries known as the Lady and the Unicorn in which images of the senses are symbolically represented through the Lady and the Unicorn motifs and other symbols that expand the imagery within each tapestry. The five senses depicted are taste, smell, hearing, touch and sight, with a final tapestry called the *Mon Seul Désir* (My Only Desire), which Elizabeth Delahaye (2007) proposes could be considered as a sixth sense closest to the soul or spiritual world (44). These images emerged from the medieval 'hierarchy of senses' which moved from the most material (touch) to the most spiritual, *Mon Seul Désir* (Delahaye, 2007), and although now we would find the significance of the senses a somewhat simplistic perspective on the nature of 'being' they nevertheless form part of who and what we are.

Today the senses are just one of many perspectives that have been explored in the search to uncover the mystery of what it is to be human. Within the fields of psychology, psychoanalysis and psychotherapy, from the mid-nineteenth century onwards, practitioners and theorists have developed theories of mind and theories about the unconscious and have debated the interplay of nature and nurture. From their conceptualisations and observations theories and techniques have grown and developed about the therapeutic relationship and clinical practice. In fact the therapeutic world has been very diligent in developing epistemologies and metapsychologies about the internal world and the psyche and their application within therapeutic practice.

But, however much we engage in the debates about therapeutic practice, what emerges is the underlying importance of the therapeutic relationship. The dynamics of relation and relationship form the foundation of being, and as Buber (1937) states, 'the child gains his world by seeing, listening, feeling and forming. It is in encounter that the creation reveals its formhood; it does not pour itself into senses that are waiting but deigns to meet those that are reaching out' (77). Entering into a therapeutic relationship is a form of reaching out and is the stepping into an encounter in which the intricacies of the mind and the internal world of one (the client) are explored through reflections with the other (the therapist); a relationship in which the therapist makes use of herself or himself to enable the other, the client, to understand themselves. If we accept the premise that in therapeutic work the therapeutic relationship is vital then it is crucial to consider the client's and also the therapist's state of being and examine theories of being, or ontology, in relation to the client and the therapist within the therapeutic encounter.

Ontology and Being

Ontology, as defined in the *Encyclopaedia Britannica* (2005), is 'the theory or study of being … i.e., of the basic characteristics of all reality' and existence. Heidegger (1953) gave it a central place in his work and commented that we have forgotten the question of being which concerned philosophers from Plato onwards. Heidegger revisits what he calls this forgotten struggle with the issues of being and 'being in the world' (113–130) and through complex arguments considers the ongoingness of being, that is, being over time as well as the concept of existence. Barrett (1978) comments that for Heidegger 'the whole nature of our being is time-saturated. … We begin our existence as a task, in the sense of something imposed upon us which we then take upon ourselves. Human existence is ongoing' (63), and so the realities of the struggles of life, including anxieties around death, are essential parts of being human.

But, as Heidegger (1953) argues in *Being and Time,* 'being is always the "being of being"' (8), that is, we have to consider the totality of being and the domains in which being is both experienced and expressed. Magee (1978) comments that Heidegger 'begins his investigations with an analysis of that mode of existence of which we have the most direct and immediate experience, namely our own' (60) and that Heidegger's book *Being and Time* 'consists of a painstaking analysis of conscious self-awareness, our immediate knowledge of our own existence at its most elementary' (60). Barrett (1978) refers to the way that Heidegger saw 'man as essentially an open and ongoing creature … always involved in the task of creating ourselves' (64), and this perspective relates to another key aspect of being which Heidegger (1953) explores in detail and calls 'Dasein' (*being there/existence*) (41–45). By this he means the way in which being and 'Dasein initially finds "itself" in *what* it does, needs, expects, has charge of … in the surrounding world' (116) and 'is always pressing into new possibilities' so that our 'activity is directed towards a 'towards-which' and orientated towards the future' (Dreyfus, 1988: 265).

In Heidegger's view ontology (being-ness) preceded epistemology (know-ing-ness) (McCoy Brooks, 2011: 494); however, from the point of view of the therapeutic relationship, we cannot separate the two in that we are aim-ing to know and make conscious the unconscious and the unknown but are inevitably caught up with the being-ness of the other. The interaction between being-ness and knowing-ness is dynamic and in Heidegger's view meaning is disclosed through a process 'of openness to being' (McCoy Brooks, 2011: 508). Heidegger's view differs, as McCoy Brooks points out, to that of Jung's in which Jung focused on *a priori* meaning but the important point here is that meaning emerges through an understanding of being. There is a danger of get-ting stuck in an argument as to whether meaning, or indeed the self, is inher-ent or socially constructed. What is more useful to examine is the impact and repercussions of the various states of being which we embody and which we encounter with the other in relationship.

Being is, therefore, a dynamic that is intrinsic and influences us all and, as therapists, if we are to understand the other, the client, in a therapeutic endeavour then awareness of our engagement with the dimensions of being is important. Such ideas go beyond theories of mind and require us to confront and consider theories of being in the vast and rich tapestry that being is. Being contains the elements of our physical, emotional, rational, irrational, nurturing, sexual, relational, thinking, creative, social and spiritual selves and the possi-bilities and potential contained within these, and many other, aspects of life.

The Therapeutic Relationship

In this book we will not be pursuing the depths of Heidegger's (1953) philo-sophical arguments about ontology, but what Heidegger identified is that ontology, the study of being, is vital in considering 'being in the world' (52–62) and being with others and that the concept of 'being of being' (8) is a crucial perspective in considering what it is to be human. As Colman (2008) points out, 'the totality of our being is made up of the totality of our action in the world' (355). Our senses, as the medieval tapestries depict, are part of our being but if we take the concept of the 'being of being' to its broadest meaning it is clear that it must be the sum of many parts; parts which include our physical, emotional, affective and relational selves and our states of mind as well as our realities and limitations. Within the thera-peutic relationship we, as therapists, need to aim to understand the broader warp and weft of the internal world of the other as well as the intricacies of the individual's patterns of relating. Our being is, therefore, a complex set of interacting phenomena combining the internal world and the structures of mind which we have developed: our senses, our capacity to relate and our capacity to be emotional and affect laden within ourselves and in relation to others. These human capacities and ways in which we inhabit our 'being of being' are expressed through emotion, relationship, creativity, spirituality, our senses and through our whole being.

When therapist and client meet in the consulting room or whenever two people meet they encounter, consciously and unconsciously, the being of the other or, as Heidegger would suggest, the 'being of being' of the other in a way in which both are affected. Jung comments:

> for two personalities to meet is like mixing two different chemical substances: if there is any combination at all, both are transformed. In any effective psychological treatment the doctor is bound to influence the patient; but this influence can only take place if the patient has a reciprocal influence on the doctor. (Jung, 1929: para163)

He later states that 'a person is a psychic system which, when it affects another person, enters into reciprocal reaction with another psychic system' (Jung, 1935: para 1). In such a relationship the therapist needs to engage with and understand the 'being of being' of the other in order to gain as full a sense of the other, the client, as possible and enable a shift from 'being' to 'knowing' (Colman, 2008: 361) and ultimately understanding.

Laing identifies ontology, and the work of Heidegger, as significant in his book *The Divided Self* (Laing, 1960). He considers the importance of 'ontological security and ontological insecurity' (39); in other words, the security and insecurity of being in relation to tackling the 'hazards of life' in terms of the 'social, ethical, spiritual and biological' (39). WPF Therapy (formerly the Westminster Pastoral Foundation), also recognised ontology, the study of being and the 'mystery of what it is to be a human being' (Black, 1991: 96), as important in the training of counsellors and psychotherapists. Such a perspective requires the therapist to be willing to develop a depth of understanding of the attributes of being that, in many ways, go beyond the theories of the internal world or psyche. The challenge is to look in greater detail at what being means at an individual, relational, social and cultural level, to consider what shapes people's lives, what is meaningful to them and gives life meaning, and what enables the development of what has become known as self-reflexive consciousness of the 'kind that is specific to human beings and consists of being aware of being aware' (Colman, 2008: 351).

Introduction to This Book

What this book explores is how being and relating are inextricably linked and how the being that we are is expressed and known through our interaction with others. This book emerges from the authors' interest in ontology and the way that it has informed and influenced their therapeutic work as well as from a desire to explore what is meant by the 'being of being'. The topics focus on what we have considered to be important aspects of being and ones that are essential to consider within the therapeutic encounter with the totality of the being of another.

The book begins with a consideration of the therapeutic relationship including an exploration of speaking and not speaking as well as engaging with Buber's (1937) exploration of the I-Thou and I-It and the therapeutic relationship. It goes on to explore aspects of being such as, generosity, love, shame, loneliness, life and death, and in the final section considers the self, diversity, sexuality, creativity, religion and values and the role and importance of rites of passage. The authors' perspectives emerge from their own 'being of being' and reflect their own views and a range of theoretical perspectives.

Conclusion

This book is not about answers but about important questions in relation to what being and relating are and how being is expressed within the therapeutic encounter and needs to be resourcefully engaged with in order to fully understand the other. This goes beyond the therapist's willingness to engage in a process of understanding the client via the transference and countertransference and unconscious communication, as it involves a willingness to hold the 'big picture' alongside the detailed intricacies of intra-personal and inter-personal relating. Therapy in its deepest sense is about working with, and understanding, the breadth of human experience (conscious, unconscious, personal, social and cultural) and working with the other in helping them come to terms with, understand and express themselves more fully and develop their ability to relate to their own being.

What this book aims to consider is the 'states of being' that we encounter within ourselves and within others and to reflect on them in relation to the broader consideration of being. The authors explore a range of perspectives and theories about how various 'states of being' affect the individual and consider their importance within the therapeutic relationship.

It is not possible in any one book to cover every aspect of being, as that would be like trying to convey the universe on a grain of sand. We are aiming to hold a lens to aspects of being to try to convey the complexity and importance of the ways in which our 'being of being' is experienced and expressed. The hope is that this book, and the ideas within it, will broaden the understanding of being and of being human and place the study of being, ontology, in a more central place within therapeutic work and therapeutic understanding.

References

Barrett, W. (1978) 'Heidegger and Modern Existentialism' in Magee, B. (ed.) *Men of Ideas. Some Creators of Contemporary Philosophy.* (Oxford and New York: Oxford University Press).

Black, D. M. (1991) *A Place for Exploration.* (London: The Westminster Pastoral Foundation).

Buber, M. (1937) *I and Thou.* (Edinburgh: T & T Clark). 1970.

Colman, W. (2008) 'On being, knowing and having a self', *The Journal of Analytical Psychology,* 53, (3), 351–66.

Delahaye, E. (2007) *The Lady and the Unicorn.* (Paris: Réunion des Musées Nationaux).

Dreyfus H. (1988) 'Husserl, Heidegger and Modern Existentialism' in Magee, B. (ed.) *The Great Philosophers.* (Oxford and New York: Oxford University Press).

Encyclopaedia Britannica (2005) *Encyclopaedia Britannic 2005 Ultimate Reference Suite (Browse),* DVD. (London: Encyclopedia Britannica (UK) Ltd).

Heidegger, M. (1953) *Being and Time.* Stambaugh, J. (trans.) (Albany: State University of New York Press). 2010.

Jung, C. G. (1929) 'Problems of Modern Psychotherapy' in *The Practice of Psychotherapy, CW 16.* (London and Henley: Routledge & Kegan Paul). 1981.

Jung, C. G. (1935) 'Principles of Practical Psychotherapy' in *The Practice of Psychotherapy, CW 16.* (London and Henley: Routledge & Kegan Paul). 1981.

Laing, R. D. (1960) *The Divided Self.* (London: Penguin Group). 1969.

Magee, B. (1978) *Men of Ideas. Some Creators of Contemporary Philosophy.* (Oxford and New York: Oxford University Press).

McCoy Brooks, R. (2011) 'Un-thought out metaphysics in analytical psychology', *Journal Analytical Psychology,* 56, (4), 492–513.

2

The Healing Relationship

Michael Elfred

In her book, *Somewhere towards the End*, Diana Athill claims that

Always we are being reflected in the eyes of others (Athill, 2008: 84).

Athill's statement succinctly sums up the problem and potentiality of human relationships. Physiologically speaking, we have our origins in the most intimate union: we come from within another person, our mother, and even when physically separated at birth, we develop a sense of self and well-being by what we see reflected in mother's eyes (Winnicott, 1971: 147). There is also a considerable weight of evidence from neuroscience that lack of strong early positive bonding adversely affects brain development (Schore, 1994). Schore puts forward a considerable body of evidence to show that the child's first relationship, with mother or primary carer, acts as a template for the imprinting of circuits in the child's emotion-processing right brain, and this affects the shaping of the infant's capacities to enter into emotional relationships later in life. Mother's face and emotional expressions are highly significant in determining the emotional development of the child. Gradually, other people impinge on the mother–child dyad and a wider set of significant relationships develop and have to be negotiated as the sense of 'me and not me' evolves. Our earliest socialisation depends on the quality of the relationships which develop within the family. Our early relating profoundly affects the kind of relationships we make in later life and when early relating has in some sense malfunctioned then this can profoundly inhibit the formation of adult liaisons.

An Historical View

In his study of human development, Eric Rayner (1986) defines the two basic ways in which things can go wrong with regard to relating both internally and externally. The most serious form of this emotional crisis is a psychosis, which

Rayner defines as follows: 'In such a breakdown, if the person remains fixed so that his self and internal fantasy are confused with external reality then he is said to be in a psychotic state' (Rayner, 1986: 142). Rayner goes on to compare the psychotic state with the neurotic state in the following way:

> If, on the other hand, the person goes into crisis but fundamentally maintains differentiation between fantasy and reality, yet still fixedly repeats his old ways of relating self to others, while at the same time struggling yet not quite succeeding to adapt to the new situation, he is in conflict and is said to be in a neurotic state. (Rayner, 1986: 142)

It could be said that, to some extent at least, all human beings are neurotic in so far as they are a prey to fantasies about relationships and situations which, objectively speaking, are not true. It would appear from Rayner's definition that there is more hope of releasing the neurotic client from their state than the psychotic client. As we shall see, within the psychotherapeutic world, there have been and are conflicting views on these states and the extent to which a relationship with a psychotherapist can help to cure or heal the resultant conditions.

Before we attempt to address these fundamental questions, let us look at the nature of how the human mind was understood prior to the rise of modern psychological thinking. The prevailing basic assumption in the west concerning the human mind was that it was, in the main, a conscious reality or at least that conscious thinking was the most powerful and developed form of human functioning and was therefore the best means of addressing the ills of humankind. This had its early origins in Platonic thought where reason, thinking and consciousness were considered to be the route to connection with eternal reality delivering an individual from the limitations and illusions of sense perception (MacDonald Cornford, 1969). This mindset reached its climax in the writings of Descartes who argued that the one thing that was beyond doubt was that there was a mind doing the doubting – hence, 'I think therefore I am' (Descartes, 1984). For Plato, the ills of mankind were largely due to ignorance and the cure was that of gaining knowledge of eternal realities, which lay beyond sense perception and were abstract in nature.

In Christianity, mankind's ills were seen not so much in terms of ignorance but rather in terms of sinfulness; the problem was therefore basically a moral one. The church developed a system of confession and sacramental healing in response to this. From this perspective, mankind's ills stemmed from a moral disease, original sin, which was dealt with by baptism; ongoing sin being subsequently dealt with by confession and absolution. In addition to the sacramental administration of what the Church called the cure of souls, there was a recognised tradition of addressing the inner reality of the human soul via mystical experience. There was also spiritual direction, as a means of finding inner healing; this involved the development of a meaningful conversation and relationship with a confessor. Many of the mystical writers of the Middle Ages seem to anticipate what would develop later in psychological thinking. Following the comparison John Welch makes in his book, *Spiritual Pilgrims, Carl Jung and Teresa of Avila*, one might almost describe Teresa of Avila as a Jungian before Jung (Welch, 1982).

The rise of modern psychological theories challenged the earlier assumptions by stressing the existence, importance and power of the unconscious. For Plato, when someone acted in a problematic way this was due to ignorance and what they needed to experience to facilitate a cure was education. Christianity offered a sacramental system of confession to facilitate a moral cure alongside spiritual direction and mystical experience. In contrast to this tendency to see both the problem and the cure as a largely conscious, intellectual or moral phenomenon, psychoanalytical thinking came to stress the importance of a compensatory or alternative emotional experience, which addressed the deep unconscious roots of the problem. For modern psychoanalytic thinking the basic issue was neither intellectual nor moral but rather a matter of emotional disturbance with conscious and unconscious origins. A cure or healing could only be effected when the contents of the unconscious were confronted, addressed and its conflicts resolved through a relationship with a psychotherapist.

Freud's Perspective

Freud developed a way of approaching mankind's emotional illness through accessing the unconscious, which has often been referred to as 'the talking cure'. This description is accurate in so far as the various leading disciplines within the therapeutic world which have developed from his original work, or in some cases in reaction to it, involve a relationship between the client and the psychotherapist, which originates in a conversation. However, there is a wide disparity of opinion about just how that cure works and also its limitations. Freud thought that conflicts occurred because the basic instinctual drives connected with human biological development became arrested usually due to shame or guilt connected with sexuality. When this happens Freud envisaged a blockage in the flow of psychic energy, so that an individual's emotional development could not proceed properly (Rycroft, 1972). In brief, Freud argued that a person develops an ego (a sense of 'I') in order to mediate between the demands of the 'id', that part of the psyche which seeks the satisfaction of primal drives and instincts, and the need for socialisation of these instincts demanded by the 'super-ego', which he viewed as an internalisation of parental pressures and values (Freud, 1933). Freud gives us a picture of a gargantuan struggle where the ego utilises various defences against the acknowledgement of unacceptable memories and desires, particularly those of a sexual or of an aggressive nature. If the ego develops satisfactorily, and this is dependent largely on a favourable environment being provided by the parents then the infant can learn to tolerate the frustration of the inevitable delay in gratification of their desires. Things go wrong when the ego cannot tolerate the pressures of life and so resorts to the repression of uncomfortable or unmanageable thoughts and feelings. These unacceptable thoughts and feelings are banished to the unconscious and may form the basis of neurotic or psychotic behaviour.

Central to Freud's understanding of how the ego develops is the resolution of what he calls the 'Oedipus Complex' (Freud, 1900). For Freud, this complex arises because of the infant's sexual fantasies and desire for the parent of the opposite sex and the consequent sense of rivalry with the parent of the same sex. In this unequal triangle the ego experiences a significant wound that needs to be healed by entering into a different relationship with the parents. This early wounding of the ego is healed when the infant is able to tolerate being excluded from the sexual coupling of the parents and can move to a position of identification with the parent of the same sex. Referring to the Greek myth Oedipus Rex (the king who unknowingly murders his father and marries his mother) which gives this central complex its name, Freud wrote the following:

> His destiny moves us only because it might have been ours – because the oracle laid the same curse upon us before our birth as upon him. It is the fate of all of us, perhaps, to direct our first sexual impulse towards our mother and our first hatred and our first murderous wish against our father. (Freud, 1900: 364)

For Freud, the resolution of this tripartite relationship forms the basis for the resolution of all the demands that the ego will experience in later life. If the Oedipus Complex is satisfactorily resolved then the adult may learn to manage complexity in relationships and the capacity to both love and work. The resolution of the Oedipus Complex is thus the primary experience of the ego healing itself. The aim of the therapeutic relationship therefore is to facilitate this inner healing through the psychotherapist's interpretations of the unconscious material as it emerges in the form of transferences in the sessions. The client is encouraged to acknowledge and work with their psychic defences and a cure is effected when the individual is able to become ordinarily neurotically unhappy. The tool of healing within the Freudian therapeutic relationship is interpretation; this is the main agent to bring about change (Rycroft, 1958). The psychotherapist listened to the free associations or the telling of dreams by the client and this material gave the psychotherapist access to the client's unconscious fantasies which could then be interpreted so that the client could acknowledge and confront what troubled them. The dysfunctionality which caused the client to be dominated by fantasy would thus be addressed, enabling them to realise that they had to live with the ordinariness of human life with its attendant frustrations and unhappiness. For Freud, therefore, the unconscious containing as it does repressed aspects of the psyche, memories of early traumas and things of which the individual is ashamed, is largely a problematic reality.

The Ideas of Balint, Winnicott and Bion

Other practitioners, however, have taken issue with Freud's basic assumptions. Balint, for instance, wants to speak in terms of what he calls a 'basic fault'. In geology an irregularity in the overall structure of a rock might lay hidden but, when subjected to a critical amount of stress, it would cause a fissure to occur, which would then affect the overall structure. Balint is arguing that it is not so much the freeing of something present or the lifting of repressions which will bring about a cure, rather it is the realisation that something is missing in the first place – there is a basic fault in the material, this cannot be cured as such for there is nothing to cure, but the damage caused by the fault might be healed. He writes the following:

> We are accustomed to think of every dynamic force operating in the mind as having the form either of a biological drive or of a conflict. Although highly dynamic, the force originating from the basic fault has the form neither of an instinct nor of a conflict. It is a fault, something wrong in the mind, a kind of deficiency which must be put right. It is not something dammed up for which a better outlet must be found, but something missing either now, or perhaps for almost the whole of the patient's life. An instinctual need can be satisfied, a conflict can be solved, a basic fault can perhaps be merely healed provided the deficient ingredients can be found; and even then it may amount only to a healing with defect, like a simple, painless scar. (Balint, 1968: 21)

Balint seems to be arguing that if a basic fault exists then stresses that activate the fault can lead to breakdown occurring. Balint also questions to what extent the Freudian use of interpretation is valid for those who fall into psychosis. Balint argued that schizophrenics and addicts, also those with deep narcissistic wounds, could not tolerate the frustrations inherent in Freud's approach and would therefore be unable to use the interpretations of the psychotherapist. So, for Balint, Freud's approach is inherently limited to those whose ego is strong enough to be able to cope with interpretation (Balint, 1957). He also argued that the area of the basic fault predates the Oedipal Complex, which is a tripartite issue; the basic fault has to do with a dyadic relationship. Balint believed that clients suffering from schizophrenia or addiction or deep narcissistic disturbances exhibited either ocnophilic behaviour, where they desperately cling to negative internal objects, or philobatic behaviour, where they avoid such dangerous objects by a false self-sufficiency (Balint, 1957). Balint seems to argue that it is doubtful that a cure as such can be affected but rather healing is offered by a kind of psychological mothering which aims at the avoidance of a reproduction of the cause of trauma during the therapeutic relationship. Regression which inevitably occurs during treatment can be benign and can enable recognition of unacknowledged needs. It is however only benign if it exposes the needs rather than satisfies them. Through this two-person relationship it becomes possible to re-establish a primary love relationship. If this is successfully done then the recognised basic fault can be healed and it becomes possible for the client to let go of a compulsive clinging to negative internal objects and also be freed from a false omnipotence.

Balint's views are in accord with other practitioners who have stressed the importance of the earliest relationship with the mother or primary carers who provides the original environment for psychological development. Winnicott and Bion stressed the importance of holding and containing for the process of psychic development and the subsequent healing of the psyche when the initial environment has failed. For Winnicott, the mother and the baby are a dyad in which the good enough mother establishes a creative space where the baby can learn to play (Winnicott, 1971). Through this space infantile idealisations can be worked through and relinquished enabling the ego to integrate with reality. This pattern is repeated in later life. When the psyche feels under threat it needs the creative space in order to heal itself. This space facilitates recovery by offering a place where holding occurs. Through the experience of being held, the individual recovers and is able to function again and regain the capacity to be alone. Bion expands Winnicott's basic presuppositions making containment a central element of the healing relationship. Bion sees the psychotherapist's mind as a container for the raw projections of the clients (Bion, 1965; 1970). The psychotherapist endures and modifies the projections prior to handing them back to the client. This way of approaching the emotional healing of human ills has moved away from Freud's original model. The psychotherapist is not like a skilful surgeon knitting together a broken bone or a psychologist releasing a blocked emotional pipe so that the psychic energy can flow in the right direction but more like a good enough mother providing a compensatory experience by creating a healing space and bearing the sadistic attacks inherent in the transferences and projections of the emotionally injured client. As the psychotherapist survives this process, the client is enabled to come to terms with reality and it is this which constitutes the healing process. The psychotherapist survives by not being overwhelmed by the material which is projected onto them in the transference realising that it is largely a fantasy. This realisation enables the psychotherapist not to be drawn into collusion with the client. Also available to the psychotherapist are their own feelings about the client, their countertransference. This too can be used to gain an insight into the conflicts within the client's inner world. By recognising what might be their own material and what might, through projective identification, be the client's, the psychotherapist can receive communications concerning how the client feels. Thus transference and countertransference are powerful elements within the healing process.

Jung's Ideas

Jung developed a rather different attitude to the unconscious than Freud's seeing it not only as a repository for repressed psychic material but also containing the potentiality of the self; in other words, the psyche strove for wholeness and within that process was the potential for healing. Jung argued that if the conscious element of the psyche became unbalanced because of being out of touch with reality then the unconscious would move to restore the balance (Jung, 1934: para 330). Whilst acknowledging that the personal unconscious did contain repressed material, which he termed the shadow, everything a person did not want to be (Jung, 1938/40: para 131), Jung argued that the self contained a vast reservoir of psychic potential, which had a positive aspect to it as well as a negative. Jung used the term archetypes to describe the psychic potential contained within the self. This way of thinking has resonances with Plato's eternal forms. Like the Platonic forms, which are the pattern of physical reality, archetypes form the patterning of psychic reality. However, there is a fundamental difference in so far as Plato saw the eternal forms as perfect or one might say conflict free, all light, whereas for Jung the archetypes, these primal drives, have both a dark or negative and a light or positive aspect to them as they manifested their content to the mind. For Jung, the language of the unconscious was therefore a dynamic language evolving from the self, the dynamics of the opposites and the archetypes and not a language of rational thought as is the case with the conscious mind. The internal healing of a person is therefore dependent on their being able to relate to the archetypes in both their positive and negative aspects. If this is achieved then there is a healing of the breach between the conscious and the unconscious and a helpful integration is the outcome, which in turn enables an expansion of the personality. Jung called this expansion of the personality individuation (Jung, 1939: para 490). Jung did not see the ego as the centre of the psyche; this position was held by what he called the self. The self was the central archetype which strove towards psychic integration or wholeness. Thus, for Jung, a successful analysis not only enabled a person to love and work (Freud's aim) but also involved them becoming more truly themselves, the individual they were intended to be. For Jung, emotional disturbances offered the individual the opportunity to grow. Jung defined individuation in 1928 in the following way:

Individuation means becoming an 'in-dividual', and, in so far as 'individuality' embraces our innermost, last, and incomparable uniqueness, it also implies becoming one's own self. We could therefore translate individuation as 'coming to selfhood' or 'self-realization'. (Jung, 1928: para 266)

This acknowledgement of a fuller sense of identity is an internal matter and a delicate business. Because of this, Jung argued, the psyche needed to protect itself from the often unsympathetic responses of the outer world and it did this by developing a persona, a kind of mediating shield between external and internal reality. The persona is the personal image which the psyche allows the world to see. If it is to be healthy then it needs to be flexible and adaptable not rigid. The flexible persona acknowledges that the individual plays many roles, allowing different aspects of the psyche and the self to be expressed depending on the requirements of a given situation. A person who is on the road of individuation is someone who is able to own and engage with the shadow aspects of their personality and who has thus been able to develop a flexible persona which is open and able to change rather than a persona which is rigidly defensive in the face of the challenges of everyday life. For Jung, neuroses were helpful indicators of what needed to be addressed if the psyche were to be healed of its troubling divisions. Individuation was the route to this healing though he acknowledged it had inherent limitations; it never reached a final resolution – 'the united personality will never quite lose the painful sense of innate discord' (Jung, 1946: para 400).

Like Freud, Jung also saw dreams as a way of accessing the unconscious but he took a rather different line, arguing that, whilst dreams may reveal the contents of the personal unconscious they may also be revelations of more helpful archetypal potential, which can be accessed through the images contained in the dream. Jung sought to bring out the meaning of a client's dream by a process of amplification. This was done by resorting to mythology, religious stories, fairy tales and other associations, which Jung thought were pictorial representations of archetypal potentials. The client's dream could be enlarged through such comparisons and the potential for self expression and healing of the psyche thus released. Also shadow aspects of the psyche, aspects which had previously been projected onto an external object or person, might well be revealed through the dream. If this was the case then the client was, through the dream and the associations they were able to make during therapy, being given the opportunity to own their own unconscious material and to withdraw the projection thus expanding their personality. In writing of the powerful potential for healing, which can come through the therapeutic relationship as client and psychotherapist engage together with the dream material, Jung claimed:

> To the patient it is nothing less than a revelation when, from the hidden depths of the psyche, something arises to confront him – something strange that is not the 'I' and is therefore beyond the reach of personal caprice. He has gained access to the sources of psychic life, and this marks the beginning of the cure. (Jung, 1933: para 280)

For Jung, the psychotherapist and the client journey together and both are changed through their interrelatedness (Jung, 1929: para 136), and he stresses the importance of the quality of the psychotherapist's personality in this process.

Jung was also interested in what went wrong in a person's psychological life in its later stages as well as what went wrong or was missing in early childhood. An inability to adapt to the changing phases of the life cycle was of particular interest to him, particularly changes in the second half of life. Jung articulated his conviction of why things go wrong for people in later life and how he thought healing could be effected when he wrote:

> Among all my patients in the second half of life – that is over thirty-five – there has not been one whose problem in the last resort was not that of finding a religious outlook on life. It is safe to say that every one of them fell ill because he had lost what the living religions of every age give to their followers, and none of them has been really healed who did not regain his religious outlook. This has of course nothing whatever to do with a particular creed or membership of a Church. (Jung, 1933: 264)

It was Jung's conviction that the first half of life was orientated towards adaptation to the external world, educating oneself, getting a job, finding a partner or marrying, having children, etc, but that in the second half of life the orientation changed and became more directed to the inner life. Failure to realise this would mean being stuck in later life in a mindset which, whilst appropriate to the earlier stages of development, should have become redundant.

But what did Jung mean by his statement about the problems of the second half of life and their solution being basically a matter of a religious approach to reality? I would offer a twofold answer to this question, although no doubt there might be other ways of understanding Jung's statement. First, those who are involved in religious communities have access to the myths and rituals, which both articulate and enact archetypal realities and which Jung used therapeutically to amplify his clients' dreams; in other words, they have templates which can help them through the ills of life. Whilst this does not cure such ills in the sense of making them go away, it does offer an existential solution in the sense that ways are found to cope with and creatively use the problems life inevitably throws up. In that sense the myths and rituals and the individual's relationship to them are a tool for self healing. When access to these tools is denied then a person is left to work things out for themselves in isolation. It was Jung's conviction that if this were the case then the individual is much more likely to be a prey to raw archetypal influences.

Second and more fundamental is the centrality in religious practice of sacrifice, which Jung interpreted psychologically. Jung held that for progress to be made and healing achieved the ego had to renounce or sacrifice the self-cherished psychological attitudes in much the same way as a religious adherent would sacrifice something of personal value to a god. This painful loss however has a purpose and can therefore be seen as meaningful. This psychic sacrifice enables the ego to exchange a limited and enslaving view of reality for an expanded and healthier view: 'Jung sees the necessity for sacrifice not as a remnant of archaic superstition but as an essential part of the cost we pay for being human' (Samuels et al. 1986: 132/133).

What is indicated above is an internal and healing relationship between the ego, the centre of consciousness and the self, which is the central and uniting archetype of the entire personality. We can therefore see that in the Jungian model the psyche is perceived as having a facility to self heal. The role of the psychotherapist is to facilitate this self healing, but how does this work, how is healing achieved in the therapeutic relationship? Jung was at pains to emphasise that the relationship should be seen as a 'dialectical process'. Psychotherapy was a two-way interaction and should not be seen, as is often the case in the medical world, as a doctor, who was well, seeking to treat a client, who was sick. The psychotherapist has their own particular issues and difficulties and these play their part in the process. If the psychotherapist wants to see themselves as a healer then they must first acknowledge that they are themselves in need of healing. Other theorists have attempted to illuminate the therapeutic relationship by reference to ancient healing arts and the Greek Myth of Chiron, the double wounded centaur, the teacher of the secrets of healing (Meier, 1967). Jung asserted that the psychotherapist has their own psychic wounds and this has become generally accepted in most therapeutic disciplines. As a result the practitioner has to undergo their own therapy in order to become sufficiently self-aware of their own personal emotional wounds, which may become activated in the interaction with the client, particularly if the client has similar emotional wounds, and avoid consciously or unconsciously exploiting or using the client for their own ends or gratification (Jung, 1913: para. 536). The client, in the transference, projects their unwanted psychic material onto the psychotherapist who receives and holds the material until such time as it can be given back and owned by the client. In this process, the psychotherapist recognises what is happening and either consciously or unconsciously passes this awareness back to the client.

In psychodynamic theory and practice working with the transference is at the heart of the matter. Sitting in a room with a stranger (the psychotherapist) who does not reveal anything about themselves leaves the client little option but to give vent to their fantasies and fears and thus the client projects unconscious material onto psychotherapist. As the content of the transference is recognised by both psychotherapist and client, the emerging unconscious material can be worked with. When the psychotherapist also recognises and utilises their countertransference an additional powerful tool is available to the therapist which can help the client gain self knowledge and emotional healing. The anonymity of the psychotherapist thus enables the client to become more self aware.

Sociological Aspects of a Healing Relationship

So far I have concentrated on the healing relationship, as it is manifested in a one-to-one reality between client and psychotherapist. But other relationships exist, which also have the power to heal. The social matrix in which an individual grows up can contain, encourage and heal the individual or it can re-enforce an unhealthy self image. Within societies, there are often painful divisions which can be manifestations of acting out unhealthy projections. If an individual is stuck in a paranoid-schizoid (Klein, 1975) way of being then they need an object to be the focus of their projections, that is, an enemy often viewed as if they were inferior or subhuman.

A powerful example of an attempt to bring about social healing is the 'Truth and Reconciliation Commission', which was held in South Africa in the aftermath of the end of Apartheid. Its expressed aim was that those who had been so badly abused by this political system could have their story heard. This being heard is closely akin to the psychotherapist listening to the client's story and is an important element within any healing relationship. In the Truth and Reconciliation process perpetrators of violence could also speak of what they had done and seek amnesty. Archbishop Desmond Tutu in his foreword to the Commission's report wrote the following:

> Amnesty applicants often confessed to more gruesome crimes...yet their assumption of responsibility, and the sense that at least people were getting some measure of truth from the process, resulted in much less anger. For the sake of our stability, it is fortunate that the kind of details exposed by the Commission did not come out in a series of criminal trials, which – because of the difficulty of proving cases beyond reasonable doubt in the absence of witnesses other than co-conspirators – most likely would have ended in acquittals. (Tutu, 2003: 1)

Archbishop Tutu viewed the Commission as a means of bringing healing to both individuals and to a divided nation. Liberation came through an exposure to the truth about what had happened to people, their voice was heard, feeling that they are taken seriously; their pain acknowledged was a healing experience. Summing up the process Archbishop Tutu said:

> We have been privileged to help to heal a wounded people, though we ourselves have been, in Henri Nouwen's profound and felicitous phrase,

'wounded healers'. When we look around us at some of the conflict areas of the world, it becomes increasingly clear that there is not much of a future for them without forgiveness, without reconciliation. (Tutu, 2003: 1)

Conclusion

How might we define the constituent elements which would exist in a relationship which facilitates healing? What are we looking for in the face of the other? First, it must be a relationship in which a person feels both heard and held; only then can an individual transcend the history which holds them captive. Second, it must be a relationship where unconscious communications and projections are received and processed. Third, it must enable the individual to grow emotionally by embracing reality in a way that would not be possible without the existence of the relationship. Fourth, it must foster concern for the other so that the other is accepted as they actually are and not merely used as an object of fantasy. When relationships between two people or a group of people contain these elements then they promote what might be called wholeness. People's painful symptoms are not magically cured but their distress is worked with and thus becomes a tool for the self healing of the psyche. Such relationships can be found and formed in a multitude of settings: with a friend, with a lover, with a psychotherapist, in a therapeutic group, in a church and in a group aiming at reconciliation after political conflict. As Jung succinctly put it, 'we meet ourselves time and again in a thousand disguises on the path of life' (Jung, 1946: para 534).

References

Athill, D. (2008) *Somewhere Towards the End*. (London: Granta Books).

Balint, M. (1957) *The Doctor, His Patient and the Illness*. (London: Tavistock Publications).

Balint, M. (1968) *The Basic Fault,: Therapeutic Aspects of Regression*. (London: Routledge). 2006.

Bion, W. R. (1965) *Transformations*. (London: William Heinemann).

Bion, W. R. (1970) *Attention and Interpretation*. (London: Tavistock Publications).

Descartes, R. (1984) 'Meditations on First Philosophy' in *The Philosophical Writings of Descartes* Vol. II. Cottingham, J. (trans.). Cottingham, Stoothoff, and Murdoch (eds). (Cambridge: Cambridge University Press).

Freud, S. (1900) *The Interpretation of Dreams*. Penguin Freud Library 4. (Harmondsworth: Penguin). 1976.

Freud, S. (1933) *New Introductory Lectures on Psychoanalysis*. Penguin Freud Library 2. (Harmondsworth: Penguin). 1991.

Jung, C. G. (1913) 'General Aspects of Psychoanalysis' in *Freud and Psychoanalysis, CW4*. (London: Routledge). 1993.

Jung, C. G. (1928) 'Relations between the Ego and the Unconscious' in *Two Essays on Analytical Psychology, CW 7*. (London: Routledge). 1990.

Jung, C. G. (1929) 'Problems of Modern Psychotherapy' in *The Practice of Psychotherapy, CW 16*. (London and Henley: Routledge & Kegan Paul). 1981.

Jung, C. G. (1933) *Modern Man in Search of a Soul*. (London: Ark Paperbacks). 1984.

Jung, C. G. (1934) 'The Practical Use of Dream-Analysis' in *The Practice of Psychotherapy*. (London and Henley: Routledge & Kegan Paul). 1981.

Jung, C. G. (1938/40) 'Psychology and Religion' in *Psychology and Religion: West and East, CW 11*. (London: Routledge) 1991.

Jung, C. G. (1939) 'Conscious, Unconscious and Individuation' in *The Archetypes and the Collective Unconscious, CW 9 (1)*. (London: Routledge).

Jung, C. G. (1946) 'The Psychology of the Transference' in *The Practice of Psychotherapy, CW 16*. (London and Henley: Routledge & Kegan Paul). 1981.

Klein, M. (1975) *Envy and Gratitude and Other Works 1946–1963*. Masud R. Khan (ed.). (London: The Hogarth Press).

MacDonald Cornford, F. (1969) *The Republic of Plato*. (London: Oxford University Press).

Meier, C. (1967) *Ancient Incubation and Modern Psychotherapy*. (Evanston Illinois: Northwestern University Press).

Rayner, Eric. (1986) *Human Development*. (London: Unwin Hyman).

Rycroft, C. (1958) 'The Function of Words in Psychoanalytical Situation' in *Imagination and Reality*. (London: Hogarth Press).

Rycroft, C. (1972) *Critical Dictionary of Psychoanalysis*. (London: Penguin Group).

Samuels, A., Shorter, B., and Plaut, F. (1986) *A Critical Dictionary of Jungian Analysis*. (London and New York: Routledge & Kegan Paul).

Schore, A. (1994) *Development and Psychopathology*. (Cambridge: Cambridge University Press).

Tutu, D. (2003) 'Chairperson's Foreword' in *Truth and Reconciliation Commission of South Africa Report, Vol. 6*. http://www.info.gov.za/otherdocs/2003/trc/rep.pdf 2011.

Welch, J. (1982) *Spiritual Pilgrims, Carl Jung and Teresa of Avila*. (New York: Paulist Press).

Winnicott, D. W. (1971) *Playing and Reality*. (London: Tavistock Publications Ltd).

3

Not Speaking: Thinking More about the 'Talking Cure'

Meg Errington

Infant Joy.
'I have no name.
I am but two days old'
What shall I call thee?
'I happy am,
Joy is my name.'
Sweet joy befall thee.

Pretty joy!
Sweet joy but two days old.
Sweet joy I call thee:
Thou dost smile,
I sing the while,
Sweet joy befall thee.

Infant Sorrow.
My mother groan'd! my father wept.
Into the dangerous world I leapt:,
Helpless, naked, piping loud:
Like a fiend hid in a cloud.

Struggling in my father's hands,
Striving against my swaddling bands,
Bound and weary I thought best
To sulk upon my mother's breast.
                    William Blake. (1789)

Introduction

I want to begin this chapter with these complementary poems by William Blake. They depict two mental states he describes as 'contrary' states which he has called 'innocence' and 'experience'. The poems are, in my view, an account of the pain and loss we all face in moving from a pre-symbolic world into the world of language. The French psychoanalyst, Jacques Lacan, would have called this the movement from an imaginary realm into the realm of the symbolic. In my view, the poems describe well what Lacan might have meant by these two realms of experience (Lacan, 1953/54).

Both poems are seemingly about birth and new born infants. The first poem 'Infant Joy' is an idyllic portrayal of a mirroring relation between a mother/other and an infant. The poem achieves something remarkable in its ability to use language to imagine the preverbal connection between mother and infant at the beginning of life. The infant revels in an undifferentiated unity and lack of identity, which is joyous. There is an illusion of 'oneness' between two people; it is difficult to know who is speaking, who is who. The loving mother/other echoes and mirrors her infant's joyful state, although she knows it cannot last. This mother knows there will be a fall from this state of grace but she hopes for gentle disillusionment for her infant 'sweet joy befall thee'. There is an absence of clear boundaries between self and other and the language of the poem is personal and idiosyncratic. For this infant, there are no names and sentence structures are inverted. The infant creates his own world, organising language and his relations according to his own principles. Lacan would describe this as the realm of 'the imaginary'.

'Infant Sorrow' describes a very different birth. The infant is born into a world of three people. Father is present and the infant must share mother. Not only must he share mother but also he must share meaning and use words in a proper way. This is the world of the symbolic. The world of this poem is frightening and dangerous. It is a world of despair and grievance. Blake has no illusions about a world in which we are subject to the rules and structures of language and Oedipus. In the symbolic world we are subject to language, we must use names; in Lacan's terms to enter 'the Name of the Father' (1954/55). This concept of Lacan is of course about the real father who intrudes into the mirror relation between infant and mother. But it is also a description of the introduction and structure of symbolic signification. Language becomes associated with loss; loss of the sensual experience of the nursing couple and loss of a myth of undifferentiated unity. Language introduces the demand to share; to share mother and to share meaning in an accepted discourse. The poet discovers once again in the writing of the poem what that means; it is constricting, like being 'bound in swaddling bands'. Lacan wrote that 'man is the subject captured and tormented by language' (Lacan, 1955/56). Blake reveals in the poem a phantasy of triumph over this unpleasant state and his solution is to 'sulk'. The word is shouted triumphantly and emphatically as a climax to the poem. Language remains a constraint rather than a possibility and he will not connect or relate in a world of three where two cannot become one. Blake presents us with the essential paradox of language; the very form which permits communication and dialogue also recalls the pain of death, disconnection and rivalry. It is this paradox of language that I want to explore in this chapter. In my view it is from these painful realities clients retreat in their sulking and silence and distortions of language in the consulting room. The task of psychotherapy with adolescents whom I shall be discussing in this chapter is to reconcile them to language and all that it stands for.

Talking and Not Talking

To begin at the beginning, the most extreme case of refusal to enter the symbolic world of language is the autistic child. Francis Tustin (1986), a psychoanalyst of the British School, observed that it is not only in poetry that sulking can be observed at the beginning of life. In her book, *Autistic barriers in Neurotic Patients* she wrote:

> Psychogenic autistic children seem to be in a massive unmitigated primal sulk....shot through with umbrage and black despair. This has caused them to be unrelated to the mother and to people in general. They avoid looking at people and communication by language is scanty or often not present at all. (Tustin, 1986: 20)

Many of the children she wrote about were completely mute. Tustin believed that an experience of traumatic bodily separation lay at the heart of autism. Tustin wrote

> the fall from the sublime state of blissful unity with the mother who in earliest infancy is the sensation dominated centre of the infants universe is part of everyone's experience. However for some individuals for a variety of reasons different in each case the disillusionment of coming down to earth from this ecstatic experience has been such a hard and injurious one that it has provoked impeding encapsulating reactions. (Tustin, 1986: 20)

Stella Acquarone (2007), a contemporary Lacanian analyst, builds on Tustin's work but sees the traumatic 'separation' between mother and infant as being of a different kind. She sees the demand being made on the baby as being able to become 'emotionally born' by being able to share the mind of the mother. The infant must tolerate a sense of 'you, me and the others'. She comments:

At birth the baby is required to integrate a physical fact, that they and their mother are not one but two. Neither they nor the mother has a choice about this.....the baby is also forced to integrate a psychological fact...that they are not one but two. Psychological separation might be so unbearable for either or both mother and baby that they refuse to acknowledge the separation by refusing to communicate.... the baby is soon forced to integrate a psychodynamic fact: that the mother's mind is full of 'others'...rivalling what the baby may have thought to be an exclusive relationship. The one has now become three'. (Acquarone, 2007: 219)

For Acquarone resisting communication is an unconscious resolve:

Consciously, pre-autistic babies cannot process communication with others because to do so would cause them to violate an unconscious resolve they have placed over their deepest fear: they are no longer at one with the 'other'. Not communicating with others is a deeply felt state that self-soothes. The lack of intimacy and the need to regain/maintain this state could be seen as a retraction into themselves. (219)

Acquarone joins up her thinking in a powerful way with Francis Tustin. She has a theory of the autistic complex which elaborates the infant's emotions and emotional development. She says, 'For many years, I have been exploring the impact that the other occupants of the mothers mind make on her baby's emotions. In other words, how does the general psychodynamics of "you me and the others" affect the baby's emotional development and how in particular does a baby's emotional make-up be such that the other occupants of mother's mind could be felt as unbearable?' (Acquarone, 2007: 216). Acquarone refers to a powerful image that Tustin uses in her work, 'the nest of sucklings' or 'the swarm of stinging rivals'. In Tustin's theory, this was the autistic child's fantasy that they were in competition with predatory rivals at the other side of the breast who wanted to snatch the nipple away from them and take away their chance of life and sustenance. For Tustin, this was a reason why infants would not relate to others. Acquarone asks the question, how could the autistic children in Tustin's practice feel the occupants of mother's mind as predatory rivals? To paraphrase Acquarone:

The awareness involves an awareness of others in mother's life. If there were to be a premature rivalry with the occupants of mothers mind we would have a very primitive and very powerful inhibitor of emotional development. For autistic children finding a way out on their own, of a premature rivalry with the others in mother's mind is impossible. This is what it means to be trapped in the autistic spectrum. The infant refuses to share the mind of the mother. (Acquarone, 2007: 216–217)

The refusal to share the mind of the mother...to allow the possibility of a two in a world of three or more forecloses on the possibility of entering the symbolic realm for the autistic child. Autistic children remain like the infant in 'Infant Joy' using language (if at all) in highly idiosyncratic ways in an illusory attempt to avoid the pain of loss of mother's body and to cling to a phantasy of sole possession. They reject father and all that he stands for...a world of language, of rules and of symbolic triangulation. Francis Tustin believed that there could be autistic barriers in neurotic clients. It is interesting to consider the case of Leo in the light of the above.

The Case of Leo

Leo was an angelic looking boy as though late emerging from latency. He was referred to me because he had 'pretended' to shoot a teacher in the head with a toy gun one day in class and she had for a moment believed the gun to be real. The class had been traumatised. Several teachers had informed me that they thought he was 'autistic'. He would have terrible tantrums in class, once jumping up and down on his English book in front of his peers because he got a bad mark. He then refused to speak to the teacher for weeks.

He was assessed by the child psychiatrist who laughed at the diagnosis of autism. My supervisor thought he might be a bit 'Aspergerish'. He was consistently preoccupied by thoughts of other students who came to see me and would badger me constantly with empty, formulaic questions, 'Who comes miss? What do they talk about?' He communicated to me through the form of elaborate stories like a much younger child. He spent the early months of our work telling me stories about animals he owned; cats, dogs, then iguanas and snakes and a crocodile. The 'bitey', angry nature of the animals was not lost on me. I was surprised, however, and a bit alarmed one day, at a meeting with other staff to hear one teacher who prided herself on her excellent relations with the students telling us all about Leo's large and interesting collection of pet animals and I realised something of his power and plausibility. This came to a head during the time of the Tsunami in Thailand when Leo acted out very dramatically. He told one of his teachers a story of a relative who had died there. The teacher was so upset and moved by the story that she had rung Leo's mother to say how sorry she was and of course his mother said they didn't have any relatives who had died in the Tsunami.

A common dilemma working in an organisation with students, unlike working with adults in private practice, is hearing things or knowing things which the students don't want you to hear about or know about. A school is a symbolic realm of rules, laws and shared relationships. It is always noticeable the students who can create for themselves the illusion of the dyad and who block out the wider world of school. This is always an indication of a determined retreat from reality. It is interesting to speculate how long it would have taken Leo to tell me what he had done, if ever he had. Because of the dangers of this illusion continuing ad infinitum, I have a practice of always informing students when I start working with them that I will never gossip about them or talk about them to anyone without discussing it with them first but that if I hear anything from my end, things that people say about them, then I will tell them. This is usually completely forgotten about or ignored by the student but sometimes it is the only way of introducing the notion of my separate mind. Some sessions after this incident, when he had not told me about it but was about to launch into a story about how his auntie had a swimming pool in her garden, I let him know that I knew what had happened about his story of the Tsunami. The sweet child disappeared and an enraged adolescent took his place; 'I hate this fucking school' was the last thing he said to me for weeks. He did however come for his sessions and either sat and said nothing and faced the wall or communicated through writing notes on tissues or scrap paper saying things like, 'You are just like all the others' or 'I hate this fucking school'. He had tried to maintain a state of me and you but no others. In his imagination he had claimed exclusive possession of my mind. He had experienced my revelation on two levels, as his being in competition with a swarm of stinging rivals – 'this fucking school' that he had tried to both investigate and eliminate in the room with me. It took many months to explore his state of grievance until we could reach the loss underlying his sulky rage. He was able to tell me that his parents had split up and his sister had been chosen to stay with his 'adored' father while he was staying with his mother. The murderous rivalry he experienced in relation to his rivals for my attention at school had reactivated more primitive terrors and longings for sole possession of both parents. The pretend shooting was simultaneously an attack on the others in mother's mind and an attempt to kill her and have father to himself. It was no small thing to convey the enormity of this emotional experience in language.

Margaret Tonnesmann (2005), a contemporary psychoanalyst of the British School, makes a distinction between two possible kinds of verbal relating in the psychoanalytic encounter. One is at an 'Oedipal level',

> if the patient is engaged in a personal verbal relationship…. then the setting becomes a backcloth and becomes a surround that is taken for granted and not specifically referred to. At times during therapy the verbal interpersonal relating breaks down and some disturbance in the analyst patient relationship becomes apparent. The surround becomes more important and the communications have ceased to be of an interpersonal verbal kind. Instead analyst and patient are engaged in an emotionally highly charged encounter…it means that the patient has regressed to an early pre-verbal trauma'. (Tonnesmann, 2005: 195)

Rather than thinking of this as a regression to a preverbal trauma, I would see the breakdown in the flow of speech as being something of a retreat from meaning which the client perceives will be enraging or impossible to bear.

Learning to Speak

None of us can remember how we learned to speak. Language acquisition is a developmental given for most infants. In most cases children learn to speak in an invisible, almost miraculous way, not imitating parents but following what Chomsky called universal rules of grammar which occur in every language and according to Stephen Pinker make language acquisition 'an instinct' (Pinker 1994). Yet we need help to activate this instinct. Oliver Sacks (1989) in his book *Seeing Voices* about his work with deaf children describes the importance of communication between mother and child so that the child becomes 'a user of language'. The innate ability we have to acquire language must, he says, be "activated' by,

> 'someone in possession of linguistic power and competence.... The origin of questioning, of an active and questioning disposition in the mind, is not something that arises spontaneously, de novo, or directly from the impact of experience; it stems, it is stimulated by, communicative exchange... it requires dialogue, in particular the complex dialogue of mother and child.' (Sacks, 1989: 63)

The mother has, he says, 'a terrible power' to communicate with her child.

For Lacan, the acquisition of language is itself traumatic. Philip Hill (2002), a contemporary Lacanian, describes the highly charged emotional experience that he believes is behind the process of negotiation between mother and child as the child acquires language:

> The helpless infant requires insurance, a guarantee, some tool of negotiation over which he possesses some control. The event he needs to ensure against is that of his Mummy no longer managing his sensations; she should be the gratifier of his needs, the provider of pleasure and remover of unpleasure, that is pain. Ironically the baby is best able to establish the guarantee and discover what mother demands by becoming a language user. Not least because when baby presents a sensation need, mother increasingly delays gratification and instead feeds him a morsel of language. The baby eats language because he has a requirement for pleasure, or for pain to be removed and the mother has her requirement for jouissance, to have her child say 'I love you'. So the good mother tortures her baby, delaying his pleasure, increasing his pain depriving and frustrating until her symbols are swallowed. Torture invariably has the

aim of producing speech from the suffering victim. If torture victims speak it is primarily to plead 'What do you want?' of their torturer, of the one who has power over their sensations. The victim may say whatever she believes her torturer wants to hear. So it is with mothers and their infants. Sometimes children deny their mother's wishes: sometimes victims of torture are defiant. The price initially set for helping the helpless infant is the insistence that the infant comes to have knowledge of the mother's demands and desires and above all that he speaks. (Hill, 2002: 181)

Speaking becomes a mark of separation and love for mother. The ability to go beyond the level of experiencing speech as a demand and to become reconciled to language is the emotional achievement required of the child. The child shows his love for mother in this way. But in order to separate and use language, in Hill's account, the child must be able to tolerate a degree of pain and unpleasure. Hill sees language as the marker of separation '...we are separate from mother when we speak our mother tongue'. This is of course the demand we make as psychotherapists. For some clients at some times, words become symbols of pain and the harsh reality of separateness...a demand to suffer. Sulking becomes a triumph over this suffering. My experience with sulky and sullen clients is that they must emerge from a period of enraged grievance and be able to express their pain and loss in words. Grievance must be replaced by grief if change is to occur.

In *Beyond the Pleasure Principle*, Freud (1920) described his observation of watching his eighteen-month-old grandson in the process of discovering language in what has become known as the 'fort/da game'. Freud observed him throwing a toy out of his pram, exclaiming 'fort' (gone away) then hauling it back in again crying 'da' (here). This is the birth of the symbol and entry into the symbolic. Freud saw his grandson registering and mastering his mother's absence through language (Freud, 1920). Terry Eagleton the literary commentator describes the 'fort/da game' as 'the first glimmerings of narrative',

Fort/da is perhaps the shortest story we can imagine: an object is lost, and then recovered. But even the most complex narratives can be read as variants on this model: the pattern of classical narrative is that an original settlement is disrupted and ultimately restored. From this viewpoint narrative is the source of a consolation; lost objects are a cause of anxiety to us, symbolising certain deeper unconscious losses, (of birth, the faeces, the mother) and it is always pleasurable to find them put securely back in place (Eagleton, 1983: 185).

Loss can drive the narrative of our lives impelling us forward to pursue substitutes for the imagined lost paradise; of the womb, of the mother's body or of the possession of the parent. Language is the paradigm substitute. We substitute words for things, and a whole world is opened up to us. At best, we become reconciled to sharing and to the world outside us. Through language, we become reconciled to our losses. Language will never connect us in relationship as we imagine we were connected in the lost pre-symbolic unity but it is all that we have. Blake, after all, despite his frustration over the constraints of 'the swaddling bands' of language which make him want to sulk and turn away, thinks better of this and he does not. Instead he writes a poem which in its intense emotional engagement and mastery of subjection to language and the losses this stands for helps us to re-experience the extraordinary possibilities and consolations of language.

Anna O and the 'Talking Cure'

That is why Anna O's description of psychoanalysis is so lasting and resonant. Anna O has been influential in naming psychoanalysis 'the talking cure'. It might seem then as though she talked easily and effortlessly in her treatment. However, reading the case study again, it is striking to note that this was far from the case.

At the time in their *Studies on Hysteria* of which Anna O's case is one, Freud and Breuer (1893) were documenting the importance of speech in psychoanalysis. Speech was important in an obvious way…as a way of two people communicating with each other but the function of language was paramount in the process of becoming conscious. The *Studies on Hysteria* articulates microscopically the importance that Freud gave to language in moving from an unconscious state to a state of consciousness through freeing 'the operative force of the idea which was not abreacted in the first instance by allowing its strangulated affect to find a way out through speech' (Freud and Breuer, 1893: 69).

In Freud's view the symptom was evidence that we were 'strangled' and we must put in words the hidden ideas and feelings which had caused the symptom in the first place. The expression of emotion is given equal weight. Even though Freud later replaced his theory of recollected real trauma with the exploration of unconscious phantasy, the ability to 'put affect into words' and to 'talk things out' is still today at the heart of 'the talking cure'. Jacques Lacan called this the achievement of 'full speech' and he saw this as the aim of psychoanalysis (Lacan, 1953/43: 107). Jean Michel Quinodoz describes the case of Anna O as 'paradigmatic' and comments that 'Anna O's therapy will remain in the annals as the first successful treatment by the cathartic method as it was then called and the one that launched Freud on the road to discovering psychoanalysis' (Quinodoz, 2004: 14).

Anna O began treatment with Breuer in 1880 when she was 21 years old which according to Peter Blos would be considered 'late adolescence' (Blos, 1972). One difficulty in rereading the case is Breuer's (Freud and Breuer, 1893) use of hypnotic technique in his treatment of her, which Freud later rejected in favour of 'free association'. The way in which Breuer conducted the case was as much like a family physician as a psychoanalyst, since he visited her at home to conduct her 'treatment', at one point as much as twice a day. Anna O had entered treatment with Breuer after becoming ill with anorexia and after developing a nervous cough while nursing her 'adored' father who was ill and who subsequently died six months into her treatment. Her relationship with her mother was described as 'poor'. Anna O's illness was dramatic and took the form of multiple symptoms…a paralysed right arm, frightening hallucinations, anorexia, chronic splitting of the personality and what Breuer describes as absences but what we now might think of as acute dissociated states. Over the hundred years, since the case was written, there have been many subsequent criticisms of how Breuer conducted the case, not least from Freud himself. Freud later told James Strachey, who edited Freud and Breuer's *Studies on Hysteria*, that he believed Anna O had a 'strong unanalysed positive transference' to Breuer 'of an unmistakeably sexual nature' (Freud and Breuer, 1893: 95). Anna O did not just describe her treatment as a talking cure but as 'chimney sweeping', the sexual connotations of which Breuer did not fully take on board and certainly not in relation to her attachment to him.

However, what Breuer did catalogue most clearly was a powerful symptom in its own right which he described as 'the deep ongoing functional disorganisation of her speech' (Freud and Breuer, 1893: 77). This does not receive much attention in later commentaries yet what Breuer describes seems to be a psychotic state of mind which is manifest in her language disturbance. Breuer describes her as seeming most of the time to be in a 'dream'. The way she communicated with him was of such a metaphorical and condensed nature particularly when she was describing her terrifying hallucinations which rendered her speechless with terror.

Breuer details her disturbances of speech, minutely as though they are highly significant. Rather than speak to him Anna O mostly communicated through telling child-like fairy stories which began with a girl sitting at her father's bedside. Most extraordinarily, for long periods she refused to speak her native language (German) 'her mother tongue' – speaking only English which Breuer could understand but not her nurse. We might think of this as a highly sophisticated way of keeping Breuer to herself and keeping nurse/mother out. At one point Anna lost her ability to use grammar. Breuer meticulously notes this showing an expert understanding of grammar himself: 'she lost her command of grammar and syntax; she no longer conjugated verbs, and eventually she used only infinitives, for the most part incorrectly formed from weak past participles' (Freud and Breuer, 1893: 77) In Lacanian terms she was refusing to become subject to language and refusing to enter 'the Name of the Father'.

She became dumb for two weeks at one point. At another time she invented her own language from a mish-mash of foreign languages. Breuer interpreted this, seeing her refusal to speak and her distortions of language as having an emotional base:

> For two weeks she became completely dumb and inspite of making great and continuous efforts to speak she was unable to say a syllable. And now for the first time the psychical mechanism of the disorder became clear. As I knew she had felt very much offended over something and had determined not to speak about it. When I guessed this and obliged her to talk about it, the inhibition which had made any other kind of utterance impossible as well, disappeared. (Freud and Breuer, 1893: 78)

It is striking the attention that Breuer pays to Anna O's not speaking. He documents carefully the instances when Anna refuses to speak, 'she lost the power of speech (a) as a result of fear after her first hallucination at night, (b) after having suppressed a remark another time (by active inhibition), (c) after having been unjustly blamed for something, (d) on every analogous occasion (when she felt mortified)' (Freud and Breuer, 1893: 94).

Breuer describes the lengths he went to, in order to persuade her to talk, at times sounding like a mother cajoling a sulky toddler. 'When.. she was in a bad temper she would refuse to talk and I was obliged to overcome her unwillingness by urging and pleading and using devices such as repeating a formula with which she was in the habit of introducing her stories' (Freud and Breuer, 1893: 83).

Rather than seeing this as a preverbal trauma, a Lacanian reading would indicate a problem with moving into the symbolic realm. For Lacanian analysts there is no 'preverbal'. Language exists before us; we are born into a world of language. The French psychoanalyst Francoise Dolto (1995) believes that children understand language as soon as they are born. The word infant means 'without speech' and my own view is that in adolescence speech disturbances in therapy reveal an unconscious desire to retreat to into an imaginary state, away from the difficulties and changes which are required to move into adulthood. Schizophrenia would be an extreme case of this. Anna O conveys her dilemmas through dream-like images rather than conventional speech. Her distortions of speech show her problem of 'you me and the others' and her attempt to create an imaginary relation in which two can become one. She struggled to be a two in a world of three. We know that Breuer's wife had a child during Anna's analysis with him and that Anna was powerful in claiming a great deal of Breuer's attention. She ran circles round him and he acted out and accommodated her demandingness rather than understanding what it stood for. He was able to interpret her anger to a point but he did not understand her fear. Her hallucinations with their florid symbolism of snakes biting her father, of her fingers turning to snakes and her imagining that she had snakes in her hair seem to display the kind of biblical and mythological symbols of sexual and forbidden temptation, the fear of punishment (from a Medusa type figure) and expulsion from the Garden of Eden which have existed for all time in various guises. Breuer describes her as being 'remarkably free from thoughts of a sexual nature' (Freud and Breuer, 1893: 83), and he seemed unaware of the symbolic significance of her communications tracing them back to real events (his understanding of the snakes she had hallucinated biting her father was that she had seen some in her garden). Lacan would describe her as being remarkably able to articulate her own disorder (Lacan, 1955/56). Her distortions of speech and language reveal a terror of sexuality and all that it stands for. Just as for Adam and Eve, after sex, there is no escape from the expulsion from the garden and the inevitability of death. In my view the case study shows a desire to retreat from the sorrows and terrors of adult sexuality as well as a longing for the father she cannot have.

In reality, the pre-fall world which Anna O and the autistic child attempt to re-find is a hell as much as a heaven. It is a world dominated by what Bion called 'nameless dread' in which meaning cannot be made (Hinshelwood, 1995: 353). Perhaps that is why Anna O responds to Breuer's attempts to make meaning of her terrors and her anger despite his shortcomings as an analyst. That he was able to make meaning of any kind seemed to calm her. Naming her feelings and linking her hallucinations to events in the past freed her even temporarily from 'torment'.

Concluding Reflections

Anna O's description of her experience of psychoanalysis as 'The Talking Cure' is well known, but it interests me that over a hundred years after Anna O, a fifteen year old inner city school boy who worked with me for a year, should describe his experience of psychotherapy in a similar way to her. He was surprised and pleased that talking was so helpful to him, a process he described as soul healing. Like Leo, his sense of grievance was expressed against the symbolic world of school and its rules and laws. Ray found talking very difficult. He learned a way of communicating through coming to therapy. Ray came to see me after his father's sudden death. His father's death was made more difficult because Ray's parents had divorced three years earlier and this was an unresolved and painful issue for him.

What was characteristic of Ray, like many adolescents I have worked with, is the way in which talking seemed like an impossible demand. His teachers described him as being angry and sulky. He had very much wanted to come and see me but once in the room he was uncomfortable and at a loss. He would sit with his head in his hands and be unable to speak. He would appeal to me with a kind of mute longing. He had shown signs of real disturbance before coming to see me writing suicide notes in class and hearing voices telling him to jump downstairs. He was hopeless about the future and attempting to retreat from thoughts of 'the upstairs' in terms of his parents and his own sexuality. The beginnings of our sessions were always characterised by what Bion described as 'nameless dread' on both our parts; a fear that we would not be able to put into words his overwhelming feelings and confusion. As our relationship developed, Ray became less aggrieved at having to speak and showed a willingness to experiment with language. Over time, we developed a method of communication which involved him spending some time in the session when he would write something, random thoughts or ideas in a kind of free association, a poem perhaps, usually expressing his pain over his father's death or his feeling that he had always had a poor relationship with his father. I would read back to him what he had written and we would begin a dialogue and he would begin to speak. This dredging up of language, this struggle to articulate what seems inarticulable, is often the work of psychotherapy.

For many adolescents the means of 'cure', talking, saying what comes to mind, is the very difficulty the client brings to the work or experiences in the course of the work. It was a revelation to see Ray discover that language was not only a signifier of loss and difference. He embraced speaking and writing as a way of loving and mourning his father. He discovered in Eagleton's (1983) terms 'the consolations of narrative'.

References

Acquarone, S. (ed.) (2007) *Signs of Autism in Infants*. (London: Karnac Books).

Blake, W. (1789) *The Complete Writings*. Keynes, G. (ed.) (Oxford: Oxford University Press) 1966.

Blos, P. (1979) *The Adolescent Passage*. (Madison: International Universities Press).

Dolto, F. (1995) *Tout est Langage*. Gallimard. (ed) (Paris and New York: Vintage Books).

Freud, S. (1920) *Beyond the Pleasure Principle*. Vol. 11. (London: Pelican Freud Library). 1984.

Freud S. and Breuer, J. (1893) *Studies in Hysteria*. Vol. 3. (London: Pelican Freud Library) 1974.

Eagleton, T. (1983) *Literary Theory*. (Oxford: Basil Blackwell).

Hill, P. (2002) *Using Lacanian Clinical Technique – An Introduction*. (London: Press for the Habilitation of Psychoanalysis).

Hinshelwood, R. D. (1989) *A Dictionary of Kleinian Thought*. (London: Free Association Books).

Lacan, J. (1953–54) *The Seminar of Jacques Lacan Book 1*. Miller, J-A. (ed). (Cambridge: Cambridge University Press) 1988.

Lacan, J. (1954–55) *The Seminar of Jacques Lacan Book 2*. Miller, J-A. (ed.). (Cambridge: Cambridge University Press) 1988.

Lacan, J. (1955–56) *The Seminar of Jacques Lacan Book 3*. Miller, J-A. (ed.). (London: Routledge) 1993.

Pinker, S. (1995) *The Language Instinct*. (London: Penguin Books).

Quinodoz, J-M. (2005) *Reading Freud*. (London: Routledge).

Sacks, O. (1989) *Seeing Voices*. (London: Picador).

Tonnesmann, M. (2005) 'Transference and Countertransference, An Historical Approach' in *Introducing Psychoanalysis*. Budd, S. and Rushbridger, R. (eds.) (London: Routledge) 2005.

Tustin, F. (1986) *Autistic Barriers in Neurotic Patients*. (London: Karnac Books).

4

The I-Thou Relationship

Stephen Gross

Introduction

Martin Buber's (2004) celebrated notion of the I-Thou relationship can be employed as a paradigm to explore more freely the dyadic relationship that exists between therapist and client. Despite his longstanding hostility towards all psychotherapies and his rejection of the notion of the unconscious, his emphasis on the centrality of dialogue in true human relationship has a profound significance for the therapeutic encounter and then beyond the consulting room into the social and political spheres.

Martin Buber

Martin Buber was born in Vienna in 1878 into a traditional central European Jewish family. Without question the most significant event of his formative years and very probably his entire life was his mother's abandonment of him at the age of three. It is arguable that such an experience was more than tangential to his later philosophy of relationship which constitutes the foundation of his most famous work *I and Thou* written in 1923 and published in English in 1937. I shall return to this below.

The influence of Hasidic Judaism and the mystical elements of its thought were crucial to Buber throughout his life and are evident in much of his writing. In 1901 he wrote his first important philosophic essay, *Ueber Jakob Boehme* (Buber, 1901) on the issue of the relation of the individual to the world and later *Daniel: Dialogues on Realization* (Buber, 1913) which was regarded as a more original work reflecting his immersion in mysticism as well as his deep interest in Eastern religions. This work particularly provided early evidence of the more relational philosophy that was to come to full fruition in 1923 when he wrote *I and Thou* (Buber, 2004) and later when he published *Between Man and Man* in 1947. In facing accusations that his work was not altogether free of mystical influences Buber averred, 'The clear and firm structure of the I-Thou relationship familiar to everyone with a candid heart and the courage to pledge it, has not a mystical nature' (Buber, 2004: 97).

I-Thou

The I-Thou relationship which underpins the major body of Buber's thinking and philosophical output is throughout contrasted with its antithetical conceptual twin the I-It. At the very beginning of *I and Thou* Buber writes:

> To man the world is twofold in accordance with his twofold attitude. The attitude of man is twofold, in accordance with the twofold nature of the primary words which he speaks. The primary words are not isolated words but combined words. The primary word is the combination *I-Thou*. The other primary word is the combination *I-It*; wherein, without a change in the primary word, one of the words *He* and *She* can replace *It*. (Buber, 2004: 11)

These opening lines from *I-Thou* immediately attest to Buber's belief that the individual does not exist as an isolated being disconnected from the being of others but is and remains always in some state of relationship with others. As relationship can arguably be regarded as the very bedrock of therapeutic practice and much of its theory, the significance of Buber's ideas to psychotherapeutic thought begins to become apparent.

In his *I-Thou* Buber distinguishes the three spheres in which the world of relation and encounter is built. The first of these he identifies as our life with nature as represented by individual objects such as a tree or rock in which the relationship is experienced pre-verbally. The second, with which this chapter is primarily concerned, is what Buber calls our life with others in which the relation takes on the form of speech and the 'solid give and take of talk' (Buber, 2004:79). As Goldenburg and Isaacson point out, 'It is important to recognise that for Buber 'speech' or 'saying' is used as a metaphor for a way of being in the world' (Goldenburg and Isaacson, 1996: 119). The third sphere Buber calls our life with spiritual beings. This relation, 'being without speech' (Buber, 2004: 78), reveals itself and creates language through the response of creating, thinking and acting with our being. After outlining these three spheres, Buber reminds us of his roots in Jewish mysticism: 'In every sphere in its own way, through each process of becoming that is present to us, we look out toward the fringe of the eternal *Thou*; in each we are aware of a breath from the eternal *Thou*; in each *Thou* we address the eternal *Thou*' (Buber, 2004: 79).

Whilst this chapter sets out to consider some of the vital components of Buber's *I-Thou* in relation to clinical practice, it is approached here from an essentially humanistic perspective in which only the human character and potential of the therapist/client encounter is examined. In addition, whilst fully acknowledging the spiritual dimension in subjective being and relation-ship, I am not considering here the realm of the transcendent. On this point Sue Morgan-Williams draws our attention to the first English translation of *Ich und Du* in 1937 (2004) when 'Du' was translated as 'Thou' with all of its accompany-ing 'danger of sacralisation and mystery'. She goes on to cite Kaufman's 1970 translation of 'You' instead of 'Thou' which she suggested was 'more easily associated to Buber's ideas of intimacy, spontaneity, dialogue, mutuality and intersubjectivity etc.' (Morgan-Williams, 1995: 82–83).

Throughout this chapter I will be drawing some comparisons between Buber's key concepts and those of some of the major figures from the domain of psychotherapy. However, it seems important to say that such comparisons can be no more than superficial for whilst Buber was certainly prepared to consider some of his ideas within the context of a therapeutic relationship, he was first and foremost a philosopher who set out to construct a philosophy of being and relationship. The notions of 'psyche' and 'the unconscious' were quite alien to his thinking. In fact Buber was trenchantly dismissive of all analytical psycho-therapy which he claimed was a psychological reductionism which 'saw the soul, with which psychology and psychoanalysis was said to concern itself, as something lifted out of the relationship of the world, isolated and abstracted' (Morgan-Williams, 1995: 87).

Healing, as Buber understood it, could never be achieved through the inter-pretation of an individual's psychological pathology but occurred through a special meeting between therapist and client and of 'the Between' which, for Buber, was an important aspect of relationship. He considered that the objec-tive of therapy, the regeneration of a stunted personal centre from which the client is unable to engage fully in a true meeting with the world, could not be achieved (Buber, 2004: 99). Here, as throughout his 'I-Thou', Buber fails to recognise the potential for a profound meeting in relationship within psy-chotherapy and the subsequent beneficial transformation of both client and therapist alike.

Perhaps Jung, above all other psychotherapists, challenges Buber's intransi-gent stance with his teleological or purposive, as opposed to reductive, orienta-tion towards psychological disturbance. Buber additionally failed to recognise Jung's belief in a mutually transformative experience through dialectical inter-action between two individual psyches (Jung, 1935).

For Buber, true relation is being able to see the whole, but it is possible to see the whole without being able to say 'Thou' through a retreat from open dialogue with the other into 'solicitude'. Buber argued resolutely against Heidegger's stance on solicitude, which he regarded as 'monological' (as opposed to dia-logical), where the subject is closed off to the other, and regarded Heidegger's notion of existence as something only completed in self being or in 'self as a closed system' (Morgan-Williams, 1995: 81). Buber regarded relation in its essence as only emerging through an open and direct being with others:

In *mere* solicitude man remains essentially himself, even if he is moved with extreme pity; in action and help he inclines towards the other, but the barriers of his own being are not thereby breached; he makes his assistance, not his self, accessible to the other. (Buber, 2002: 201)

Buber and Psychoanalysis

Whilst it would be quite misleading to suggest that both writers are in their own fashion saying the very same thing, those familiar with the work of psychotherapist Donald Winnicott (1957: 88) and his celebrated adage that there is no such thing as a baby will possibly be reminded of Buber's 'In the beginning is relation as a category of being, readiness, grasping form, it is the *a priori* of relation, the inborn Thou, inborn because in the womb the child is enfolded in natural relation, the bonds of which are broken at birth' (Vermes, 1988: 47). We cannot readily translate these remarks of Buber's into the rather more literal sense in which Winnicott, especially among object relations theorists, regards the mother/baby dyad, but they nevertheless carry a considerable poignant resonance. In reflecting upon Buber's 'the bonds of which are broken at birth' we are reminded of his mother's early abandonment of him. For Buber, whoever enters into personal therapy, which is itself of course a seeking out of relationship with a particular other, is most likely to be the individual of 'a stunted personal centre', who has striven till then unsuccessfully to secure themselves in personhood.

Buber maintained his unshakeable antipathy towards psychotherapy because of what he regarded as its essential reductionism and with that its primary concentration on the individual, in this case the client, as opposed to the relationship between therapist and client. By doing so, he ignored the profound psychological engagement which underpins therapeutic endeavour. However the psychotherapist may very well, in defending against Buber's indictment, draw attention to Buber's early childhood experience of maternal abandonment as a pivotal determinant in the positioning of relationship at the very heart of his philosophy. The psychotherapist may at the same time view Buber's accusation of therapy as psychological reductionism as his defence against an interpretation which may have undermined his essential idea, the fulcrum of all of his mature work.

This experience of early maternal abandonment was one from which Buber almost certainly never fully recovered. Such cruel destruction of the young child's sense of internal security and trust in the external world would most probably have contributed to his conviction that the I-Thou relationship could only be sustained for a very limited period of time before sliding back into an I-It, only to be reconstituted in what would become at best an ever-oscillating process. We are reminded here of Melanie Klein's similar notion of the paranoid-schizoid and depressive position in 'Some Theoretical Conclusions Regarding the Emotional Life of the Infant' (Klein, 1952). Kaufman describes it in the following way:

> It is not true that a genuine relationship to another human being can be achieved only in brief encounters from which we must always relapse into states in which the other human being becomes for us merely an object of experience and use.

He goes on,

> If one takes this dichotomy seriously and identifies with the person who championed it instead of treating it scholastically one realizes that it reveals a deep malaise in the writer. In Buber's case it seems safe to surmise that he was permanently damaged by his mother's abandonment of him. (Kaufman, 1992: 257)

Whatever we may think of Kaufman's explanation for Buber's belief in the transience of the I-Thou encounter, and no doubt Buber himself would be the first to cite it as the perfect example of the psychological reductionism against which he railed, Kaufman does introduce the idea of a 'genuine relationship' which does open out the enquiry somewhat beyond the parameters as defined by Buber.

The Between

No exposition of Buber's mature philosophy, however rudimentary, can fail to consider his idea of the Between which might be perceived as its very pulsing heart.

Not only does the Between seem to ensure absolute centrality in his conception of relationship but also can be understood as its supreme realisation to which we all ultimately aspire. It is, claimed Buber, the place where spirit is both found and lived. The Between is that place established by two persons who move towards each other from out of their own separateness, their own I, in a readiness to embrace the other as the Thou. In doing so each I undergoes a transformation and is only fully realised knowingly in the place of the Between which, as a consequence of this meeting of two separate beings, is itself something other than either of them *and something both other and greater* than the mere sum of their interaction. Here again Buber evokes thoughts of Winnicott (Winnicott, 1953; Davies and Wallbridge, 1981), in this instance his notion of transitional space, transitional objects and transitional phenomena. We might also consider Jung's idea of mutual transformation taking place within an analytical space or interactional field.

Buber, by the time he had come to write *I and Thou*, had moved away from his earlier mystical inspired notion of the individual self becoming totally dissolved in the other. Whilst retaining the belief in the existence of the individual I in the place of the Between, he argued that in fact it was neither objective nor subjective and something greater than its constituent parts. It was also necessary for Buber to reject the idea of psychologism, (that is the belief that psychology is the foundational explanation of all human experience), in his understanding of relation. Instead he favours an ontological explanation in which each individual reaches out towards the being of the other and in which neither is appropriated by the other.

An impressively succinct summary of the Between is given by Wood:

> The Between is the presence, the immediate bridging and encompassing subject and object. Though the Between comes only through man it is that which grounds man to man. The Between is identified as spirit and spirit in turn is identified as man's relation to that which transcends the world. (Wood, 1969: 112)

A further and original illumination of the significance of Buber's the Between is given by Geering:

> He was concerned with human understanding. Whereas the traditional theologian believes the answer to the question 'What is man?' has to be revealed by God, and the humanist believes the answer is to be found in man himself, Buber contended that the answer is to be found in the realm of the between, in the relation of person with person. (Geering, 1983: 21)

It is perhaps this capacity of Buber's to transcend the established categories of both theology and psychology in his attention to being in relation which renders him so important a thinker to all interpersonal therapies. Whilst he has been most readily embraced by the existential schools as one of their primary intellectual inspirations, the import of his essential philosophy for all psychological schools of therapy cannot and should not be ignored. It is perhaps Buber's concern with dialogue that signifies his presence within all therapeutic contexts in which therapist and client will turn, the one to the other, in a movement of address and response.

Dialogue

The late Jungian psychotherapist and group therapist Louis Zinkin (1996: 343–354) acknowledged the importance of dialogue to Buber's idea of the I-Thou relationship and how such a notion brought him together with such otherwise diverse thinkers as Carl Jung, who believed in dialogue between the individual's conscious and unconscious mind, and the Russian literary theorist

Mikhail Bakhtin in his conception of the relationship between the individual and society. The following quote from Bakhtin highlights its relevance to both Buber and all relationally centred therapies:

> Truth is not born nor is it to be found inside the head of an individual person, it is born between people collectively searching for truth in the process of their dialogic interaction. (Bakhtin, 1984: 110)

By the time he had come to write *Between Man and Man* in 1947 Buber had come to distinguish two fundamental attitudes or movements of the individual towards the other. The first of these he named 'reflexion' in which the subject turns away from the other back towards himself into a life of monologue or self-engagement. The second is that of the turning towards the other and in doing so opening himself up to a meeting with the other into the life of dialogue and thereby evolving as a person as distinct from an individual.

As Goldenburg and Isaacson (1996: 124–125) inform us, Buber moved increasingly away from the idea of relation to that of dialogue in what they term his 'root metaphor'. Dialogue for Buber was based on an interaction of address and response where address is to be open to the voice or call of the other and, in knowing that one is being addressed, a readiness to respond. Such response may take many forms but it is always an assumption of responsibility to that which calls. Dialogue, we should not forget, was for Buber not just about man's relation with his fellow man but with the entire world, that of nature and of the spiritual.

> It by no means needs to be a man of whom I become aware. It can be an animal, a plant, a stone…Nothing can refuse to be the vessel for the Word. The limits of the possibility of dialogue are the limits of awareness. (Buber, 202: 12)

The Application of I-Thou

Having provided a broad overview of Buber's concept of the I-Thou relation, I want now to consider its possible application to the therapeutic encounter between therapist and client with particular emphasis on those clinical practices that adopt a psychotherapeutic approach.

The question being posed is to what extent it might be possible to establish an I-Thou relation in the consulting room. The answer I anticipate will appear far from conclusive. The direct and faithful application of a highly abstract conception of human relationship, of teasing complexity and ambiguity, to the concrete reality of the consulting room can ultimately be no more than a speculative leap, as opposed to anything approaching a testable hypothesis.

It is important to recall that Buber himself *did not believe* that the I-Thou relation could be sustained for more than a very brief period which led him to refer to such a state of affairs as 'the sublime melancholy of our lot' (Buber, 1970: 68). As Kaufman puts it, 'when we experience, observe or think about another human being this is proof of the melancholy lapse from I-Thou into I-It for the other has then become a mere object for us' (Kaufman, 1992: 262).

This very transient nature of the I-Thou relation as Buber himself conceived it renders it not merely melancholic in nature but even tragic as it would seem to be our inescapable state of being as conscious subjects. It is perhaps nothing other than that elusive or at best fleeting condition of being that is sought by all but achieved by few. As the poet T. S. Eliot memorably put it, 'humankind cannot bear very much reality' (Eliot, 1963: 180).

It may however be the case that not all readers will agree with Buber's pessimistic contention that the I-Thou relation can only be sustained for the briefest of periods. As noted earlier, Kaufman suggested that Buber's early abandonment by his mother destroyed for ever his capacity to believe in anything more enduring. It may be, however, that any belief in a more sustainable I-Thou connection can really be no more in itself than a matter of faith, something in which we would like to believe as a possible ideal vision of human intercourse at the extreme point of intersubjectivity.

Certainly by implication in Buber's uncompromising dismissal of what he regarded as reductive psychologism, and with it the entire psychotherapeutic perspective of both theory and practice, he was also rejecting any notion of the unconscious. Given what psychological theory has to say about such unconscious processes of projection and introjection in our experiences with others, it becomes very difficult to consider Buber's I-Thou as much more than an idealised abstraction. For Buber, whatever the personal determinants, there emerged a need, it could be argued, to at least consider the possibility of an exalted state of intersubjective being, that is the state of I-Thou, however short lived, which evolved into philosophic expression in his mature writings. It is tempting to enquire as to how many of us, including Buber himself, can, with anything approaching certainty, claim to have experienced the I-Thou state of relation with another as he himself defined it.

How then might a practising psychotherapist of whatever school approach Buber's I-Thou relational aspiration? Founded on the Kantian (1785) principle of regarding the other as an end rather than a means, it would surely constitute a fundamental tenet of probably all psychotherapeutic practice, however they might be defined. As I suggest below, the significance, if not the absolute centrality, of the relationship between therapist and client, is now little short of universal in all psychotherapies. The quality of relationship based on the openness, compassion, concern, respect and responsibility of the psychotherapist is seen generally as a prerequisite if genuine healing of the client is to occur. I want therefore to propose two, albeit rather crude, variations on Buber's I-Thou which could conceivably be taking place in the consulting room.

The first of these, which is much closer in essence to Buber's notion, I will call the 'spectrum' view which is more likely to work for therapists of all theoretical colours. In this case we might imagine the psychotherapist, during the course of one session or cluster of sessions, moving continuously along a spectrum of interaction with their client. At the one end they may enter, however fleetingly, into an I-Thou state whilst at the further pole their engagement will be detached and objective as they consciously struggle to make sense of their client's 'clinical material'. In reality, it will be most likely that the psychotherapist is constantly moving from one point on the spectrum to another. Sometimes the shifts will be slow, gradual and imperceptible while at other times something will happen in the room that will pitch the psychotherapist into a markedly different place. This kind of fluid movement is perhaps what most psychotherapists would most readily recognise even in the absence of the I-Thou concept.

Even if Buber was mistaken about the capacity of the I-Thou state to survive beyond a brief period, it would seem that given the purposive intent of the client's initial engagement with the therapist, that is to make some change to their life, and Buber himself identified the true task of therapy as 'healing through meeting in and of the Between'; the I-Thou moment however fleeting will nevertheless constitute a significant occurrence in the therapeutic process for therapist and client.

The second of these variations I term 'the both and', which would seem to be more applicable to the experience of the psychotherapist. In this case we can talk of an I-Thou context or relational environment, something redolent of the Greek *temenos* or temple sanctum, created by *the very act of coming together in encounter* of client and therapist, that is, the one who calls and the one who is called. Where such meeting occurs between caller and called then an I-Thou relation is immediately brought about at the deepest levels of intersubjectivity and remains unbroken for the duration of the therapy. Once again it is Jung who offers the best example of this when he talks of a psychological container created together by therapist and client and the importance of the encounter between the two (Jung, 1929: para163).

What has been suggested then is that by considering these two 'variations' it is possible to imagine that despite Buber's emphatic dismissal of psychotherapy, within all therapeutic contexts irrespective of clinical orientation, the I-Thou relation can be achieved, however fleetingly. It is after all almost certainly the case that all therapists, at least those who choose to work with an open-ended or long-term approach with clients, are themselves impelled to a greater or lesser degree by a reaching out for relationship. As a 'wounded healer', the therapist, however unconsciously, is seeking some of their own healing through their meeting with the wounded other. The place where, according to Buber, such healing occurs is named the Between. Even if we disregard the two approaches outlined above, in accommodating the possibility of the I-Thou within any therapeutic relation, Buber's own uncompromising attitude towards all psychotherapy seems overly harsh. There is much to suggest that his perception of them is based on either a superficial familiarity or misunderstanding. There are a number of elements of the I-Thou to be found in both the theory and practice of all psychotherapy.

Somewhat paradoxically, and underlying Buber's objections to such therapies, is that he seems to have overlooked the living, palpable reality of the therapist/client encounter and the ensuing relationship between them which ineluctably unfolds. It is as if he embraced the cartoonist's image of the 'blank screen' therapist sitting impassively at the head of the couch furiously scribbling in their notebook. It is therefore hardly surprising that he was so dismissive of the possibility of the psychotherapist ever being able to move beyond the I-It position with their clients.

One final thought on the application and relevance of the I-It and I-Thou concepts to psychotherapeutic practice. It would appear, beyond dispute, that it is considered to be both vital and necessary that empathy, the human capacity to both understand and to imaginatively enter into the feelings of another in this case the client, is an integral feature of the therapist's makeup. This being the case then it must be assumed that he or she is already predisposed towards engaging with the other as a Thou, as this is implicit in the very definition of the word. The major obstacle therefore to the therapist and client effectively establishing an I-Thou relationship would appear to be the client's resistance to opening themselves up to the offering of the therapist, a consequence of which could well be that not only does the client reduce themselves to an It but they also render the therapist likewise. In order to become a Thou the client must be open to receiving the empathic gift that the therapist is offering.[1]

Buber and Jung

Whilst Freud himself, at least in his early clinical practice, came some way to embodying Buber's crude misconception, it was not long before others among his peers were understanding the therapeutic encounter somewhat differently, none more so than Freud's one time 'heir apparent', Carl Jung.

Despite Jung's unshakeable belief in the reality of the human psyche with its collective as well as individual unconscious content, concepts which had no place in Buber's thought, he, like Buber, believed that the therapeutic relation must be of a dialectical nature if healing is to occur in the client (Jung, 1981). Buber himself was first and foremost a philosopher and theologian, primarily interested in the nature of human existence as a dialogic relationship between two individual subjects. Jung on the other hand was a psychologist with a profound interest in religion, whose richly expansive understanding of the human psyche grew out of his lifelong practice as a psychotherapist. Jung believed that a real relationship was necessary to bring about genuine therapeutic change.

Unlike Freud and most of his Viennese followers, Jung talked in terms of healing rather than cure (Chapter 2) and with it the wholeness of personality:

> Psychotherapy is at bottom a dialectical relationship between doctor and
> patient. It is an encounter, a discussion between two psychic wholes in which
> knowledge is used only as a tool. The goal is transformation – not the one
> that is predetermined but rather an indeterminable change. (Jung, 1986: 89)

It is also interesting to note that for Jung, as well as for Buber, the ideas of both
'healing' and 'wholeness' figure very prominently in their writings. It is perhaps
of no little significance that both these thinkers, however dissimilar their ultimate vision of the human subject, could be described as holding a deeply religious attitude towards the world, however unconventional and independent.
Such an attitude may very well account for some very similar if only limited
elements within the totality of their thinking.

I-Thou: A conclusion

The greatness of Buber's I-Thou notion is that encapsulated within these two
monosyllabic interconnected pronouns rests a totalising, that is an all including
vision of human relation, of the meeting together of two independent subjects
through an intersubjectivity. This I-Thou notion need not however merely be
applied to the encounter between one individual and another, but to the individual in relation to a collective other and also to the relation between collectives
themselves. That is to say it has far reaching social and political implications.

For example, the issues posed by the hostility towards immigrants and asy-
lum seekers, especially those perceived as embodying excessive 'otherness'
would lead, in Buber's terms, to them to being viewed as I-It. Predicated on
the Kantian principle of the right to universal hospitality (Derrida, 1997: 11),
the capacity of the host nation or community to move from an I-It to an I-Thou
position in their attitude to the stranger would facilitate a transition from hostility and rejection to the generosity of sharing and acceptance of those who call
by those who are called. This would require an opening up of the self to a new
kind of encounter of giving and receiving. In Buberian terms the shift from the
Other as 'It' to being addressed as a 'Thou', is redolent, though not synony-
mous with, Klein's movement from the paranoid-schizoid to the depressive
position (Klein, 1988).

At the point of considering these two Buberian concepts on the levels of the
social and the political I introduce a most interesting and highly pertinent third
term from the academic psychologist Philip Zimbardo, that of the It-It. In discussing the subject of dehumanisation, he writes:

To use Martin Buber's terms, humanised relationships are "I-Thou" while dehumanised relationships are "I-It". Over time, the dehumanizing agent is often sucked into the negativity of the experience and then the "I" itself changes, to produce an "It-It" relationship between objects, or between agency and victim. The misperception of certain others as subhuman, bad humans, inhuman, infra human, dispensable, or "animals" is facilitated by means of labels, stereotypes, slogans and propaganda images. (Zimbardo, 2007: 223)

Human history right up to recent times has been repeatedly scarred by examples of this compelling but equally disturbing 'third term'.

Martin Buber's *I-Thou* carries a clarion reminder to each one of us of the possibility, and with it the responsibility, of true and profound relationship with the other. As Walter Kaufman impressively claimed for Buber's *magnum opus*:

The book will survive the death of theology for it appeals to that religiousness which finds no home in organised religion and it speaks to those whose primary concern is not at all with religion but rather social change. (Geering, quoting Kaufman, 1983: 9)

Both at the level of the individual and of the collective Buber's notion of I-Thou remains indispensable to our awareness of the potential for real relationship out of open dialogue both in the consulting room and in the world at large: the personal and the other.

Note

1. For an exploration of the theme of Generosity, see Chapter 5.

References

Bakhtin, M. (1984) *Problems of Dostoevsky's Poetic*. Translated by Emerson, C. (ed.). (New York: Collier Books Macmillan).

Buber, M. (1901) 'Ueber Jakob Boehme', *Wiener Rundschau*, 12, (June), 251–253.

Buber, M. (1913) *Daniel: Dialogues on Realization*. (Leipzig: Insel).

Buber, M. (2002) *Between Man and Man*. Smith, R.G. (trans.). Introduction by Friedman, M. (London and New York: Routledge).

Buber, M. (2004) *I and Thou*. Smith, R.G. (trans.). Postscript by the author. (London and New York: Continuum).

Davies, M. and Wallbridge, D. (1981) *Boundary and Space. An Introduction to the Works of D.W. Winnicott*. (London: Karnac).

Derrida, J. (1997) *On Cosmopolitanism and Forgiveness*. (London and New York: Routledge). 2001.

Eliot, T. S. (1963) *Collected Poems 1909–1962*. (London: Faber & Faber).

Geering, L. (1983) *The World of Relation. An Introduction to Martin Buber's I and Thou*. (Wellington: Victoria University Press).

Goldenburg, H. and Isaacson, Z. (1996) 'Between persons: the narrow ridge where I and Thou meet', *Journal of the Society for Existential Analysis*, 7, (2), 118–130.

Jung, C.G. (1929) 'Problems of Modern Psychotherapy' in *The Practice of Psychotherapy*, *CW16*. (London and Henley: Routledge and Kegan Paul). 1981.

Jung, C. G. (1935) 'Principles of Practical Psychotherapy' in *The Practice of Psychotherapy*, *CW16*. (London and Henley: Routledge and Kegan Paul). 1981.

Jung, C. G. (1981) *The Practice of Psychotherapy*, *CW16*. (London and Henley: Routledge and Kegan Paul).

Jung, C. G. (1986) *Psychological Reflections*. (London: Ark Paperbacks).

Kant, I. (1785) *Groundwork of the Metaphysic of Morals*. Paton, H. J. (trans.). (New York: Harper & Row). 1964.

Kant, I. (1972). *Perpetual Peace: A Philosophical Essay*. Campbell Smith, M. (trans.). (New York and London: Garland Publishing).

Kaufman, W. (1992) *Discovering the Mind*. (New Brunswick: Transaction).

Klein, M. (1952) 'Some Theoretical Conclusions Regarding the Emotional Life of the Infant' in *Envy and Gratitude and Other Works*. (London: Vintage). 1997.

Klein, M. (1988) *Love, Guilt and Reparation and other works 1921–1945*. (London: Virago Press).

Morgan-Williams, S. (1995) 'All real living is meeting', *Journal of the Society for Existential Analysis*, 6, (2).76–96.

Vermes, P. (1988) *Buber*. (London: Peter Halban).

Winnicott, D. W. (1953) 'Transitional Objects and Transitional Phenomena' in *Playing and Reality*. (Harmondsworth Middx., and New York: Penguin Books). 1980.

Winnicott, D. W. (1957) 'Further Thoughts on Babies as Persons' in *The Child, the Family and the Outside World*. (Harmondsworth Middx., and New York: Penguin Books). 1976.

Wood, R. E. (1969) *Martin Buber's Ontology*. (Evanston: NorthWestern University Press).

Zimbardo, P. (2007) *The Lucifer Effect: How Good People Turn Evil*. (London: Rider/Ebury Press).

Zinkin, L. (1996) 'A dialogic model for group analysis: Jung and Bakhtin', *Group Analysis*, 29, 343–54.

Part II

The Personal and Interpersonal

In Part II, the chapters concentrate on aspects of being that clients and therapists bring to the consulting room. The themes revolve around the personal and the interpersonal in the therapeutic relationship including the inner world issues that both client and therapist grapple with and which impact on our sense of our own being and can inhibit or affect our relationship to ourselves and to others.

The chapters all reflect aspects of our being and being with others. Stephen Crawford, in Chapter 5, examines Generosity, Christine Driver writes about Love, John Rignell explores Shame and Gabrielle Brown considers Loneliness. The final chapter in this section, by Lynsey Hotchkies and Neil Hudson, invites the reader to reflect on the issue of mortality and the importance of this in relation to therapeutic work and our sense of being and not being.

The chapters, in their explorations, open out these issues, provide insight on the themes and raise important questions for us to consider in relation to our therapeutic work and also in our relationships with ourselves and others.

Part II

The Personal and Interpersonal

5

Generosity

Stephen Crawford

Introduction

In her paper 'On the Necessity for the Analyst to be Natural with his Patient', Paula Heimann describes how a supervisee of hers, a psychiatrist undertaking a psychoanalytic training, reported a session with his patient, in which the patient had arrived 'wet all over and blue from cold'. Heimann says that her supervisee worked with the patient's material, made correct interpretations, but 'did not feel comfortable with his actions'. Heimann writes:

> So I asked him what he felt when he saw the patient completely wet and blue in the lips. Didn't he think of offering the patient something hot to drink? The student immediately confirmed that this had in fact been his first impulse. And he would have done so with a patient in his psychiatric practice, but while in psychoanalytic training he thought he was only permitted to give the patient interpretations. (Heimann, 1978: 313)

It seems clear that on this occasion, Heimann would not have condemned her supervisee if he had offered his patient a hot drink, but I can imagine psycho-therapists having a lively discussion about this. What should the supervisee have done? He seems to have felt bad for not giving a drink, although he does not, from what we are told, think about his feeling as perhaps having a meaning in the countertransference. To offer the hot drink might be seen by some as infantilising, or possibly seductive, or as demonstrating a fear of the patient's potential aggression if no gesture is made towards his cold and wet state. One can wonder about why the patient was not better prepared to meet the by no means unusual weather conditions. This is undoubtedly his responsibility. On the other hand, for some, including Heimann perhaps, not offering a hot drink might be seen as an exaggeratedly cold interpretation of analytic distance and neutrality.

It is not my intention now to try and formulate a 'correct' response to this situation, but more to use this example to begin opening up some of the themes that I am interested in exploring. Heimann says in her paper: 'It is true that many analysts do in fact insist that an analyst can only offer interpretations' (Heimann, 1978: 313–314). In most situations, this is likely to be true, but I think it may be illuminating to consider the language we often use as psychotherapists when talking about our work: for example, we *offer* interpretations, we *provide* a setting for the psychotherapeutic work, we *make ourselves available* to work with our patients and to be on the *receiving* end of their projections, and we attempt to process these projections before *offering*, or *giving*, something back to the patient in our comments and interpretations.

This brief examination of the kinds of thing that psychotherapists say about what they do in sessions shows that they do see psychotherapy as involving exchange, giving and receiving, as well as taking and using, or making use of, and of course, sometimes refusing. Following on from this, I am arguing that it is important to think about this aspect of psychotherapy, that is, its connection with giving and receiving, in relation to ideas about generosity, or indeed its lack. This connection refers to the availability of the therapist to receive from the patient and give something back, to be attuned to and thoughtful about what the patient has to say, to be mindful of the patient and what he or she brings into the therapy, and mindful as well of the therapist's own feelings, reactions and responses. This is my main point in this chapter: that to be a psychotherapist requires what I shall call a capacity for generosity and this involves what we offer and give, what we receive and how we do this.

Other analytic writers have also been making this idea explicit, rather than implicit. For example, two books published in 2004 that explore difficulties of feeding and eating in children and adolescents had the subtitle, *The Generosity of Acceptance*. In the introduction to these books, the editors write that the title

> applies primarily to the struggle of some patients to accept from another, but it also refers to the need of clinicians to accept generously the sometimes violent projections of their patients. The gift of help often involves a risk of rejection, and the chapters in these two volumes vividly describe the courage and generosity it takes to persevere with patients suffering from severe eating disorders. (Williams et al., 2004: xiv)

The idea of accepting projections highlights something important for my theme, namely the efforts therapists make to try and understand their experience in the consulting room, to allow it time and space in their minds. This is an aspect of the therapist's availability and attention which requires effort and commitment to sustain. I would imagine that most of us are familiar with moments in sessions when we feel under attack from a patient, and yet it would be unrealistic of us not to expect that patients will sometimes subject us to uncomfortable and painful experiences and perhaps we can only hope that they will come to recognise this in time, as Winnicott suggested in 'Hate in the Countertransference':

> The analyst must be prepared to bear strain without expecting the patient to know anything about what he is doing, perhaps over a long period of time. To do this he must be easily aware of his own fear and hate. He is in the position of the mother of the infant unborn or newly born. Eventually, he ought to be able to tell his patient what he has been through on the patient's behalf, but an analysis may never get as far as this. (Winnicott, 1947: 198)

The Therapeutic Relationship

Freud established an enduring framework for psychoanalytic work, and his ideas about the therapist's neutrality and the importance of the treatment being 'carried out in abstinence' (Freud, 1915: 165) are still relevant today. But he also understood that analytic work involves an openness to exchange, and this is shown by his statement that the analyst 'must turn his own unconscious like a receptive organ towards the transmitting unconscious of the patient' (Freud, 1912: 115). His concerns about this function of the analyst lay in what he saw as the danger that the analyst's own complexes and resistances would obstruct and distort the reception of the patient's material, unless the analyst had themselves been psychoanalysed. In contemporary understandings of the psychoanalytic process, this is where the therapist's attention to countertransference comes in.

As psychoanalysis has developed over the last century, patients have been identified whose difficulties are thought not to be primarily to do with conflict and repression, and who are therefore less likely to be helped by the ordinary analytic work of making the unconscious conscious through interpretative work. Instead their pathology is linked to difficulties in their very early development, and for them, it is widely believed that 'non-interpretive and relationship factors are more important' in their treatment (Baker, 1993: 1224).

This distinction is reflected in the greater attention now paid to the relationship between therapist and patient, including the transference and countertransference dynamics, and it is this attention to the therapeutic relationship that has opened the way for thinking about the qualities a therapist needs in order to be able to do this work, including as I am arguing a capacity for generosity. While Freud was able to suggest that an analyst should model him or herself on 'the surgeon, who puts aside all his feelings, even his human sympathy' (Freud, 1912: 115), it seems to me that this is no longer seen as what is desirable for most psychoanalytic practitioners who attempt to be in touch with and make use of their countertransference.

Freud described psychoanalysis as an 'impossible' profession (Freud, 1937: 248), and it is true that the demands on psychotherapists can be high throughout their professional lives. Trainings are arduous, lengthy and expensive; private practice can be isolating and insecure, and the work itself can be draining.

In this context, it is important for practitioners to reflect on the difficulties of sustaining a psychotherapy practice over time. In simple terms, there does need to be a degree of balance between what one gives out, and what one gets back, and one needs to think about the emotional cost involved in maintaining the kind of availability and openness to experience that I am seeing as part of the generosity of the therapist, with each new patient over time. The therapeutic task is often associated with parenting, particularly in the object relations approach, but one big difference is that for most parents, their children do grow up and leave home, even if there will be a continuing relationship. For the therapist, patients who leave are replaced and the process is constantly being repeated, until retirement. And yet, each patient is different, and when therapeutic work goes well, there are rewards as John Klauber expressed very clearly when he wrote about the relationship in psychoanalysis:

> The most neglected feature of the psychoanalytic relationship still seems to me to be that it is a relationship. ... Patient and analyst need one another. The patient comes to the analyst because of internal conflicts that prevent him from enjoying life, and he begins to use the analyst not only to resolve them, but increasingly as a receptacle for his pent up feelings. But the analyst also needs the patient in order to crystallise and communicate his own thoughts, including some of his inmost thoughts on intimate human problems which can only grow organically in the context of this relationship. ... It is from this mutual participation in analytic understanding that the patient derives the substantial part of his cure and the analyst his deepest confidence and satisfaction. (Klauber, 1976: 200–201)

In writing about generosity, I am venturing into issues of ethics in relation to practice, and there is always a danger of being seen as moralising if one does so. However, I cannot imagine that anyone would now want to dispute that there is an ethical dimension to psychotherapy, that the working relationship between people that it involves takes place subject to ethical requirements and responsibilities, and that any practitioner would ignore this at their peril. In a broader philosophical context, I am concerned with questions of our 'being with others' and with the quality of human relationships (Macquarrie, 1973).

What Is Generosity?

I think it is easier to define meanness, one of the opposites of generosity, than generosity itself. Dickens, in *A Christmas Carol*, created Scrooge as an epitome of miserliness, and describes him as follows:

O! but he was a tight-fisted hand at the grindstone. Scrooge! A squeezing, wrenching, grasping, scraping, clutching, covetous, old sinner! Hard and sharp as flint, from which no steel had ever struck out generous fire; secret and self-contained, and solitary as an oyster. (Dickens, 1994: 8)

In psychoanalytic terms, this is a vivid portrait of a form of narcissism.

The novel tells the story of Scrooge's transformation, a transformation that is fuelled by the visits of four ghosts: his former business partner Marley, then those of Christmas Past, Present and Future. Death is a powerful presence throughout and Scrooge is shown the sadness and emptiness of his own life, together with an appalling vision of his own possible death, alone and unloved. Everything he is shown has a cumulative effect so that his cold heart melts, and he emerges from the prison of his narcissism, beginning to think about others, enjoying their company and accepting responsibilities towards them too.

Scrooge is in effect given a powerful warning, and in Dickens' narrative the warning is effective. Scrooge is transformed, not simply someone doing the right thing, or going through the motions, in order to save themselves. Generosity is not simply a matter of giving. How one gives matters too. It is perfectly possible to give for selfish reasons, or with a manipulative intent, seeking something in return, and in such cases I think the generosity is diminished.

In fact, once one starts to look at questions of motivation, it is not difficult to find oneself faced with a question of whether true generosity exists at all, and this question does seem to have been on the minds of contemporary Darwinists. For them, as Matt Ridley puts it in his book *The Origins of Virtue*, the 'thing that needs explaining about human beings is not their frequent vice, but their occasional virtue' (Ridley, 1996: 38). But as Ridley recognises, this is a reformulation of an old debate amongst philosophers, over whether 'man is basically nice if he is not corrupted, or basically nasty if he is not tamed' (Ridley, 1996: 251), and this debate intersects and overlaps with questions of nature versus nurture. If we think about Freud, he certainly saw instincts as in need of taming and thought that this happens through a combination of internal and external forces but also recognised that they could be tamed too far (Freud, 1923).

While Klein's account of infantile sadism might seem to give support to the idea of human badness, her picture of development also includes the depressive position, which undoubtedly involves recognition of the other and the desire to behave well towards them (Klein 1935). On the other hand, Winnicott's picture of the infant and his or her good enough mother could be taken as supporting the view of human goodness, but to say this would be to lose sight of his great interest in the existence of aggression, and his efforts to account for this without recourse to an idea of a death instinct (Winnicott, 1985; 1990). In psychoanalysis, human life is seen as inevitably involving both goodness and badness, although different theories try and account for this in different ways, and being good is generally thought of as a developmental achievement involving self-awareness and awareness of others, but I shall return to this idea later.

Some years ago now, I had an experience while driving in London which highlighted some of the complexities around generosity, both in relation to questions of motivation and also with regard to the experience of the recipient. I was stopped at a red traffic light at a major junction. A young man approached my car carrying a window cleaning tool in his hand. I indicated that I did not want my windscreen cleaned, but he ignored me and began soaping the window and then cleaning the water off. I was feeling cross, intruded upon and imagining being pestered for payment. At the same time, I felt anxious that he might not finish the job, or in some way damage my car. However, I began to notice that, in fact, he was doing a good job, lifting the windscreen wipers carefully to clean under them too and cleaning the whole windscreen quickly and efficiently. I was then surprised by the fact that he simply walked away when finished without asking for payment. The lights changed and I drove off, feeling angry still, but also confused and guilty. There had been no pressure from the man and he had cleaned my windscreen well. I felt I had been given a gift that I hadn't wanted or asked for, and yet which was nonetheless useful. In my guilty feeling, I was unable to accept what in the end felt like his generosity, although it was certainly possible that he knew it was a way of leaving me feeling bad, and perhaps him feeling good.

Generosity in Relation to Virtue and Love

To help explore the notion of generosity further, I have turned to philosophical discussions of virtue. Aristotle wrote of two virtues that seem relevant to generosity. One is usually translated as liberality, relating to issues of getting and spending, the other is magnanimity, relating to issues of behaviour, honour and dishonour. The French philosopher André Comte-Sponville in his book *A Short Treatise on the Great Virtues*, suggests that generosity 'lies at the crossroads' of these two, saying

> ...the magnanimous person is neither vain nor low, the liberal person is neither miserly nor prodigal, and a person combining both qualities is always generous. (Comte-Sponville, 2003: 93)

It is part of Aristotle's account that he considers virtue to be an average 'between two kinds of vice, one of excess and the other of deficiency' (Aristotle, 1976: 101–102). So, generosity can be taken to excess or be deficient, too great or too little, and from here it is possible to see how one could construct a pathology of generosity which I shall attempt later.

In his exploration of virtues and of generosity in particular, one of the questions that interests Comte-Sponville is how to distinguish between generosity and love. He notes that love invariably involves giving while generosity doesn't necessarily involve love. He writes:

> One might prefer, of course, for love to suffice. But if it could, would we need to be generous? Love is not in our power and never can be. Who chooses to love? What power does the will have over a feeling? Love doesn't come on command, it can't be ordered up. Generosity is different: if we want to be generous, we can be. Love doesn't depend on us, that is its great mystery and why it lies outside the realm of virtue. ... Generosity does depend on us, however, which is why it is a virtue and distinct from love even in the act of giving, in which it so resembles love. (Comte-Sponville, 2003: 96)

My view here is slightly different, in that I think generosity is not only a matter of will but also a capacity that is achieved when development goes reasonably well. On the other hand, many of us would recognise Comte-Sponville's description of love as not being in our power, but perhaps there is also a kind of loving that is related to development and can be worked at. This is something that Nina Coltart wrote about in her paper 'What does it mean: "love is not enough"?' She suggests that psychoanalytic work can be thought about as involving 'the practice of the capacity to love' (Coltart, 1993: 126) and envisages love as a capacity that can be exercised and developed through effort and attention. She writes:

> I think that good psychoanalytic work is fed at its roots by the capacity to love...love may well be the matrix of a piece of work...I mean that it is the only trustworthy container in which we may have to feel hatred, rage or contempt for varying periods of time (Coltart, 1993: 121).

To my mind, Coltart's idea of 'the practice of the capacity to love' could be usefully reformulated in terms of the capacity for generosity, since I think that love is not always the right word to describe my feeling and attitude in my ordinary work as a psychotherapist. My feelings for a patient may sometimes include loving feelings; but in terms of my day-to-day work with my whole caseload, it does seem to me to be more accurate to speak in terms of a generosity that involves my willingness to be there and my attempt to be open, available and involved in the psychotherapeutic work.

I think this formulation of the place of generosity has some similarity to what the Jungian analyst Kenneth Lambert wrote about as the agapaic attitude of the analyst, where agape is a kind of non-erotic love, sometimes translated as 'charity' (Lambert, 1981). Perhaps generosity as a term has the advantage of being more neutral and down to earth. A capacity for generosity is not to do with being worthy, or saintly. Rather, as Winnicott said, we need to know about our hate, fear, anger and resentment, if we are to be able to contain these feelings and still be able to help our patients when in the grip of them, rather than act them out (Winnicott, 1947). Richard Kradin seems to be taking a similar view of generosity to mine, when he writes that 'the question analysts must ask themselves is not whether we "love" our patients, but whether we have the capacity to be generous towards them' (Kradin, 1999: 232); while for Neville Symington, love 'is so easily misunderstood' that he prefers 'to break it up into component parts and talk of generosity, gratitude and forgiveness' (Symington, 2008: 489). Phillips and Taylor identify generosity as an aspect of kindness and argue that both generosity and kindness involve a 'sympathetic expansiveness linking self to other' (Phillips and Taylor, 2010: 4).

Generosity in Relation to Some Psychoanalytic Theories of Development

While I have not found a discussion in Freud of generosity, one place where his theories relate to this theme is in his discussion of sexuality. Freud described bodily based erotogenic zones as part of his account of infantile sexuality and of sexual development (Freud, 1905). These were the oral, anal and genital zones. In terms of bodily function, it is clear that consideration of the oral and anal zones includes questions of what is taken into the body, and what is put out of it. Freud also described the anal character, which he saw as marked by a trio of personal qualities, namely, the tendency to be orderly, parsimonious and obstinate (Freud, 1908). This description in its extreme fits the character of Dickens' Scrooge as given above, prior to his transformation, and is undoubtedly of value in understanding difficulties in giving, or giving up.

With the development of object relations theory, a much greater emphasis was placed on the mother–baby relationship, including the baby's experience of the breast and of feeding, or being fed. In Fairbairn's theory, development is conceptualised in terms of the individual's passage from infantile to mature dependence, such that 'an original oral, sucking, incorporating and predominantly "taking" aim comes to be replaced by a mature, non-incorporating and predominantly "giving" aim compatible with developed genital sexuality' (Fairbairn, 1941/94: 35). Thus for Fairbairn, giving has an association with maturity and healthy development.

In Klein's theory with its strong emphasis on the infant's relation to, and phantasies about, the breast, her description of paranoid-schizoid and depressive positions lead her to think about envy and gratitude, and to make an explicit connection to generosity:

We find in the analysis of our patients that the breast in its good aspects is the prototype of maternal goodness and generosity as well as of creativeness. ... A full gratification at the breast means that the infant feels he has received from his loved object a unique gift which he wants to keep. This is the basis of gratitude. Gratitude includes belief in good objects and trust in them. It includes also the ability to assimilate the love object – not only as a source of food – and to love it without envy interfering. The more often this gift received is fully accepted, the more often the feeling of enjoyment and gratitude – implying the wish to return pleasure – is experienced. Gratitude is closely bound up with generosity. For inner wealth derives from having assimilated the good object, and this enables the individual to share its gifts with others. (Klein, 1956: 215–216)

In other words, generosity relates to the feeling of having something to give, gratitude for what one has been given, and also, an idea of someone that one wants to give to. In this way, we can see how generosity is fundamentally contrasted with narcissism and can be seen as related to the depressive position.

The struggle to be generous emerged strongly with a patient who I shall call Jane, whose childhood was marked by severe neglect and cruelty from her parents. Married with a daughter of 11, she was describing how she had reacted when out shopping with her daughter, and trying out some cosmetics. The shop assistant had made a fuss of her daughter and given her some free samples. Jane had suddenly felt angry and envious, and was barely able to contain these feelings, and her desire to have the samples for herself. It was not difficult to link her reaction to her childhood experience of neglect and deprivation, and her continuing effort to cope with what she feels it can cost her emotionally to be a different kind of mother to her daughter, compared to how her own mother was with her.

While Winnicott hardly ever used the term narcissism, his thinking about mothers and babies is centrally concerned with the movement made by the infant from what he calls a subjective world to a world that is objectively perceived. This is surely about the overcoming, or perhaps outgrowing, of the narcissistic state. At the beginning, the infant is absolutely dependent on the mother, who, in the good enough situation, meets the baby's needs in such a way that the baby has an illusion of omnipotence, of things being where he or she wants them, when he or she wants them. Gradually, elements of failure can be tolerated by the baby, bringing about an experience of disillusion and a realisation of separateness, of me and not-me, as part of a move towards independence (Winnicott, 1960a). Where mothering has been good enough, the infant's true self (Winnicott, 1960b) has been able to find a place in which to exist and initiate its spontaneous gestures, which can be thought of as gifts back to the mother, providing a basis for exchange and play.

Through his concept of the true self, Winnicott located an original creativity, or at least the potential for this, within the infant, rather than seeing creativity arising from the infant's experience of the breast. At the same time, the infant needs the good enough mother at the stage of absolute dependence if this true self is to have the opportunity to come into being and grow. Winnicott preferred to talk of the 'capacity for concern' (Winnicott, 1963) rather than the depressive position, and this capacity was for him rooted in the infant's experience of having an opportunity to contribute its spontaneous gesture, and for this to be received and recognised. Just as Winnicott writes of a capacity for concern, it seems to me that it is possible to conceptualise a 'capacity for generosity', and that this too is a sign of health.

My own capacity for generosity was tested in working with a patient I shall call Simon, when working through issues of dependence and independence in relation to his wish to end therapy which I found myself disagreeing with. As it seemed to me, there were a number of reasons why it would be useful to continue working together, and I had a strong sense of the work being unfinished. In fact, Simon did not disagree but expressed the thought that if he did not leave then, perhaps, he would never be able to leave. In other words, his wish to end seemed to arise from his fear of dependence. Much as I interpreted this, he remained determined to end. I began to feel that in the transference I was in the position of a father who was claiming a relationship with his son, and I knew that Simon's real father had abandoned the family when Simon was still an infant. It thus seemed that Simon's ambivalence towards the father who had left him was being evoked between us. When I spoke about this to Simon, he seemed to find it meaningful, and the atmosphere between us changed from one of considerable polarisation to one of greater shared understanding. I had felt in a dilemma which was to do with being able to find a way of expressing my disagreement about the ending, without becoming angry or insistent, while recognising Simon's increased separateness and that he might still decide to leave.

In more recent psychoanalytic writing, I find Neville Symington's work on narcissism relevant to my theme of generosity. Symington thinks that narcissism is not simply about trauma, or deprivation, or failure of maternal care, but also includes the response of the individual to the trauma, so that there can be a reaction that leads to narcissism, or an opposite reaction that allows for relationship and emotional growth. He conceptualises the reaction away from narcissism as being towards an object which he calls 'the lifegiver' (Symington, 1993: 35). In this account, opting for the lifegiver seems to be a way of saying 'yes' to life, generating a basic openness and receptivity that may underly a person's relation to other people and the world; in later writing, Symington has identified generosity as a 'source of sanity' (Symington, 2008: 488).

Drawing on the above, I want to briefly put forward some thoughts on the pathology of generosity. Borrowing from Aristotle, one can think of excesses or deficiencies of generosity and the deficiencies centre on a group of related themes: narcissism, anal character and schizoid personality, all of which imply difficulties in recognising and relating to other people as human beings similar to oneself. Narcissism can involve an isolated and bubble-like existence in which outside influences are kept to a minimum, and so receptivity is restricted, thereby limiting opportunities for growth. It may also involve an assumption of being at the centre of things and of being entitled, so that much is taken but without acknowledgement of who or where it has come from. To the extent that eating disorders can be thought of as involving a 'no-to-life' position, they, and their sufferers, have a place within this group too, as may people who have suffered trauma, or who are depressed.

The compulsive caregiver described by Bowlby (1998) seems to be a case of excess in giving, combined with a deficiency with regard to the individual's own needs which are projected into the person being cared for. By contrast, a capacity for generosity where individual acts may be unmarked by compulsiveness, or a hidden agenda, is, I think, an indicator of health and maturity.

Generosity and Therapeutic Work

I have suggested that a capacity for generosity is a necessary part of a therapist's personality, which helps him or her to maintain their availability and openness to the experience of the patient. At the same time, while I see the relationship between therapist and patient as central to the therapeutic work, I also believe that this relationship is not one of equals but has a basic asymmetry, which requires a boundaried and ethical approach in the therapist. To speak of generosity in relation to clinical practice does feel a little dangerous, however. Perhaps it is too suggestive of giving presents or slipping into a way of relating that lacks a necessary distance. To me, this would not be a true generosity in the context of the therapeutic setting, and I hope it is clear that this is not what I am advocating. Nor am I suggesting that therapists should not be able to be firm. To be available does not imply being weak, nor does it imply being masochistic, even though I think we do sometimes have to suffer and survive a patient's attacks without retaliating. Perhaps it is being true to what we believe in that means the suffering that any of us can experience in a session does not have to be masochistic or self-destructive. In addition, I think that it is sometimes necessary for therapists to take a longer term view with a patient, as I think parents must too with their children.

I also want to emphasise that the therapist's capacity for generosity needs to be applied to themselves, so that they do not submit themselves to demands that are too great. Glen Gabbard has written about therapists who have broken the usual boundaries of the therapeutic setting in an attempt to 'save' a patient who is suicidal, often at great cost to themselves, and without providing the patient with effective help. He reminds us that as therapists we harbour a good deal of ambivalence about our work, even 'unconscious hatred', and says that the 'analytic role at times is experienced as a strait-jacket from which we long to escape' (Gabbard, 2003: 258). It is generous to ourselves and our patients to be mindful of this.

Conclusion

At the beginning of this chapter I took an example from Paula Heimann's paper on being natural, and perhaps now I should say what I think about it. On the one hand, I would not want to say that I would never, under any circumstances, give a patient a hot drink. But on the other hand, I don't think that I would have done so in the situation as she described it. I might have wanted to indicate the bathroom that is available for patients and the towel therein. And then of course, there would be the listening out for any consequences of such an action, in the way that we all actively try and follow the movement of the transference and of our own countertransference.

Giving a hot drink is not really the kind of generosity I have had in mind in writing this chapter. I have been much more thinking of generosity as a capacity that therapists bring to their work with patients, which consists of their availability, openness and willingness to engage with the patient, as well as the effort involved in sustaining this capacity over time and through periods of difficulty and hostility. I think it is something that we cannot necessarily expect to find in the patient but can recognise it as a sign of development if it emerges in the course of a psychotherapy. On the whole, I am arguing that generosity be thought of as a structural element within the therapeutic situation, part of what the therapist brings into the setting, rather than as something associated with specific acts.

I also think that generosity has a place in our professional lives as a whole, including our relationships with colleagues, and our professional and training bodies. Here it seems to me that we have to cope with some uncomfortable realities. One is that, as psychotherapists, we are all rivals, as well as colleagues, not unlike siblings. Another is that new siblings are likely to keep coming along. I think we have to try and accommodate both of these facts while at the same time allowing that we may feel threatened by them.

My conclusion is that a capacity for generosity is necessary for us all in our work as psychotherapists, but it is not sufficient. We also need our theoretical knowledge, our skills gained in training and after, and a range of other qualities such as patience, courage, firmness and resilience. But generosity is important. If for a moment, you put yourself in the place of the patient, you would surely want to be able to say that you had experienced your own therapist as generous, generous with their thinking and their interpretations, and perhaps especially in giving their attention and being willing to try and understand you and your emotional life.

Acknowledgements

The original version of this chapter was written for an FPC(WPF) Psychoanalytic Psychotherapists' Study Day, and I am grateful for the comments of my colleagues on that occasion. I am also grateful to David M. Black for commenting on a subsequent version and to Dr Salman Akhtar for his interest in my work on this subject and for letting me read his forthcoming paper on 'Normal and Pathological Generosity'.

References

Aristotle (1976) *Ethics*. (London: Penguin).

Baker, R. (1993) 'The patient's discovery of the psychoanalyst as a new object', *International Journal of Psychoanalysis*, 74, 1223–1233.

Bowlby, J. (1998) *Attachment and Loss Volume Three: Loss, Sadness and Depression*. (London: Pimlico). First published in 1980.

Coltart, N. (1993) 'What Does It Mean: 'Love Is Not Enough'?' in *Slouching Towards Bethlehem: And Further Psychoanalytic Explorations*. (London: Free Association Books).

Comte-Sponville, A. (2003) *A Short Treatise on the Great Virtues: The Uses of Philosophy in Everyday Life*. (London: Vintage). First published in 1996.

Dickens, C. (1994) 'A Christmas Carol' in *The Christmas Books*. (London: Penguin Popular Classics). First published in 1843.

Fairbairn, W. R. D. (1941/94) 'A Revised Psychopathology of the Psychoses' in *Psychoanalytic Studies of the Personality*. (London: Routledge). First published in 1952.

Freud, S. (1905) 'Three Essays on the Theory of Sexuality' in *SE.VII*. (London: Hogarth Press).

Freud, S. (1908) 'Character and Anal Erotism' in *SE.IX*. (London: Hogarth Press).

Freud, S. (1912) 'Recommendations to Physicians Practising Psycho-Analysis' in *SE.XII*. (London: Hogarth Press).

Freud, S. (1915) 'Observations on Transference-Love' in *SE.XII*. (London: Hogarth Press).

Freud, S. (1923) 'The Ego and the Id' in *SE.XIX*. (London: Hogarth Press).

Freud, S. (1937) 'Analysis Terminable and Interminable' in *SE.XXIII*. (London: Hogarth Press).

Gabbard, G. (2003) 'Miscarriages of psychoanalytic treatment with suicidal patients', *International Journal of Psychoanalysis*, 84, (2), 249–261.

Heimann, P. (1978) 'On the Necessity for the Analyst to Be Natural with His Patient' in *About Children and Children-No-Longer*. (London: Routledge). 1989.

Klauber, J. (1976) 'Elements of the Psychoanalytic Relationship and Their Therapeutic Implications' in Kohon, G. (ed.), *The British School of Psychoanalysis: The Independent Tradition*. (London: Free Association Books). 1986.

Klein, M. (1935) 'A Contribution to the Psychogenesis of Manic-Depressive States' in Mitchell, J. (ed.), *The Selected Melanie Klein*. (Harmondsworth: Penguin). 1986.

Klein, M. (1956)' A Study of Envy and Gratitude' in J. Mitchell, J. (ed.), *The Selected Melanie Klein*. (Harmondsworth: Penguin). 1986.

Kradin, R. (1999) 'Generosity: a psychological and interpersonal motivational factor of therapeutic relevance', *Journal of Analytical Psychology*, 44, 221–236.

Lambert, K. (1981) *Analysis, Repair and Individuation*. (London: Academic Press).

Macquarrie, J. (1973) *Existentialism*. (Harmondsworth: Penguin).

Phillips, A. and Taylor, B. (2010) *On Kindness*. (London: Penguin). First published in 2009.

Ridley, M. (1996) *The Origins of Virtue*. (Harmondsworth: Penguin).

Symington, N. (1993) *Narcissism: A New Theory*. (London: Karnac).

Symington, N. (2008) 'Generosity of heart: source of sanity', *British Journal of Psychotherapy*, 24, (4), 488–500.

Williams, G. et al. (eds) (2004) *Exploring Eating Disorders in Adolescents: The Generosity of Acceptance Volume 2*. (London: Karnac).

Winnicott, D. W. (1947) 'Hate in the Counter-transference' in *Through Paediatrics to Psycho-Analysis*. (London: Hogarth Press) 1975.

Winnicott, D. W. (1960a) 'The Theory of the Parent–Infant Relationship' in *The Maturational Processes and the Facilitating Environment*. (London: Karnac). 1990. First published in 1965.

Winnicott, D. W. (1960b) 'Ego Distortion in Terms of True and False Self' in *The Maturational Processes and the Facilitating Environment*. (London: Karnac). 1990. First published in 1965.

Winnicott, D. W. (1963) 'The Development of the Capacity for Concern' in *The Maturational Processes and the Facilitating Environment*. (London: Karnac). 1990. First published in 1965.

Winnicott, D. W. (1985) *Playing and Reality*. (Harmondsworth: Penguin). First published in 1971.

Winnicott, D. W. (1990) *The Maturational Processes and the Facilitating Environment*. (London: Karnac). First published in 1965.

6

Love and Relationship

Christine Driver

Love is a poem with many stanzas

Introduction: Life, Love and Relationship

Life is inseparable from relationship. Whether that is at the level of physical requirements or emotional need we all need another and the 'need for attachment and connection with others is universal and inborn' (Lasky and Silverman, 1988: 1). However, within the seeking of relationship, love is a question that haunts everyone. Clients come to therapy looking for it and individuals in life search for it. It is elusive, sought and valuable. When an individual finds themselves in a relationship or seeks one out within a therapeutic environment what is often hoped for and anticipated is something that will touch them as a person and change them in some way but as Colman (1994) points out 'Love can be a heaven but it can equally be a hell, as terrible and ensnaring in one form as it is delightful and enchanting in the other' (500).

Many have tried to define love, and write longingly, contentedly, regretfully and sorrowfully about it. Poets use words as the conscious symbols of a profound experience that reaches into the unconscious, evokes the emotions and awakens the imagination in relation to a longed for yet elusive state of 'being': that of being in love and its counterpart of being loved. It is a complex emotional experience and state of being that incorporates generosity, compassion, empathy, concern, charity, sexuality, creativity, and, in a relationship, evolves through the vicissitudes of conflict, hate and more intricate emotions. In fact much of human life is preoccupied with love; looking for it, reacting against it or curious as to how others manoeuvre in and out of it. But, however we view love it is a dynamic that comes from deep within our emotional selves and links to aspects of the self that seek expression.

The expression, integration and understanding of aspects of the self are part of the life-long process of individuation that occurs within and through relationship with others. It is within relationship, especially the therapeutic one,

65

that the potential for processes of awareness and discovery of aspects of the self lies. Love is a powerful catalyst for this process. Falling in love entails, in part, the seeking of something in the other; a fantasy that the other will make one complete or that life is not manageable without the loved one.

John Donne intimates this in his poem 'The Ecstasy' in which he describes love and ecstasy as an escape from the body and a merging with the 'divine' and he touches on something of the power and life-changing capacities of love when he writes:

> When love with one another so
> Interanimates two souls,
> That abler soul, which thence doth flow,
> Defects of loneliness controls.
>
> We then, who are this new soul, know,
> Of what we are composed, and made,
> For th' atomies of which we grow
> Are souls, whom no change can invade.
>   (Donne, 1633: 53–56)

Donne's use of the word 'interanimates' beautifully signifies the sheer intensity of love when it activates the depths of the self. However, this state of being is generated from an illusion that the other can lift one out of the conflicts and realities of ordinary life into a place where they no longer exist. What remains hidden within such fantasies is the meaning inherent within the affects and the unconscious forces that come into play when love and the erotic are activated.

Psychoanalytic Ideas about Love

From the moment of birth what the infant seeks is another for the provision of basic human needs, nurture, love and relationship. In the unfolding patterns of life these needs stay with us in an underlying quest to find a sense of belonging through sustaining and loving relationships. In a now seminal book on infant development Gerhardt (2004) outlines the way that affection shapes the brain and by implication the way the individual relates to and perceives the world in adult life. Research such as that into attachment theory (Holmes, 1993; Knox, 2003) and neuroscience, (Solms and Solms, 2000; Damasio, 2000; Wilkinson, 2006; Hart, 2008) all emphasise the importance of relationship on brain development and affect regulation and reinforce the idea originally propounded by Jung (1935: 3) and considered in detail by Wiener (2009) that it is through relationship that an individual is affected and changed.

The issue of love within the therapeutic relationship has a long and controversial history. Freud primarily wrote about love in 'Three Essays on Sexuality'

(Freud, 1905),' On Narcissism' (Freud, 1914) and 'Instincts and their Vicissitudes' (Freud, 1915a) and, as Bergman (1988) points out 'Freud suggested that it be reserved for the relation of the total ego to its object' (655). Freud (1915b), in his examination of transference love, stressed the importance of holding an analytic attitude in handling 'the most dangerous mental impulses' (170) and clearly emphasises the danger of love and desire in the consulting room but, as Bergman (1988) points out, Freud never really addressed 'how sex, a drive, becomes love, an emotion' (654).

Bergman (1988) goes on to cite the development of psychoanalytic thinking about love and concluded that 'it consists in a hope that the lover will heal the wound inflicted by the less than good enough early objects' and that 'the lover as healer is an important aspect of love and contributes to making the healer loveable' (669). Within the context of psychotherapy Gerrard (1996) comments that clients 'need to arouse the loving feelings of their psychotherapist in order to reach a sense of their own lovableness' (163). Wrye and Welles (1994) distinguish between narcissistic and non-narcissistic aspects of falling in love and identify the importance of preoedipal dynamics as the body-based sensual matrix which form erotic precursors in their own right (34). They identify the significance of the maternal erotic transference and pre-genital dynamics and, they contend, 'the maternal erotic transference is frightening to male and female clients alike insofar as it threatens to suck them back into the intense body feelings towards the early mother and is thus a threat to separateness' (Wrye and Welles, 1994: 162). In contrast, oedipal and genital issues bring in the powerful dynamic of sexuality into the erotic transference. Wrye and Welles (1994) see the erotic transference as a 'transformational opportunity' (204) and that it is the 'double helix of analytic theory and countertransference, which serves as the frame of comprehension through which constructions are created' (224). This enables the slow working through of the erotic transference and countertransference, the integration of 'tenderness and aggression' and the development of 'mutuality, love and genuine intimacy' (224). For them, 'the storytelling itself...and...the relationship in which the analyst and the analysand construct each other in the process of making meaning is...also critically important' (Wrye and Welles, 1994: 17).

Lasky and Silverman (1988) and subsequently Mann (1997; 2002) provide detailed and comprehensive overviews and explorations of love in the therapeutic relationship. Mann (1997) maintains that Winnicott and Bion 'do not consider, or at least ignore, the erotic component of the mother–infant couple, and that when this model is applied to the analytic process the same oversight occurs' (123). Mann's perspective is that, 'through the erotic, the psyche seeks growth. It provides the mechanism and the impetus to transform our unconscious life' (9) and that 'what our patients need is the therapist's understanding in order to liberate the optimum range of their emotional experiences, so that they can have more satisfactory and loving relationships outside therapy. Their erotic fantasies need to be freed from their pre-Oedipal and Oedipal fixations' (Mann, 1997: 23).

Jung also examined love and writes about this fundamental and archetypal predisposition throughout his Collected Works. He makes the important statement that 'love, in the sense of *concupiscentia* (covetousness), is the dynamism that most infallibly brings the unconscious to light' (Jung, 1955/56: para 99) and that love is 'one of the mightiest movers of humanity' (Jung, 1911/12: para 98). Colman (1994), a Jungian analyst, examines love as 'an experience of initiation, a developmental event in its own right' (497), and he considers the potential for regression in relation to erotic love and comments that 'what is sought without can only be found within. In the end love's bliss is an illusion' (508) and that 'in addition to the regressive elements emphasized in psychoanalytic views of love, encountering the erotic spirit involves an initiation process culminating in the transformation brought about through the painful loss of love's illusions' (513).

Love and the Therapeutic Relationship: Jung and the Alchemical Metaphor

Love in the therapeutic relationship therefore needs to be carefully understood and navigated in terms of its meaning. Jung saw the imagery and symbolism of art, alchemy, religion and culture as expressions of psychic processes and realised that the medieval woodcuts (Jung, 1946) depicting the alchemical process[1] symbolically and metaphorically illustrated a relational and psychological journey that 'tells a love story' (Wiener, 2009: 81) and a 'process going on between two people' (Edinger, 1994: 40).

The images describe a journey which begins with an unconscious coming together of the core components of all the individual personal elements of the self and unwinds through challenging confrontations with eros, captivation, merger, disillusionment, darkness, death of the ideal and the gradual emergence of conscious awareness and the potential for integration of aspects of the self that previously remained hidden in the unconscious. Being pulled towards the desire for merger with the other is one of the powerful aspects of falling in love. Edinger (1994) identifies that when two people merge the dynamic between them ceases and there is, as a consequence, a loss of identity and a kind of psychological death. However, here, as Edinger (1994) points out, is a turning point. Either this process is repeated again and again in different relationships, with the unconscious continuously seeking external satisfaction, or development and individuation occurs through the painful process of disillusionment, awareness and insight. The alchemical images of the Rosarium Philosophorum (Jung, 1946) therefore provide a symbolic means of understanding the dynamics inherent in falling in love and the way in which self-awareness, understanding and integration can enable a true development of the self.

This alchemical metaphor assumes that insight and the development of the self occurs through a cycle of love, loss, disillusionment and insight. Haule (2010) points out, 'there is always a struggle in romantic love between oneness and separation' (168) and the need to find a place in which 'unity will respect their individuality and a new sense of individuality that will respect their unity' (Haule, 2010: 70). The danger and struggle of falling in love is of losing the self through idealisation of, and merger with, the other but love can also enable discovery about the self through the processing of the struggle with the relationship.

What begins as a passion and a fantasy has to evolve through the intricacies of reality, and this is the challenge for each individual within any relationship but especially the therapeutic one. In both, the individual is reaching out for something of which they are, as yet, unconscious but because it is unconscious it is powerful, as it represents the search for the expression of the self through projection onto and into the other.

Love and Illusion

Love can be fuelled by projections as well as by a search for unexpressed aspects of the self and is based on the conscious and unconscious illusion that the other can fulfil something within the self. Love feels, and is, real and yet the paradox is that often it is also an illusion in relation to the other and yet can be transformational. Freud attacked 'the role of illusions in human affairs' (Palmer, 1999: 72) but Winnicott (1971) saw a positive and transformational aspect of illusion in that it occurs via an 'intermediate area of *experiencing*, to which inner reality and external life both contribute' (3). Winnicott's concept of the transitional object relates to this intermediate area of experience in which the question 'did you conceive this or was it presented to you from without?' (Winnicott, 1971: 14) applies equally to falling in love in terms of the question 'is the loved other one's own creation or does it correspond to reality?'

The movement between illusion and disillusionment is, as Winnicott points out, never complete and within any relationship the transitional space contains the potential for a transformational experience. Bollas (1987) refers to the potential of the mother–infant relationship to be transformational and argues that later feelings about the self emerge from this. He comments that 'in adult life, the quest is not to possess the object; rather the object is pursued in order to surrender to it as a medium that alters the self' (14). However, as both Winnicott (1971) and Bollas (1987) indicate, transformation occurs through the dynamics between illusion, disillusion, desire, the relating of inner and outer experience and reality. Love could therefore be seen to take place in an in-between and transitional area and in the dynamic between I and Thou and I and It, (see chapter 4 by Stephen Gross), such that when the ego is in dynamic relationship to the self a dialectical experience between 'self and not self' (McFarland Solomon, 2007: 282) occurs which can be transformational and facilitate self-realisation.

Agape and Eros

Love, as Lambert (1981) and Hopwood (1991) point out, is not a one-dimensional phenomena but encompasses the aspects of Agape and Eros and that 'we need Eros, the life-giving spirit of love, as well as the reflective thinking of agape to come together' (Hopwood, 1991: 21) in order to achieve openness and under-standing with and for the client and to enable the achievement of this capacity within the client themselves.

Agape

Empathic and agapaic love is an essential ingredient of the therapeutic encounter and links to generosity as described by Stephen Crawford in Chapter 5. Lambert (1981) comments, 'The motive power that keeps the therapeutic encounter alive and moving is..... in my view the agapaic capacities of the analyst' (161), and Hopwood later points out, 'there can be no love which does not call forth an active caring towards the one who is loved. There must be an active concern for the life and growth of the one whom we love' (Hopwood, 1991: 17). This applies as much to the therapeutic relationship as it does to any interpersonal relationship. Within the therapeutic encounter there must be a desire to engage with empathy and agapaic concern with clients for the process to be creative and helpful.

For example, a client who came to me for therapy idealised and envied thera-pists and was frequently angry at me because he felt I could not be a 'proper' therapist because I did not live in Hampstead in London where several of the major training institutes are situated. Hampstead was, for him, the home of 'proper therapists' whereas he experienced the area where I lived as impover-ished, diverse and messy. The constant onslaught and attack on myself and my capacity as a therapist was both difficult and enlightening. My professional self could see that the client was actually attacking the impoverished, diverse and messy part of himself that he did not wish to own. My personal self, however, felt affronted, frustrated and angry at the constant attack on my professional capabilities. Such feelings with clients can be generated in numerous ways and the capacity to hold and contain in order to understand is intrinsic to analytic work. However, this capacity is something that not only comes through train-ing and personal therapy but is also based on the therapist's attitude to the client. Such an attitude requires a capacity to be psychically available for the client, to hold the client in mind, to retain an ego-related position in relation to oneself and the other, to maintain an analytic attitude and not act out id, super-ego or retaliatory responses. All of these are aspects of agapaic love in relation to another within the therapeutic encounter.

Therapy is not a process 'done' to another, it is a process carried out 'with' another in which the therapist is a tool through which understanding of the internal and relational precepts that the client operates from can emerge. Undertaking this role from the perspective of agapaic love is essential so that a talion response or the expression of raw and unprocessed feelings is not activated within the therapist and the negative transference dynamics can be contained and processed.

Eros

Eros and the erotic is potentially a much more dangerous affective state of mind than agape, but its significance is that it fully engages the self of the client. The danger, as Freud (1915b) identified, is that this can just stimulate a resistance in which the client (and possibly the therapist) is unable to think. However, if the therapist can sustain an analytic stance within and through the power of the affects involved then the therapeutic work can lead to awareness and the development of insight and meaning.

For example, Pamela came into therapy following a difficult and unrecipro-cated relationship which left her feeling depressed and anxious. It soon became evident that in the transference she was 'falling in love' with me. She would turn on the couch so that she could gaze at my face. She would hide under the blanket so that she could fantasise that she was inside me or in bed with me. She drew pictures of the two of us together and longed to hear my voice. The days between sessions were hard for her to bear and she found it difficult to survive breaks. Through such regressive enactments Pamela ensured that she was in my mind more or less constantly. She metaphorically and symbolically got inside me. This was fuelled by her love and longing to merge and be part of me and a fantasy that if I was part of her she would feel whole. My counter-transference left me feeling fascinated by, and curious about, her and a simul-taneous longing to be close to her. I also recognised that powerful homoerotic feelings were present between us which required me to hold onto my analytic attitude and simultaneously be both part of the client's internal drama as well as be separate from it. To avoid getting submerged and lost in the dynamics I needed to find meaning in the transference, my countertransference and the client's narratives and comments to me.

This longing to merge and be one is intrinsic to the passion of falling in love. It might have a regressive or narcissistic core but the yearning is to fulfil a desire and to feel whole. It is also both a physiological and psychological urge and significant in the mysterious journey of relationship with another. Jacoby (1984), in referring to Buber's work, comments that the 'I-Thou relation means immediate presence,...and...the I-It attitude means making an object of any-thing or anyone outside of oneself in order to think about it or to use it' (63) and goes on to link the I-Thou to Eros and the I-It to Logos in which 'Eros is our uniting feeling-link with other people, with nature or with ourselves' (63). The significance of this within the analytic relationship is not so much the falling in love, although that is an important generator of a dynamic, but of how the next phase is handled in relation to the death of the illusion, disillusionment and the integration of the parts of the self that are unconsciously felt to be in the other.

For Pamela I held the door to understanding and meaning in relation to her self. I was the magical other who held the key to the unconscious shadowy underworld and who knew how to access and understand the internal dramas and dark places which her vivid and frequent dreams revealed. These dreams often depicted dramas with devil-like figures and death, and she was desperate to receive my understanding of them and also to relieve her of the fears and anxieties that they generated in her. Her projection on to me of a fantasy of who I was and what I could do was symptomatic of that of a child to a mother who can make the world a safe place or a lover who would make her feel whole.

In the transference I was the person she wanted to be and I was aware that she activated in me a countertransference to her as being the sort of person I would like to be. Unconsciously and consciously a longing was generated between us that was partly based on envy but mostly on longing, love and an illusion of completion. For Pamela this originated from an upbringing where there had been a denial of, and defence against, negative feelings, an emphasis on 'being happy' and an underlying assumption that this would create 'heaven on earth'. 'Being happy' was what Pamela felt was both her right and her predisposition. The night fears and frightening dreams represented the range of unhappy, dark and depressive feelings that are inherent in us all. Union with me as a woman would, she felt, enable her to have a sense of completion. Within this, there was no 'as if', no sense, at this point, of the symbolic, only a concrete sense that union would bring completion.

At one point in the therapy, however, I said something to her that upset her and made her unhappy and broke the spell leading to a long period of anguish and despair that 'heaven on earth' was not possible for her. This facing of reality led to a confrontation with her unconscious hopes and longings and the split off and unexpressed parts of herself which required integration and acceptance. This necessitated a long and painful journey through and beyond the other side of love in order to achieve an acceptance of reality and the 'dark side' of herself as well as insight and awareness.

Discussion

Paradoxically it is often when the loved object fails to fulfil expectations and disillusionment sets in that true psychological growth occurs. Loss and disillusionment generate intense feelings of loneliness and of being alone but, as Haule (2010) points out, given the right environment 'new capacities and new resources' (26) can be found. The danger of falling in love is that the ego can become overshadowed by the power of projection onto the other and the longing for merger as Jung (1946) and Edinger (1994) point out. The way forward is achieved via the journey through loss and disillusionment whereby the unconscious 'force' that led to connection with the other, for example, the therapist, can become conscious and understood. Symbolically and psychologically this requires the soul searching of the 'dark night of the soul' and the capacity to allow the unconscious aspects of the self that were merged with the loved object to come to consciousness. Here, as Freud (1915a,b) pointed out, lies the danger of the client remaining stuck in a resistance and repeating the same pattern elsewhere. However, as Winnicott (1963) and Bion (1967) later identified, it is only by failing the client (Winnicott, 1963: 344) or by developing the capacity to tolerate the frustration of desires (Bion, 1967: 112) that reflection, thought and self-awareness are achieved.

The therapist's role therefore is to maintain the analytic attitude so as to provide the client with the opportunity to engage in a process of understanding and integration in relation to the aspects the self that were enmeshed and merged with the loved one. This requires a new sort of love and a new attitude; one that is 'directed toward the still-hidden totality of the client, to the process of self-development of the person coming for help' (Jacoby, 1984: 108). For Jung, the psyche was driven and developed by the dynamics of the opposites but falling in love can lead to a cessation of this. It is only when loss and disillusionment occurs that the dynamic of the opposites is recreated through, say, love and hate, love and loss. When love 'dies' it is all too easy to fall into the opposite of 'hating' the previously loved person because they failed to live up to the hopes and expectations. However, if the opposites can be held together in a creative tension then a new way forward can be found in which ownership of what has been looked for in the other can be achieved. Jung referred to this as the transcendent function (Jung, 1916/57) in which a 'creative synthesis' of opposites creates a 'way out of what had appeared to be a locked state of polar opposition' (McFarland Solomon, 2007: 268). This represents a similar perspective to that reflected in Klein's (1975) work on the shift that takes place from the paranoid-schizoid to the depressive position and the subsequent work on this undertaken by Steiner (1993) and others.

Through the processes of understanding and integration of experience within a relationship, perspectives can change and be changed. Neuroscience identifies a similar dynamic in terms of how mind and brain function is based on experience and relationship, and that the underlying potential for the expression of the self via interaction with another is intrinsic to our nature. Wiener (2009) touches on this when she comments, 'affect has the power to regulate experience, but affect is also regulated *by* it in turn – a truly interactive matrix of connections (97) and she quotes Siegel's (1998) ideas that 'interpersonal experience may continue to influence neurobiological processes throughout the lifespan' (4). Love is one such expression of the self and can lead to insight, awareness and individuation when it can be understood, a process however, that requires loss and disillusionment to be faced and integrated.

Love and Countertransference

Falling in love is therefore activated by both conscious and unconscious forces but it is the unconscious ones that are the most powerful and potentially the most destructive, or creative, depending on how the ego deals with them. Countertransference can be a highly informative indicator of the internal and unconscious relationships with the client (Searles 1955). When used in the service of the therapeutic work this enables awareness but when the therapist fails to consider it with an analytic attitude it can form the seedbed of analytic enactments. Wrye and Welles (1994) give a considered overview of the dangers and the 'defensive constellations employed by therapists when faced with primitive erotic maternal transference' (64). These include, grandiose fantasies on the part of the therapist of their capacity to cure the client, 'anaclitic/depressive countertransference' and an 'unwillingness to let go of the patient' (65), 'erotic horror and schizoid distancing because of a fear of being invaded by the client' and 'gender issues in relation to heterosexual or homosexual erotic transferences and countertransference' (Wrye and Welles, 1994: 67).

For the therapist, such affects within the intimacy of the consulting room represents a true challenge to integrity. Perhaps the most dangerous of these is when a grandiose fantasy is evoked in the therapist that actual enactments with the client will provide a cure. Enactments may briefly satisfy the physiological urge but they confuse and conflict with the psychological ones because the unconscious self of the client is not attended to and the meaning of the power of the affects is not discovered. Indeed as Levine (2010) indicates, where such enactments have occurred, both client and therapist are damaged by them. Physical and sexual enactments with a client therefore destroy the symbolic and analytic space, they destroy the analytic attitude and destroy the possibility of the making of meaning with and for the client in relation to understanding their internal world dramas that are being actively played out via the transference and the therapist's countertransference. In the therapeutic relationship intimacy has to be combined with abstinence, however painful and difficult, for true understanding and insight to emerge.

Conclusion

Love therefore embodies Agape and Eros and can be both creative and destructive. The paradox is that the capacity to engage in the dynamics of love and the capacity to abstain from it are both necessary to the processes of individuation and creatively expressing the self. Love in the therapeutic encounter can therefore be an agent for change because it activates the deep unconscious and enables the ego to encounter the self in a breadth and depth that relating in a cognitive way with another does not achieve. However, it is a powerful and dangerous affect especially when love and Eros combine. Love and Eros are potent partners and activate the depths of the self emotionally and physiologically. They fuel the desire to merge; activate the pleasure principle and can blind the ego to reality. Love is such an upsurging that it can be experienced like a tsunami in intensity in the way it can obliterate reason and ego.

Yet here again the therapist is presented with a paradox in that when love and Eros emerge it is because the other is perceived as holding something that is desired. Such a dynamic is archetypal, a predisposition intrinsic to all, and activates physiological, emotional, and numinous dimensions, but, as Wiener (2009) points out, within the therapeutic encounter can lead to the danger of there being 'too much body or too much spirit' (83). In such circumstances the ego can split into rational and irrational states. The rational aspect of the ego holding onto reality and the irrational losing sight of reality and wanting to rush into an actual and physical enactment with the other, or holding the other as a spiritual ideal in the hope of achieving an alternative state of being.

Within the therapeutic encounter disillusionment is inevitable at some point and indeed it is an essential part of it but the psychological shifts that it entails are profound. They require sacrifice of the search for the ideal, mourning of the loss of the ideal, integration of the reality of self and other, the acceptance of limitations of the self and other and the development within the self of an integration of the opposites in what Klein (1975) would refer to as the depressive position and Jung as the process of individuation and the integration of the opposites (Jung, 1916/57).

Love can be expressed and experienced in many ways: with another, through art, music, poetry and literature; through work; through play; and through activities that activate the deeper aspects of the self and the soul. We need it to keep us psychically and emotionally active and alive, but the danger is if it takes over and we lose our rational self. Within the therapeutic encounter, we need to be aware of the diverse ways in which love is expressed and experienced in order to be open to the ways in which the psyche and the self are seeking and finding expression, meaning and the integration of aspects of the self.

Love is a term that we have to discover in its fullness for it to have real and true meaning in relation to another and in relation to ourselves. However, this is not a once and only motif but rather an ongoing cycle of entrancement, passion, love, engagement, disillusionment and discovery. As La Rochefoucauld said in the seventeenth century,

> In the human heart passions are forever being born; the
> overthrow of one almost always means the rise of another.

(La Rochefoucauld, 1665)

Note

1. Termed the 'Rosarium Philosophorum' these are a series of medieval pictures made from woodcuts that depict the alchemical process. Jung uses them as a metaphor for relational processes including the dynamics of transference and countertransference in the therapeutic relationship.

References

Bergman, M. S. (1988) 'Freud's three theories of love in the light of later developments', *Journal of the American Psychoanalytic Association*, 36, (3), 653–72.

Bion, W. R. (1967) *Second Thoughts*. (London: Maresfield Library).

Bollas, C. (1987) The *Shadow of the Object: Psychoanalysis of the Unthought Known*. (London: Free Association Books).

Colman, W. (1994) 'Love, desire and infatuation: encountering the erotic spirit', *Journal of Analytical Psychology*, 39, (4), 497–514.

Damasio, A. (2000) *The Feeling of What Happens: Body, Emotion and the Making of Consciousness*. (London: William Heinemann).

Donne, J. (1633) *Poems of John Donne*. Vol. I. Chambers, E.K. (ed.) (London: Lawrence & Bullen). 1896.

Edinger, E. F. (1994) *The Mystery of the Coniunctio. Alchemical Image of Individuation*. (Toronto: Inner City Books).

Freud, S. (1905) *Three Essays on the Theory of Sexuality. SE.VII.* (London: Hogarth Press).

Freud, S. (1914) 'On Narcissism: An Introduction' in *SE.IV.* (London: Hogarth Press).

Freud, S. (1915a) 'Instincts and their Vicissitudes' in *SE.XIV.* (London: Hogarth Press).

Freud, S. (1915b) 'Observations on Transference-Love (Further Recommendations on the Technique of Psycho-Analysis III)' in *SE.XII.* (London: Hogarth Press).

Gerrard, J. (1996) 'Love in the time of psychotherapy', *British Journal of Psychotherapy*, 13, (2), 163–73.

Gerhardt, S. (2004) *Why Love Matters*. (Hove and New York: Brunner-Routledge).

Hart, S. (2008) *Brain, Attachment, Personality. An Introduction to Neuroaffective Development.* (London: Karnac).

Haule, J. R. (2010) *Divine Madness. Archetypes of Romantic Love.* (Canada and America: Fisher King Press).

Holmes, J. (1993) *John Bowlby and Attachment Theory.* (Hove and New York: Brunner-Routledge). 2002.

Hopwood, A. (1991) 'Love and Professionalism. Love: Personal, Professional and Pathological', *Institute of Psychotherapy and Counselling Annual Conference 1991.* Unpublished.

Jacoby, M. (1984) *The Analytic Encounter. Transference and Human Relationship.* (Toronto: Inner City Books).

Jung, C. (1911/12) 'The Hymn of Creation', in *Symbols of Transformation.* (London: Routledge). 1981.

Jung, C. (1916/57) 'The Transcendent Function', in *The Structure and Dynamics of the Psyche, CW 8.* (London: Routledge). 1991.

Jung, C. (1935) 'Principles and Practice of Psychotherapy', in *The Practice of Psychotherapy, CW 16.* (London and Henley: Routledge & Kegan Paul). 1981.

Jung, C. (1946) 'The Psychology of the Transference', in *The Practice of Psychotherapy, CW 16.* (London and Henley: Routledge & Kegan Paul). 1981.

Jung, C. (1955/56) 'The Paradoxa' in *Mysterium Coniunctionis, CW.14.* (London: Routledge). 1981.

Klein, M. (1975). *Envy and Gratitude and Other Works* 1946–1963. Masud R. Khan (ed.) (London: The Hogarth Press).

Knox, J. (2003) *Archetype, Attachment, Analysis.* (Hove and New York: Brunner-Routledge).

La Rochefoucauld. (1665) *Maxims.* http://www.brainyquote.com 2010.

Lambert, K. (1981) *Analysis, Repair and Individuation.* (London: Karnac Books). 1994.

Lasky, J. and Silverman, H. W. (eds) (1988) *Love, Psychoanalytic Perspectives.* (New York: New York University Press).

Levine, H. B. (2010) 'Sexual boundary violations: a psychoanalytic perspective', *The British Journal of Psychotherapy,* 26, (1), 51–63.

Mann, D. (1997) *Psychotherapy. An Erotic Relationship, Transference and Countertransference Passions.* (Hove and New York: Routledge). 2008.

Mann, D. (ed.) (2002) *Love and Hate.* (Hove and New York: Routledge).

McFarland Solomon, H. (2007) 'The Transcendent Function and Hegel's Dialectical Vision', in *Who Owns Jung?* Casement, A. (ed.) (London: Karnac).

Palmer, M. (1999) *Freud and Jung on Religion.* (London and New York: Routledge).

Searles, H. F. (1955) 'The Informational Value of the Supervisor's Emotional Experiences', in *Collected Papers on Schizophrenia and Related Subjects.* (London: Maresfield Library). 1965.

Siegel, D. J. (1998) 'The Developing Mind: Toward a Neurobiology of Interpersonal Experience', in *The Signal: Newsletter of the World Association for Mental Health,* 6, (3–4), 1–11.

Solms, K. P. and Solms, M. (2000) Clinical Studies in Neuro-Psychoanalysis. (London: Karnac Books).

Steiner, J. (1993) *Psychic Retreats.* (London and New York: Routledge).

Wiener, J. (2009) *The Therapeutic Relationship.* (Texas: A&M University Press).

Wilkinson, M. (2006) *Coming Into Mind: The Mind-Brain Relationship: A Jungian Clinical Perspective.* (London and New York: Routledge).

Winnicott, D. W. (1963) 'Dependence in Infant Care, in Child Care, and in the Psycho-Analytic Setting', *International Journal of Psycho-Analysis*, 44, 339–44.

Winnicott, D. W. (1971) *Playing and Reality*. (Middx, England and New York: Penguin Books). 1980.

Wrye, H. K., and Welles, J. K. (1994) *The Narration of Desire*. (Hillsdale, NJ and London: The Analytic Press).

7

Shame

John Rignell

Introduction

This chapter started life as a talk given to colleagues and has developed as a result of conversations and discussions. Facilitating this kind of dialogue and the processes of mutual discovery in the solitary activity of reading and writing is more of a challenge. However, I believe it is important to encourage the reader to develop a dialogue with themselves over this topic: a dialogue that is crucial in the context of shame, an emotion that is so difficult to talk and think about. This is borne out by my experience as a psychotherapist: I cannot remember anyone I have seen at a first meeting who has complained of being burdened by shame. It would appear that it is easier to admit to difficulties with anger or guilt or a myriad of other emotions than shame. However, with many people, over the course of time, it has transpired that the problems they experience have, to some extent, been due to this irksome emotion. It is therefore my intention to stimulate a process of thinking about shame in the reader. I will have succeeded if the reader has a sense of knowing or being familiar with the subject matter but may not necessarily have thought about it. Christopher Bollas makes the point that: 'There is in each of us a fundamental split between what we think we know and what we know but may never be able to think' (Bollas, 1987: 282). I would suggest that this is particularly true in the case of shame, an emotion that leads to a paralysis of thought and can so easily remain an embodied experience, trapped within our soma, never making the transition to our psyche and thence to the liberating possibility of thought.

In this chapter, I will be looking at the experience of shame and the repercussions on our relationships with others and ourselves. Shame is evoked in relation to the other. A recurring theme in this chapter will be the ways in which shame is generated through the response of the other from infancy onwards. As will be seen, shame can be understood as a multilayered experience, more nuanced than might be thought at first glance. In order to guide the reader through this exploration, I shall begin with an examination of the differences between shame and guilt as subjective experiences. I shall go on to explore the genesis of shame with respect to the parent–infant dyad and its development on a societal level including some thoughts for the implications in the consulting room. The final part of the chapter covers two further aspects of shame. The first is an analysis of the ways in which shame can be hidden within the expression of other emotions followed by some reflections on the relational dynamic of shame.

Shame and Guilt

I wish to locate and focus on the experience of shame by contrasting it with its sister emotion of guilt. I want to take the experience of shame off the pages of the book and analyse the subjective experience. What is this feeling that is not only a state of mind but also so painfully located in our bodies? How does it differ from guilt and yet can also be confused with it? The psychoanalytic literature around guilt is immensely rich. Shame has been described as the Cinderella of the emotions, and theorists have only recently begun to rectify this imbalance. Earlier psychoanalytic writing about guilt has, at times, confused it with shame leading to further confusion amongst practitioners.

In order to find your personal answer to the distinction between shame and guilt, I would like you to reflect on an episode in your life that has evoked a feeling of guilt in you. Take a few moments...now think of an event that has led you to feel shame...again a few moments of reflection before articulating for yourself what the differences are in the subjective experience of these two emotions.

I would imagine, if it were put into words, that the experience of guilt would involve the following elements: primarily it would be a negative assessment of an event – *something* you did that you would see as bad or caused discomfort. You are able to admit to it, albeit with a sense of reluctance. Combined with this would be a sense that there is the possibility of reparation, a sense that you could make it better. The reason why you may want to repair things is an anxiety about the effect your action might have had on the relationship with the person you feel guilt towards. I would also guess that the whole experience is susceptible to being thought about.

On the other hand, regarding shame, the negative assessment is not so much about an event, but yourself. Whatever it is you have done, it makes you a bad person. It is much harder to articulate the story that gave rise to this feeling to yourself, let alone to anyone else. Added to this is the sense that it cannot be made better – there is a feeling of impotence and paralysis rather than the possibility of reparation. There could be associated feelings of anger, resentment or jealousy towards those around you or the person who stimulated the feeling of shame.

A significant aspect of shame as opposed to many other difficult emotions is the challenge it offers to find anything positive within it or any potential for future development. Shame carries with it the sense of a closed system that feeds on itself. Unlike guilt, the path towards reparation is not clear.

The Genesis of Shame

The Parent–Infant Dyad

Theoreticians (Brouak, 2002; Mollon, 1991) seeking to explain the aetiology of shame refer to Tronick's observations (Tronick et al, 1978) regarding parent–infant interaction that have become known as the still face experiments. In the experiments, a mother was asked to behave as she normally would towards her baby; she was then asked to continue to make eye contact but not engage in any other interaction. When confronted with this unusual state of affairs, the infants reacted with distress – a reaction that the researchers saw as being related to shame. Stern makes the point that, for the pre-verbal infant: 'Gazing back and forth, rather than talking back and forth is the action' (Stern, 1990/98: 49). Love and approval, acceptance and enjoyment are communicated through the look at this age. Parental ambivalence and preoccupation are inevitable obstacles that can disrupt the mutuality of this interaction.

In his seminal paper 'Hate in the Countertransference', Winnicott (1947) lists a number of reasons for this ambivalence. Crucially, he makes the point that: 'The baby is not her own (mental) conception' (Winnicott, 1947: 201). I understand this to mean that the baby the mother imagines is not the one she actually gets but is an individual in its own right, thereby necessitating a degree of accommodation on her part. This would mean that there would be aspects of the baby's personality that may be difficult for her, she would therefore need to put her own expectations and disappointments on one side for the sake of the baby's mental health. I would suggest that if the parent does not manage this negotiation and expresses disapproval or indifference consistently then shame can be the result.

In order to illustrate the nature and genesis of shame, I will use two contrasting descriptions of interactions between a mother and baby. The first, from Stern (1990/98), encapsulates a positive outcome to a potentially shame inducing experience: Joey is four and a half months old:

> Joey is sitting on his mother's lap facing her. She looks at him intently with no expression on her face, as if she were preoccupied and absorbed in thought elsewhere. At first, he glances at different parts of her face but finally looks into her eyes. He and she remain locked in a silent mutual gaze for a long moment. She finally breaks it by easing into a slight smile. Joey quickly leans forward and returns her smile. (Stern, 1990: 57)

As this rather touching episode vividly demonstrates infants are constantly looking for affirmation of their goodness. We have here an example of a responsive mother who was able to put her own concerns on one side and reciprocate her baby's wish for recognition and confirmation that he could be enjoyed.

It is helpful to contrast this with the following. Lena is eight months old and involved with playing with some bricks:

> ..she throws the block on the floor and giggles with excitement. ... she looks towards her mother, apparently expecting her delight to be met by approval and responsiveness. Instead her mother frowns at her and then turns away in irritation. Lena responds with a surprised look ... She scans her mother's face again ... She peers at her mother for another instant, looks downward at the block on the floor, reaches towards it, and cries. (Morrison, 1998: 60)

Here we have two interactions that illustrate the importance of the sensitivity of the caregiver to the baby's needs in relation to the aetiology of shame which can help us understand why some individuals are more prone to shame than others due to a consistently shaming response on the part of the caregivers. If this process is repeated often enough the result is an internal world wherein the self is hated by the self. A relationship to the self is engendered that is characterised by an almost constant carping self-criticism that serves to keep the relationship with that critical parent very much alive internally, so, paradoxically, it becomes 'good to feel bad' (Nathanson, 1992: 334). Giving up this internal dynamic would entail giving up this parent, thus the criticism insulates the infant from feelings of loss and abandonment. Pattison describes the situation as follows:

> Traumatised and unloved children, faced with their own powerlessness and their need for parental care, identify with the powerful aggressive parent. .... The child introjects the critical, hostile, punishing parent into its own psyche, creating a grandiose ego-ideal against which it measures itself and finds itself wanting. (Pattison, 2000: 112)

I believe that none of us are immune from the pain of shame. It is more a question of degree, and I will now look at the tragic legacy of shame that abuse in childhood leads to and the importance of an empathic response in order to repair this damage. It is not only in the microcosm of the parent–infant dyad that we see the operation of the shame dialogue. The same dynamics with the potential for healing or further damage can be seen on a societal level as the following example demonstrates.

Shame and Abuse

The ongoing controversy over the sexual abuse of children and the complicity of the Catholic Church in protecting the perpetrators has received much media attention. Whilst the specific circumstances of this shameful history within one institution are relevant to a particular time and place, the dynamics of the narratives I am quoting below help us to understand the workings of shame in the context of abuse. I will be using the example of the Irish government's response to the revelations of the sexual misconduct of Catholic priests in Ireland to highlight the psychological issues. The Irish government offered the potential survivors financial compensation for their suffering; this entailed a potentially traumatic exposure and retelling of their experiences. As Morrison points out, re-telling a story that evokes shame in the subject, can lead to a repetition of the original feelings associated with the trauma: 'Emotional, physical and sexual infantile and childhood traumas cause serious harm to the developing sense of self and they prime the child to re-experience shame again and again' (Morrison, 1998: 67).

The birth of shame lies in the failure to evoke an empathic response. From the victim's point of view, admitting to being abused would be admitting to this failure. Clearly, the internal logic would seem to be that because this happened to me there must be something bad about me not the perpetrator. This is a logic that, if not challenged, thought of, or talked about, renders the individual an eternal victim who can never make the reparative journey to become a survivor. The Irish state is seeking to repair the damage done through a system of redress that is outside the formal legal framework and has the power to award financial compensation. Whilst such financial compensation is welcome to the survivors, what was striking was the importance of the quality of the experience of the redress committees for the survivors.

If the experience was felt to be positive, they conveyed a very moving sense of the reparative nature of the endeavour. One female victim described how important it had been for her when the judge had said, 'I am sorry we let you down' (BBC Radio 4, 2009). An obviously powerful empathic response and experienced as such by the woman. Unfortunately, not everyone received such a sensitive response. In contrast, a male victim was asked the size of the man's penis who had abused him. Obviously, this only added to the victim's experience of violation and, we can imagine, added to the burden of his shame in being unable to evoke an understanding response in the other.

For most of the victims it appeared it was the apology, if any were forthcoming, which was vital in mending their broken lives, rather than the financial compensation. The stories of these people revolved around a withdrawal, at its most obvious from the mainstream of society, at its most tragic in suicide, but I would also argue an internal withdrawal from the self. By this I mean not feeling able to act with authenticity. This can become habitual, at its most extreme, leading to a sense of alienation from the self. Providing the other with what one thinks they want from you, not believing it possible that they would want you. The idea of withdrawal is central to the experience of shame. It invariably evokes a sense of wanting to run away and hide and for the ground to swallow one up.

When I mentioned to a friend, not in the therapy world, that I was writing this chapter, she remarked that she thought it was important as 'people kill themselves because of shame' – the ultimate withdrawal. Morrison elucidates the same idea as follows when suggesting one reason why someone might kill themselves: 'shame and humiliation spawn the feelings of hopelessness and desperation that culminate in the decision to commit suicide... With suicide comes an end to despair, the ultimate resolution of humiliation, mortification and shame' (Morrison, 1998: 193). Whilst, fortunately, we may not come in contact with this tragic withdrawal often, encountering those demonstrating some degree of psychic withdrawal is a common experience.

Implications for the Consulting Room

When my daughter was younger, she was talking about the room that I work in and referred to it as my 'insulting' room rather than my 'consulting' room. The Concise Oxford Dictionary definition of 'insult' is: 'Treat with scornful abuse, offer indignity to a person or thing'. I think my daughter had chanced on some kind of truth: that an inevitable, albeit unintended part of the therapist's endeavour, will be experienced as an insult and therefore shaming. I hasten to underline that I am by no means stating that it would necessarily be from intention but as Phillips points out when exploring the plight of the infant in oedipal terms: 'It is humiliating that the only people who can satisfy your desire from your point of view won't, and from their point of view, can't' (Phillips, 1998: 101). I would suggest that the same holds true for the relationship between therapist and client in the consulting room.

It might be tempting to surmise that shame that arises in the therapeutic space is a re-living of past experiences that evoked similar emotions. Whilst this, from a psychoanalytic point of view, is one truth, I think that for the therapist to always see shame in these terms is an avoidance of the idea that there is something inherently shaming in this particular encounter in the here and now. After all, a client is in the position of looking for and needing help over problems that may feel embarrassing or humiliating, and this puts them in a vulnerable place. They will also be required, in order to be helped to speak about these problems, to talk in an open exposing way, maybe for the first time. Given the rule of analytic abstinence and the other conventions we maintain in the service of the therapy, there is an inherent inequality in the relationship that means that the therapist is always going to know more about the client than the client will about them.

The demeanour of the therapist must also be considered here. Whilst not unheard of, it is unusual for us to lose our tempers, burst into tears or express strong emotions yet there is an expectation that our clients will. To be faced by someone maintaining a sense of quiet thoughtfulness when one is feeling overwhelmed by one's feelings, whilst a relief for some, would for many feel humiliating. Over the course of time, the growth of trust, the expression of empathy and the deepening of the relationship will do much to mitigate this, but in the early days of therapy the potential for feeling shame is ever present.

The picture is further complicated by two factors. The first being the client's early experiences and whether this has led to the creation of a particularly shame prone individual. The second being that, again shaped by earlier experiences, the way the shame is expressed will vary from individual to individual. It may not be straightforward for the therapist to understand the hidden message within the communication. These ideas do place a responsibility on the therapist to consider whether to interpret such manifestations of shame through linking them to past experiences made manifest in the present through the person of the therapist in the transference, or whether to acknowledge the peculiarity of the situation that these two human beings find themselves in.

Jacoby in his consideration of this problem comes to the conclusion that a direct acknowledgement is most helpful. He does this, 'by saying something like, "It must be an odd feeling to go to a complete stranger and to tell him personal things without hardly having said more than hello"'. He goes on to say that, 'people...are very thankful for such a comment, assuming that it is based on authentic – as opposed to routine – empathy' (Jacoby, 1994: 77).

The Deception of Shame

Up until now, I have been looking at shame when it is more or less recognisable and expressed as such. I will now look at the ways that shame can be present in an individual but expressed through other emotions. This presents us with a much more complicated picture and demonstrates clearly the insidious and destructive nature of the feeling. I shall use two clinical examples.

James

James is in his middle years; he sets high standards for himself and looks to the external world to provide him with evidence of his own worth in the form of promotion at work and reassurance from his wife that he is a good husband. He is reticent about his history, although it is clear that experiences of disappointment, particularly being overlooked in favour of a younger sibling, have led him to develop an impermeable carapace, alienated from his fellows and himself, describing himself thus: 'Inside I am not what I appear to be to other people'.

The precipitating factor that brought James into therapy was an angry incident at work that could have led to violence. His disturbance, however, was not made manifest through depression or sadness or withdrawal but expressed through bitterness, envy and a tortured seeking for revenge in which it ceased to matter whether the person to be punished was to blame or not. His office and his colleagues became increasingly toxic.

Jacoby describes the logic of such a reaction as follows:

> Rage that has been caused by early humiliations – and that is suppressed and eventually repressed because one fears punishment and the withdrawal of love – can break through in adulthood. A person with this pattern may feel justified for indulging in an outbreak of rage or may wish to seek revenge for past disgraces in the hope of restoring his dignity and narcissistic equilibrium. (Jacoby, 1994: 76)

James frequently expressed deep contempt towards those who showed any kind of psychological openness or displayed vulnerability. He demonstrated a deep lack of confidence in other people if he were to demonstrate any kind of emotional weakness: 'All that happened when my father died was people took advantage of me...tried to get one over on me at work...I just don't bother to tell people how I'm feeling now'.

James clearly states how he has become victim to the unempathic response of the other – a recurring theme in the exploration of shame. He is saying that this and earlier experiences have taught him that it is foolish to be open. Whenever he has sought to do this he feels he has been met with hostility. This leads to a state of affairs in which it becomes safer never to reveal oneself as the process of self revelation leads to attack, with the logical conclusion that one's core thoughts and feelings are unacceptable and therefore shameful. This sense of secrecy and the consequent wish to hide oneself away from others, either literally or psychologically, are irrefutable indicators of the presence of shame. If it is so unbearable to reflect on one's own nature, how much more unbearable it is to endure the examination of the other regarding one's true self.

It is interesting to reflect on the fact that James has suspicions that his boss, Sam, had slept with his wife. As Mollon points out: 'shame is concerned with comparison of self with other' (Mollon, 2002: 26). In the angry incident at work that led to him to seek help, James made allusions to Sam's sexual prowess in a most brutal and shaming fashion. He approached another member of staff who he knew to be insecure and taunted him, saying he had seen Sam making sexual advances to his wife.

This highlights James's sense of inadequacy and consequent shame in the significant areas of his life. This was exacerbated when Sam promoted a younger man to be his deputy. James's reaction was to express contempt and disdain to those around him. However unpleasant this might feel, it serves a purpose in protecting him from the feelings of shame relating to his sense of his own inadequacy.

So failures in work and love have evoked a shame response in him. However, there is a basic failure at the bottom of these experiences. According to Mollon, the core failure is 'not being able to evoke an empathic response in the other' (Mollon, 2002: 26). If this idea is followed, it suggests, as I have shown earlier, that the way in which our love is affirmed from infancy onwards is, to a large extent, governed by our ability to elicit a loving response in another who wishes and is able and ready to give it. A failure in this dynamic over time can be disastrous for the internal world of the victim evoking a profound sense of shame in the face of the inadequacy of one's loving feelings. A shame that can be masked by a hatred of the other, and a world that has diligently withheld the emotional nourishment that facilitates a subjective sense of emotional viability and being worthwhile.

Tom

I am reminded of a young man I used to see who would inevitably respond to a challenging but probably accurate piece of insight from myself thus: 'Oh you would say that, wouldn't you? That's just you being analytic, isn't it? I am talking about me now and there aren't any parallels with my past. If there are they are completely irrelevant. You are more interested in that than I am. It is simply not helpful'. His response encouraged me to reflect on shame in the following way.

We can understand his reaction from many, equally valid, standpoints; however, I am going to start with the idea that it is a response fuelled by envy. Envy in response to my capacity to think, starkly in contrast to his own lack of peace of mind and consequent inability to think. Whilst this explanation may have truth in it, I feel the understanding is incomplete. My sense is that he felt shamed in being confronted with the symbolic equivalent of the unresponsive look of the other, mentioned earlier in the description of the 'still face' experiments. In other words, my preoccupation with accurate albeit conventional psychoanalytic ways of thinking and interpretation was blinding me to the central personal issue – in this case, the shame and hopelessness engendered by the failure of yet another relationship.

This leads one to consider the entrenched nature of shame and the difficulty in finding a way to talk about it that does not lead to further entrenchment. With people not so burdened by shame, uncomfortable truths, whilst difficult to hear, can also be welcomed, especially within the context of a relationship with a trusted other. This is not the case with those in the thrall of incapacitating shame. A potentially helpful piece of insight is heard as a criticism, a judgement, or, in the words of my daughter an insult. Rather than leading to a psychic development or a helpful thought the result of such an intervention leads merely to a further entrenchment of the shame.

Jill

I will consider another clinical example to show how one type of shame can mask another more profound example of the same emotion. Shame that is originally generated in relationship with another can be perpetuated into a shame that is brought about by the sufferer's own actions. Rather than anger hiding the original shame, I will show how a self-inflicted shame can mask something more painful. However irrational this might appear at first glance, I will put forward the idea that it is preferable to feel the progenitor of ones own shame rather than be the recipient of shame you can do nothing about.

Jill has, with some difficulty, semi-extricated herself from a failing relationship. It has not been a clear clean break, and there is some question for both of them over whether they have actually separated. Maybe a tacit agreement is at work here to avoid the feeling of loss. To complicate a complicated situation further, this woman has begun sleeping with her former partner's best friend. This, she has said, is not to do with love but, she believes, is simply convenient for both of them. A weekend or so ago, she went to a party with this man and her expartner, they all ended up back at her flat and during the night she ended up in bed with the newer partner. She was caught by her expartner.

There are many ways of understanding and reading this situation. In this context I would like to consider the following. The whole scenario could not have been better designed to make her feel ashamed of herself, ashamed and guilty. But, albeit with no conscious sense of agency, it is undeniable that it is her own creation and she had control over it; at numerous points she had the opportunity to stop things. I would suggest however that somehow this shame, the shame she has brought on herself and the consequent orgy of self-flagellation it unleashed, is preferable to her than the shame she has no control over – the shame of having a mother who abandoned her at 18 months. A potent example of the paradoxical dynamic of it becoming good to feel bad as described by Nathanson (1992: 334) earlier in the chapter.

This is interesting in terms of thinking about a more nuanced understanding of shame. It is going to take time to evolve a sophisticated discourse around emotions that are difficult to think about, and clearly it is not only psychotherapy that can offer a way in to enriching the discourse of shame. However, in the same way that our understanding and hence our ability to talk about guilt or envy owes much to psychoanalytic theorists I think that a similar development is taking place around shame. I would take from the example above an idea that it is possible to differentiate between two sorts of shame, and therefore be able to talk about it in a more sophisticated way. In this way, we can help ourselves and others develop an understanding of how shame operates in our relationships both internally and in relation to others.

On the one hand there exists the shame that is engendered and evoked through the experience of the non-empathic response. The experience that brings into doubt one's sense of one's own worth when the loving gaze is not reciprocated. Crucially, an experience that is not within the subject's power to change. I would suggest that this can lead to feelings of shame brought about by the person themselves. He or she can behave in such a way that a sense of shame is evoked that is their own creation. This has two benefits, the sense of powerlessness is assuaged as the shame is brought about by ones own actions. Second, feelings of abandonment and loss are avoided. The internal logic would seem to say that it is preferable to have a shaming parent rather than no parent at all. To live with a permanent sense of shame perpetuates the bond between the self and the shaming parent. It is as if one were saying to oneself, 'I cannot be that bad if I still have my parent with me, because I feel this way I know they are still there'.

Connection and Contamination

I will conclude with some reflections on the relational aspect of shame. Shame can only be generated in the context of a relationship, and I will draw attention to a phenomenon that underlines this aspect, its contaminating nature.

It has been my contention that shame is an emotion that we are all painfully familiar with but are reluctant to think or talk about. This means that there are aspects of the experience that remain mysterious, a particular aspect of this is its contaminating nature. Interestingly, Spanish has an expression to describe this – *la verguenza ajena* – for which there is no equivalent in English. This expression means the feeling that one gets when witnessing the shame of another. This can certainly be an intense experience and one which we have all participated in but, to my knowledge, has a meaning which has not been explored.

This reminds me of another interaction with a client that, in the same way as the one above, stayed with me over time. A very withdrawn inhibited woman said to me: 'My partner asked me to kiss her with all my heart and I couldn't do it'. This was followed with a silence imbued with much pain. In this instance, it was not so much the content of what was being said but more the process that unfolded between us. A potent example of a shame dialogue.

On hearing her admission I found it very hard to look her in the face. That visceral desire to look away so characteristic when shame is in the frame is much in evidence here. The centrality of the gaze, the avoidance of the mutual look, is an essential component of shame. The difficulty in meeting the eyes of the other is a strong indication of the presence of shame, and it is interesting for those of us who are therapists to reflect on where we look when feeling it is time to articulate a wounding truth.

Broadly speaking, with the person under consideration, I felt I was left with two alternatives, either to explore with her the nature of the relationship with her partner or to accept the invitation, implicit in her gaze, to explore her relationship with me. One path, to my way of thinking, representing an avoidance of shame, the other to confront directly, and try to talk about the shame experience and its effect on our relationship and her relationship with herself.

Within this hostility there is the appeal for connection. It is a challenge to find the positive in shame, especially when it is expressed in a way that alienates. There is, however, opportunity in this paradox: the more off-putting the expression of the shame, the more alienated the individual feels and the more yearning there is for connection.

It is tempting, maybe even unavoidable, to see shame as a repudiation of a relationship with the other. Nathanson, in his introduction to Munt's *Queer Attachments* (Munt, 2007) reminds us that the opposite is true: 'Wherever you see shame (no matter how vigorously defended against) someone is hoping for reconnection' (Nathanson, 2007: xv). A helpful reminder, not only for the clinicians, to locate within ourselves, 'a renewed desire to soothe the afflicted and heal the broken interpersonal bond', rather than turn our backs (Nathanson, 2007: xv).

Any confrontation with shame, whether disguised as hostility or expressed openly, makes considerable demands on our capacity to connect and engage with human pain. We have to locate our tolerance, forbearance and understanding in order to make use of the other.

Conclusion

In this chapter, my primary aim has been to stimulate an internal dialogue in the reader about shame and open it up for consideration as a possible motivational factor regarding certain kinds of behaviour. I hope it has become clear that the seeming psychic paralysis and accompanying hopelessness in the face of this emotion is in no small part due to the difficulty in thinking about it. This difficulty is twofold involving as it does the problems in perceiving it and apprehending it in ourselves but also the painful feelings that are stimulated when we witness another's shame. I have also demonstrated how shame can be present but disguised; the pain of the experience means that it can be masked and erupt in hatred – a hatred that can be acted out both upon others and also upon the self.

Once one is able to think about shame it is possible to develop a more nuanced and differentiated articulation of it as a multi-layered emotion. I have put forward the idea that shame, in a similar way to envy, is inevitable for us all. Even good enough caregivers will have found themselves incapable of offering an empathic response all the time. It must simply be a question of degree – some individuals are more burdened with shame than others.

Jacqueline Rose in her exploration of the links between private and public worlds in *On Not Being Able To Sleep* ends her introduction, '...perhaps the best way to move forward...is to think about the things of which we are most ashamed' (Rose, 2001: 14).

This, as I hope I have demonstrated, is a valid appeal both on an individual and societal level. Whilst not minimising the difficulties in following it, I hope I have made clearer the necessity of so doing.

References

BBC Radio 4. (2009) *Law in Action.* Broadcast July 7th 2009. (London: BBC Radio 4).

Bollas, C. (1987) *The Shadow of the Object: Psychoanalysis of the Unthought Known.* (London: Free Association Books).

Jacoby, M. (1994) *Shame and the Origins of Self-Esteem.* (London: Routledge).

Mollon, P. (2002) *Shame and Jealousy.* (London: Karnac Books).

Morrison, A. (1998) *The Culture of Shame.* (Northvale New Jersey: Jason Aronson Inc).

Nathanson, D. (1992) *Shame and Pride.* (New York: W. W. Norton).

Nathanson, D. (2007) 'Foreword' in S. Munt. *Queer Attachments.* (Aldershot: Ashgate).

Pattison, S. (2000) *Shame: Theory, Therapy, Theology.* (Cambridge: Cambridge University Press).

Phillips, A. (1998) *The Beast in the Nursery.* (London: Faber and Faber).

Rose, J. (2001) *On Not Being Able to Sleep.* (London: Chatto and Windus).

Steiner, J. (1997) *Psychic Retreats.* (London: Routledge).

Stern, D. (1990/98) *Diary of a Baby.* (New York: Basic Books).

Tronick, E, A, H., Adamson, L., Wise S., and Brazelton, T. (1978) 'The infant's response to entrapment between contradictory messages in face-to-face interaction', *Journal of Child Psychiatry*, 17, 1–13.

Winnicott, D. W. (1958) 'Hate in the Countertransference' in *Through Paediatrics to Psychoanalysis.* (London: Karnac Books). (1947).

In memoriam: Dudley Rignell.

8

On Loneliness

Gabrielle Brown

Introduction

Melanie Klein's last paper, 'On the Sense of Loneliness' describes an inevitable human condition of alienation from others and from the self. For Klein, the satisfactions provided by external reality – good company and love – never mitigate enduring 'internal loneliness' derived from 'a ubiquitous yearning for an unattainable perfect internal state' (Klein, 1963: 300). The paranoid and depressive anxieties of infancy, detailed in her earlier work, leave in their wake traces of insecurity, mistrust and nostalgia. Loneliness is most acute in depressive and psychotic illness or when facing ageing and death. However, even at the best of times it is never developmentally or therapeutically resolved. Klein's is a work which affords detailed insight into the universal phenomenon of being lonely in a crowd and equally, ill at ease in our own company.

Therapists and theorists need to continue to be preoccupied with the concept of loneliness. It is a concept positioned uncomfortably at the threshold between the internal world and the domain of the social and political, such that therapists may feel helpless to have much impact. Vast and important terrains of stigma and social exclusion form the hinterland to this concept, which, although not my particular focus here, must not slip our minds.

Historically loneliness has been linked to phenomena of social isolation and social exclusion and quantified in this way (UK Government Cabinet Office, 2006). Such a narrow definition gives little impetus for understanding loneliness as expressive of internal states of mind, rather than simply secondary and reactive to external circumstances. MIND, the UK mental health charity, distinguishes between 'circumstantial, developmental and internal' loneliness in their *Coping with Loneliness* leaflet (MIND, 2004: 4). They suggest 'To feel loneliness is to be overwhelmed by an unbearable feeling of separateness, at a very deep level. To some degree, it is a totally normal emotion, a part of growing up. At birth, we all start the process of separation..., the parallel need to seek relationship begins' (MIND, 2004: 2).

I will look at loneliness as an internal state in which the quality of relationships with others is secondary to the quality of our understanding and toleration of ourselves. Both Winnicott and Klein give perspectives on the internal dynamics of loneliness and their genesis. As I discuss below, the help that we received in early life to bear and understand our own conflicts and contradictions will impact on how well we are able to use others in this task in later life. This includes how we are able to use the curiosity, responsiveness and understanding offered by therapy, and, more generally, how we can integrate and learn from experience, that of others and as well as our own.

Theoretical Perspectives

Loneliness and freedom from its misery is often linked to the theories of positive 'aloneness' and of solitude (Quinodoz, 1993;1996). Developmentally, gradual separation from the primary caregiver builds the capacity for independent and individual psychic functioning. Bowlby finds conditions which foster an independent sense of the self, requiring neither avoidance nor clinging to others to sustain the sense of a 'secure base' (Holmes, 2001). For Winnicott the 'capacity to be alone' starts with the child seeking out 'aloneness' by ignoring the presence of the caregiver (Winnicott, 1958). Being 'alone in the presence of another' allows the child uninterrupted absorption in an essential world of imagination and play, supported by increasingly internalised images of protection and attunement. Unlike Klein, Winnicott suggests the existence of an integrated core to the self and implies that feelings of loneliness are not universal. In health, contented states of 'quietude' allow unconflicted rest from communication with the external world: 'each individual is an isolate, permanently non-communicating, permanently unknown, in fact, unfound' (Winnicott, 1963: 187). I return to Winnicott's contribution below.

Aloneness in these accounts is a freedom from anxiety about our relations to others, resulting in creative inner richness and self-presence indicative of ego-strength (Storr, 1989). More recently, Quinodoz has disagreed with Klein's concept of loneliness directly. He modifies her term with the notion of 'tamed solitude', which he considers 'characteristic of affective maturity and ego strength' (Quinodoz, 1996: 48). For Quinodoz feelings of loneliness can be seen as the darkness before dawn, when internal conflict is accounted for and repaired, leading to 'buoyancy' which rides out changing internal states. Such concepts of 'solitude' inherit a Romantic tradition of the ideal conditions for creativity and enlightenment. 'Solitude' may involve suffering, but solitary suffering is productive of universal human insight. Thus, the Ancient Mariner of Coleridge's poem renders the wedding guest 'a sadder and a wiser' man through his narrative of desolation (Coleridge, 1817).

By contrast, Klein posits separation from the mother, from a symbiotic and intuitive mutuality, as the irreversible genesis of loneliness: 'However gratifying it is...to express thoughts and feelings to a congenial person, there remains an unsatisfied longing for an understanding without words' (Klein, 1963: 301). Hers is an un-Romantic view of loneliness, seen as universal, banal and inhibiting. Centrally, the antithesis of loneliness is engagement with others, stemming from an increasingly benign superego's ability to tolerate conflicting parts of the self. Engagement in generosity and reciprocity are emphasised in her work: 'Gratitude...includes the wish to return goodness received and is thus the basis for generosity (Chapter 5). There is always a close connection between being able to accept and to give, and both are part of the relation to the good object and therefore counteract loneliness...the feeling of generosity underlies creativeness' (Klein, 1963: 310).

Social Context

I will mention in passing that the strongest impetus for addressing the experience of loneliness in therapeutic work occurs in current sociological rather than psychoanalytic discourses. The experience of loneliness in society is deemed 'a greater risk for morbidity or mortality than cigarette smoking...' (Epley et al., 2008). As medical science maps the physical sequelae of emotional states, studies focussing on feelings of loneliness pinpoint 'how the social world gets under the skin' (Hermes et al., 2009). Depression, 'stress', boredom and lack of interpersonal stimulation attendant on loneliness are implicated in a range of physical diseases, from cancer to dementia, as well as in problematic salves to emotional pain, such as addiction.

Loneliness in society is difficult to measure, except as a self-reported, subjective experience. As suggested above, lack of social contact predicts rather than defines feeling lonely. For instance, studies of social isolation in aging reveal the importance of the quality of relationships and the nature of attachments, rather than their quantity (Victor et al, 2009). Exploring feelings of loneliness as social phenomena also becomes confused by a tendency to reduce the entire emotional spectrum of relating to 'being loved'. Klein sees loneliness less in intimate terms of 'love', but as a more general 'feeling...that one does not fully *belong* to oneself or, therefore, to anyone else' (1963: 302, my emphasis).

Belonging, as I will explore later, is less a state of being chosen or special, than of unconditional toleration. This includes tolerating the aggressive and imperfect sides which constitute the 'warts and all' aspect of belonging. A painful aspect of loneliness is having no one with whom to argue. We are reduced to unalleviated quarrels within ourselves, particularly in the extreme loneliness of psychosis and the self-reproaches of depression. In this vein Winnicott, in 'Hate in the Countertransference' *(1947)*, posited the enduring need to be both 'hateful' and tolerated as a precondition for being both known and loved. He typifies the genesis of this need by describing the everyday life of mother and baby: 'after an awful morning with him she goes out, and he smiles at a stranger, who says: 'Isn't he sweet?' (1947: 201).

Loneliness in society highlights our difficulties as members of groups, with conflicting and poorly integrated urges towards evasion and belonging. Bion suggested that each individual is riven with conflict and pain through an innate sense of the need to relate to others. Problems of 'groupishness' afflict us intensely, regardless of how the personal path of our group membership has played itself out. 'The individual is a group animal at war, not simply with the group', he writes, 'but with himself for being a group animal and with those aspects of his personality that constitute his "groupishness"' (Bion, 1961: 131).

Internal Loneliness

Fundamental to the 'wars' of 'groupishness' is the loss of an integrated 'perfect internal state' as individuation proceeds (Klein, 1963: 300). From that point on unresolveable conflicts between life and death drives, between reparative and aggressive forces, fissure the psyche: 'Since full integration is never achieved, complete understanding and acceptance of one's own emotions, phantasies and anxieties is not possible, and this continues as an important factor in loneliness' (Klein, 1963: 302).

An aspect of both normal and pathological psychic functioning and communication involves attributing aspects of the self to others, in a process termed 'projective identification' (Hinshelwood, 1989). In its benign form, where the psyche is relatively integrated, this plays 'an important part in the feeling of closeness' and mitigates loneliness (Klein, 1963: 310). For example, the closeness and empathy derived from a 'shared understanding' with another person. But when projection is more extreme the process becomes much like our fear of the dark – when our inner unease is perceived to bear down on us from all around. We may feel surrounded by hostility, misunderstanding and likely rejection, even in benign circumstances. As so often in Klein's accounts, the shifting landscape of our internal conflicts cast frightening shadows over external reality, and, if internal fragmentation proceeds towards psychosis, the distinction between inner and external reality, and between the self and others, becomes lost.

A turbulent internal climate makes an unstable base from which to relate to others. In addition, the superego's fear of being unable to control destructiveness inhibits our engagement with good experiences, which support internal integration, lest we spoil them (Klein, 1963: 313). When we cannot trust ourselves with our valued objects, lonely withdrawal may present the only way to curb aggressive and greedy impulses. Envy involves an active and ruthless attack upon an object recognised as good, valuable and often also loved. In these circumstances loneliness, with its more passive rueful pining, may seem the only way to limit the damage we fear our passions could inflict on those we love. In the following, I consider a client, Mrs A, who abstained from close contact because she experienced her needs as 'intolerable' and destructive. When we mistrust ourselves and feel devoid of goodness, we exhibit the distrust, meanness and the terror of being robbed of what little we have, that is so commonly associated with lonely individuals.

The clients I discuss made loneliness their primary concern. It was the presenting problem in therapy and an organising factor in their lives over many years. Marilyn Lawrence postulates that clients stay close to that which terrifies them most, in an effort to control it, using the example of the anorexic's 'dicing with death' (2008: 107). In different ways, loneliness stays close to those parts of the self which cannot be understood or 'communicated' (Winnicott, 1963) and provides landmarks to buried sites of confusion, terror of rejection or of 'impingement' and intrusion. These make a therapeutic focus on loneliness important and fruitful.

Clinical Examples

From Neglect to Loneliness

Mrs A, a woman in her 60s, came to therapy because of a habit of falling in love with unattainable men, who were gay or determinedly solitary. Her other attachments were secure and rewarding, but these unrequited loves left her feeling intensely lonely. They also confirmed a shameful image of herself as 'too needy underneath' for others to tolerate.

Mrs A presented a childhood of pining for glamorous but seldom seen parents who lived in town, while she was brought up by relatives in the countryside. She often brought an account of her childhood play. In her game she buried her rag doll, because she found it malignant, ugly and troublesome. But the chill and loneliness of the doll's entombment would haunt and preoccupy her. After a few agonised hours she would dig up the ugly doll, whereupon the cycle would repeat itself with further burial.

The doll most obviously symbolised the rejected child and served to carry projections of her 'troublesome' parts, to which parental abandonment was attributed. Klein describes an empathetic link with the projected part: 'the lost parts too are felt to be lonely' (1963: 302), which augments the general sensation of loneliness. It is also around our most 'troublesome' parts: aggression, fears, guilt and rages that the longing for understanding and acceptance from others crystallises. In this sense the discarded parts, the doll, also represented longing for her mother, as an object that would help her contain and tolerate herself.

In adulthood Mrs A idealised herself as highly self-reliant, demanding very little from another, especially her lovers. In therapy she responded with abstinence to those occasions which evoke feelings of loneliness and loss. Thus she offered me extra weeks of holiday and was uncharacteristically late for sessions for a while, inhibiting her greed by taking less time than her due. She identified strongly with an idealised image of the therapist as the insouciant mother who could do very well without seeing her child. Behind this idealisation was a more frightening image of a mother who could not begin to cope with a child's insatiable greed and resentment. Working with Mrs A occasioned chill blasts of loneliness in the countertransference, from which shared understanding and acceptance of non-ideal parts developed.

From Abuse to Social Exclusion

Lonely people often consider themselves to be much less tolerable to others than they actually are, as Mrs A illustrates above. We then hope to ease them back to a more benign reality, modify self-doubt and raise self-esteem. Such assumptions stall in the face of clients who relate to others in overtly perverse, harmful or socially unacceptable ways. Working with the conflicts and hostility of clients who may be labelled as 'self-isolating' is an important part of understanding loneliness.

Mr B came to therapy with a direct complaint of loneliness. He was, on acquaintance, a lively man living in a friendly hostel. However, he was avoided by others because he smelt strongly, for, although he washed his clothes now and again, he felt unable to wash his body. He was painfully aware of the societal opprobrium that this attracted. Mr B had suffered from psychotic episodes, where he felt his mind to be invaded or emptied by others. Behind his current difficulties lay early traumas, including sexual abuse.

The strong smell of others, be it perfume or body odour, is considered, in our culture, to be both aversive and invasive. Smell is also part of communication – with intentional, conscious and unconscious elements (Segal, 1997). Mr B identified his smell as being like his thoughts (and we might say also projections) and the metaphor continued to be useful throughout the work.

Initially, both I and the furnishings rapidly came to smell identical to Mr B. The 'unmistakeable' odour permeated and clung to the setting. Communication was then of a symmetrical, 'twin', symbiotic type: I concretely took on, twinned with, the shameful odour which signalled Mr B's loneliness and his illness. In this highly symbolic respect, difference between us was erased. Searles describes such concrete communication and wholesale projection of disturbance into another as 'Driving the Other Person Crazy' (Searles, 1959). This aims 'to find a soulmate to assuage unbearable loneliness', where the loneliness of not having been understood has already had catastrophic psychic consequences, resulting in psychosis (Searles, 1959: 267). The desolate 'nameless dread' of finding no echo in the mind of another is defended against by taking over or suffusing that mind altogether (Bion, 1962; 1970).

Mr B and I could be lonely together, as I have just described, but primarily his smell kept others, including myself, at a distance. For instance, the room in which we met smelt particularly good, thanks to the hostel baking class. But shrouded in his own odour, Mr B was having none of it. Nor could I approach him with words, for he talked volubly without pause – stereotypical of lonely individuals. There are many ways to think about these 'extraordinary protections' against contact (Mitrani, 2001) which lead from early empathic failure and intrusion to later determined loneliness. Klein suggests a longing 'to make relationships with people' inhibited by mistrust and the confusion of excessive projection (1963: 304). Glasser describes an aggressively defensive 'core complex' as a response to early trauma: 'the individual establishes a firm grip on the object but this grip also entails keeping the object at arm's length' (Glasser, 1986: 10).

As Mr B's loneliness began to acquire meaning through the therapy, he found different ways to communicate and he gradually began to wash. He was then able to join a group for those recovering from psychosis. His emotionally arid life acquired some pleasure in contact and ordinary conflict with others. This heralded a lessening of anxieties about being understood, 'there is a close link between enjoyment and the feeling of understanding and being understood' (Klein, 1963: 310).

Discussion

'Being Insulated'

Winnicott (1963) follows Klein's contention (1963) that failure of ego integration distorts the process of knowing the self. Concurrently the availability of the self to be known by others is diminished. However, Winnicott's work suggests that a split between the 'isolate' core and other parts of the ego may occur as a response to the external environment during early development, as in the split between the 'true' and 'false self' (Winnicott, 1960). Therefore, in 'On Communicating and not Communicating', contemporaneous with Klein's paper, Winnicott posits a general existential dilemma of loneliness, authenticity and relating: 'How to be isolated without having to be insulated' (Winnicott, 1963: 187).

Winnicott, and the ideas that his work has inspired, enable us to understand some forms of sociability and apparent gregariousness as defences, from which the 'real' or 'true' self is excluded (1960). Such exclusion results in parts of the self that are lonely because unacknowledged and 'insulated'. These concepts illuminate the troubling paradox of how good opportunities for relating, particularly in institutional settings, (such as Mr B's friendly hostel above), fail to relieve individual loneliness.

The 'Dead Mother' Complex

Klein, Winnicott and more recently André Green conceptualise manic attempts at communication, from childhood onwards, as defences against intense existential loneliness and internal 'deadness' (Green, 2001). A 'hole in the texture of object relations with the mother' develops when the mother is only episodically responsive to the child, due to depression or bereavement (Green, 2001: 178–9). Green terms this the 'Dead Mother Complex'. Klein gives a chilling illustration of the lasting effects of this early situation. Her case study, in the 'Loneliness' paper, presents a client who attempts to hold on to the goodness of nature by taking a field mouse home with him from the countryside (1963: 309). Once home, he forgets the mouse in his car, where it perishes. The dead mouse then comes to represent the fragility of the good empathic object under the pall of maternal depression (1963: 309). By analogy, therapists may have the experience of trying to bring to supervision the fleeting authentic connections which occur with lonely clients. The fragile liveliness of the therapy session seems to perish between the pages of the therapist's notebook. It cannot be rekindled, rendering supervision a witness to emptiness and loss.

'... A disaster not to be found'

The process of individuation has the quality of a sort of 'hide and seek' between the internal and external world of the child, in Winnicott's work. Highly charged childhood games and objects can be considered as 'transitional objects'. These objects and the response which caregivers provide to them aid the developing infant to negotiate between loneliness and relating between 'me' and 'not me', 'mine' and 'not mine' (Winnicott, 1951): 'the term transitional object...gives room for the process of becoming able to accept difference and similarity' (1951: 233–4). The excitement of the game of 'hide and seek' lies in the period of 'getting warm' – mutual acknowledgement before actual discovery, when the game ends. The skill of hiding is in remaining 'findable', as opposed to lost, lonely, beyond the pale. As in later verbal communication, remaining 'findable' involves understanding the limits of the seeker's ken. In order to play, and equally, in order to converse, we need to attune ourselves to the determinants of mutual intelligibility (Winnicott, 1963). The trauma of having little or no response, no 'seeking' from the maternal object in this complex and delicate dynamic, affects subsequent relating profoundly. Winnicott summarises this in terms reminiscent of Mrs A's solitary doll game (above): *'it's a joy to be hidden but a disaster not to be found'* (1963: 186 original italics).

Existential Objects

When the maternal object does not seek out the child at all, for instance in enduring neglect, it is the internal world of the child which is unacknowledged and lonely. An ability to tolerate separateness and difference, which playing with the transitional object initiates, is stunted, leading to distortions in relating and enduring loneliness (Winnicott, 1951: 233). Freud had observed his grandson's play with a 'found' object, a cotton reel, in the *'fort/da'* game (Freud, 1920). The game gradually enabled the child to both 'master' the anxiety that his mother's occasional absence provoked and to mourn her during such separations. When mother goes out, the dread of abandonment is 'mastered' through feeling the mother's continued empathic connection (Freud, 1920: 284). This is symbolised by the string which attaches the cotton reel to the cot, a connection which allows the child, as we may say, to 'tug at her heartstrings' as required. However, he also undertakes small acts of mourning for the ideal, ever present mother (Klein, 1963) as her difference and separateness emerge. The importance of incremental mourning in separation comes in Freud's footnote to the *'fort/da'* section in 'Beyond The Pleasure Principle' (1920: 286). Here he recounts that the early game of presence and absence undertaken by mother and child enabled this grandson to cope with the actual loss of his mother when, some years later, she died.

Elisha Davar has suggested that if the mother is completely absent or neglectful the process of incremental mourning cannot be initiated. Instead of the mediating transitional object, an 'existential object' fills her space, an object from which the child cannot then separate (Davar, 2001: 25). In the case of Mrs A, above, we see repeated idealisation of the un-responsive object which takes the place of objects capable of adapting to her needs for love, care and independence. In the presence of an 'existential object' the dramas of 'doing without' others became more engrossing than the challenges of 'being with' them. In extreme pathology, the preoccupations of eating disorders or the tides of engulfment and withdrawal in substance use, leave the client in the thrall of a concrete external object. This existential object, whilst born of neglect, confers a sense of plenitude. Clinically, the passionate embrace of the existential object makes therapeutic intervention difficult, because the place of the other is already filled (Lawrence, 2008; Weegmann and Cohen, 2002).

In the same vein, greedy hoarding of acquaintances or inanimate objects seeks to 'insulate' and shore up a lonely and disparate core – the Miser being a longstanding stereotype of the lonely individual. Collecting social contacts, such as Facebook 'friends', may also fail to bring a sense of belonging. Mr B, above, suffered this loneliness: he had gathered a large team of concerned professionals with whom he was unable ('refused to') to engage, whilst simultaneously resisting parting, that is, discharge from their care. We may say he 'hoarded' professional contacts but made little use of them. Scanlon and Adlam have extensively explored these difficulties in engagement as the meaningful 'Inarticulate Speech of the Heart' of excluded individuals (Scanlon and Adlam, 2008; 2011).

'Hoarding' of material objects has received increasing psychiatric interest, with the draft of DSM-V including a definition as 'persistent difficulty discarding or *parting with* possessions, regardless of their actual value' (2011, my emphasis). Klein had linked 'fear of parting' with loneliness and described 'a compulsive tie to certain objects'. Aspects of the self, projected into external objects or people, are felt to be torn away through parting: 'The result is an excessive weakening of the ego, a feeling that there is nothing to sustain it, and a corresponding feeling of loneliness' (Klein, 1946: 13–14). Parting from hoarded existential objects returns the client to the empty loneliness of maternal neglect.

Belonging and the Clinical Task

If therapists are to give the sense of loneliness the focus that it deserves, as a prevalent and achingly distressing state, we need to highlight how we are negotiating its presence in our professional lives. Specifically, how we keep therapeutic curiosity alive when we feel locked out by clients or equally invited to share their loneliness. In what follows I map some of the difficulties of contact with loneliness in our work and how containing structures, such as supervision, help repair our failures of integration and understanding. I centre my discussion on Klein's sense that it is the reparative activities of 'belonging' which mitigate loneliness and lead to enjoyment and creativity in our work (1963: 310).

Belonging

In Klein's paper on 'Loneliness', 'belonging/belongs' is used four times in a single paragraph, describing the painful loss of projected parts of the self (1963: 302). Although her writing cannot be reduced to autobiography, it is moving to consider the value of 'belonging' in the light of the refugee experience of psychoanalysts during the Second World War. By 1938, a few years after Klein herself arrived in England, refugee analysts made up a third of the British Society membership. 'Tearful reunions' occurred at conferences when colleagues 'dispersed far and wide, fell into each other's arms' (Grosskuth, 1986: 241). In *Love, Guilt and Reparation*, published in 1937, Klein noted that 'we speak of our own country as the 'motherland' because it symbolises the 'ever-bountiful breast' (Klein, 1937: 333). For the newly arrived refugees, issues of the location of the 'motherland' and therefore of belonging itself were painfully complex. Most had the enemy language (German) as their 'mother tongue' and were categorised as 'enemy aliens', facing formidable challenges of disorienta-tion, 'split' identifications, homesickness and loss. In this sense the pining of loneliness, with its close resemblance to feelings of homesickness, represents moments of nostalgic contact with a good 'ever-bountiful' object which can be progressively integrated into the internal world, if it can be mourned (Stubley, 2009).

For Klein 'belonging' is not a passive attribute of affiliation but an actively repeated process of internal integration and reparation, though never complete. The derivation of the word 'belonging' is 'to gather or collect', emphasising integration of split off and dispersed parts (OED, 1969). The noun 'belongings' denotes both 'one's possessions' and 'one's relatives'. Therefore, the 'belong-ings' of a therapist's ego might collate both the 'family relatives' of colleagues, supervisors, therapists and 'possessions' such as the 'brick mothers' (Rey, 1994) of our institutions, our theories, books and traditions.

Loneliness and Shame in Individual Work

Loneliness is an unpleasant emotion with which to be in touch in therapeutic work. Evasions of contact with the client's loneliness often constitute our most shameful mistakes and the failure of an easy generosity we would ideally like to embody[1]. In 1959, Fromm-Reichmann commented that 'clinicians often cannot face the loneliness of their clients and its echoes in themselves. At assessment, it may be glossed over with the less interpersonally demanding diagnosis of 'depression' (Fromm-Reichmann, 1959/1990). Beyond assessment, we may misuse the abstinent psychodynamic technique to defend ourselves, as long as possible, against emotional contact with the pressure of client's longings. Thus Brenman Pick describes how 'correct' technique gets used defensively to 'murder love and concern': 'To suggest that we are not affected by...the patient's painful efforts to reach us would represent not neutrality but falseness or imperviousness' (Brenman Pick, 1988: 163).

A further brief example from my work illustrates my panic when placed in direct contact with a client's loneliness and yearning for belonging, beyond the safe defences of technically correct neutral listening. When Mrs C arrived for her session before a holiday break, she unthinkingly put her own Yale key into the lock of my front door, where it got stuck. For a moment we both stood on the threshold in the glare of a déjà vu from our work – that the force of Mrs C's terror of being 'locked out' frequently prevented her from being invited in. I think I reacted to a long standing dread that this dilemma would appear in the transference rather than, at one remove, in her narrative. For, when I asked Mrs C for permission to write about our work, she recalled that I had 'made the situation go away' with impulsive speed, 'springing at the door with great force' to wrestle her key from the lock.

Loneliness in the Team

While we may seek to evade contact with loneliness in our solitary individual work, as members or consultants to multidisciplinary teams, therapists often find themselves being recipients of projections of loneliness and exclusion (Hinshelwood, 1986). Dynamics of loneliness and belonging play themselves out powerfully in teams and often result in one profession being excluded from meetings and case discussion. Occasions of 'non-belonging' may feel both lonely and professionally shaming or belittling. The excluded team member carries the knowledge of the failed integration of the team, with a deidealised sadness that 'the glamour has gone' from the collective endeavour of teamwork (Klein, 1963: 305).

When teams produce lonely members, conflicting projections from the client's complex inner world are acted out between professionals (Minne, 2008: 28). Exclusion of one party malignly re-enacts clients' early trauma of 'not being found', described above. In addition, the environmental conditions which enabled early abuse, neglect and acute loneliness are replicated in the creation of non-belonging members of the group. Buechler suggests that forbearance towards the pain of being excluded enables us to 'experience aloneness with a [client's team] as information, rather than as judgement' (Buechler, 1998: 110).

Supervision, Understanding and Integration

Klein states that '[when] loneliness is actually experienced [it] becomes a stimulus towards object relations' (1963: 311) on which, we may add, the therapeutic engagement is based. This stance allows us to work towards restoring projections to where they originated and ultimately 'belong'. Buechler suggests that therapists assemble an internal 'chorus' of helpful figures which support us. This professional 'chorus' strengthens our sense of belonging, even in times of loneliness.

When integration proceeds well in supervision, it enables a freely associating 'chorus' to be assembled between the helpful internal objects of both supervisee and supervisor. This richly enhances the 'belonging' of the therapist and client, enabling creative work. However, as I have argued, relating creatively to our internal objects is not without its difficulties:

> both supervisor and supervisee need to have some capacity to tolerate each other associating freely with other objects in their professional lives, such as therapists, teachers and colleagues as well as with their own minds and thoughts. ..... All of this is part of what can make supervision difficult, complex and emotionally charged, but also interesting, satisfying and effective. (Crawford, 2005: 59)

The reparative tasks of 'belonging' involve negotiation with our inherent 'problems of groupishness'. Supervision affords a space for grappling with problems of 'belonging' and relating which is rewarded in moments where both therapist and client experience 'being found'. But we must also face the disillusionment that colleagues and supervisors are not guardian angels forever perched on our shoulder. It is especially when we work with loneliness that we long for the ever present 'imaginary twin' of Klein's account (1963: 302).

Conclusion

'Aspects of the self, though intensely experienced within, continue to elude self-understanding', writes Likierman in summarising Klein's account of loneliness (Likierman, 2001: 193). If loneliness is essentially a feeling, a 'sense', then it takes considerable reflection to create understanding beyond its emotional impact. Each individual's loneliness bears the signature of a complex set of internal conflicts, splits, inhibitions and unmourned losses. Winnicott illuminates the delicate dynamics which lead to the ability to accept and understand both ourselves and others, which mitigates loneliness: 'One needs to have been *thought about a great deal by others* before one can become a 'someone'. Becoming a someone entails many births and many deaths in the metaphoric sense, and the therapist has to understand that.' (Davar, 2010: 428, my emphasis). In the therapeutic relationship, the lonely client relives the full force of their experience of not having been 'thought about'. The therapist may be cast as companion in the transference, but often, I have argued, it is in the unsettling role of perpetrator that we encounter loneliness in our work. Klein's 'On The Sense Of Loneliness' (1963) suggests that the meaning, that is the *sense* we make of loneliness, revitalises the process of integrating and tolerating the self and of enjoyment and reciprocity with others.

Acknowledgements

I am grateful for Peter Aylward's supervision and consultancy, which makes doing and thinking about psychotherapy enduringly fascinating and rewarding.

Note

1. See also Chapter 5 on Generosity and Chapter 7 on Shame.

References

Bion, W. (1961) *Experiences in Groups*. (London: Routledge).

Bion, W. (1962) *Learning From Experience*. (London: Karnac).

Bion, W. (1970) *Attention and Interpretation*. (London: Karnac).

Brenman Pick, I. (1988) 'Working Through in the Countertransference' in Botts Spillius, E. (ed.) *Melanie Klein Today*. (London: Routledge).

Buechler, S. (1998) 'The Analyst's experience of loneliness', *Contemporary Psychoanalysis*, 34, 91–113.

Cabinet Office (2006) *Reaching Out: An Action Plan on Social Exclusion*. [http://www.cabinetoffice.gov.uk/social_exclusion_task_force/publications/reaching_out]

Coleridge, S. T. (1817/1999) *The Rime of the Ancient Mariner* Fry, P. (ed.). (London: Palgrave Macmillan).

Crawford, S. (2005) 'Free Association and Supervision' in Driver, C and Martin, E (eds) *Supervision and the Analytic Attitude*. (London: Whurr).

Davar, E. (2001) 'The loss of the transitional object', *Psychodynamic Counselling*, 7, (1), 5–26.

Davar, E. (2010) 'The interplay of edges', *Psychodynamic Practice*, 16, (4), 409–29.

Epley, N., Akalis, S., Waytz, A., and Cacioppo, J. T. (2008) 'Creating social connection through inferential reproduction: loneliness and perceived agency in gadgets, gods, and greyhounds', *Psychological Science*, 19, 114–120.

Freud, S. (1920) 'Beyond the Pleasure Principle' in *SE.XVIII*. (London: Hogarth Press).

Fromm-Reichmann, F. (1990/1959) 'Loneliness', *Contemporary Psychoanalysis*, 26, 305–329.

Glasser, M. (1986) 'Identification and its vicissitudes as observed in the perversions', *International Journal of Psychoanalysis*, 67, 9–16.

Green, A. (2001) 'The Dead Mother' in *Life Narcissism Death Narcissism*, Weller, A (trans.). (London, New York: Free Association).

Grosskuth, P. (1986) *Melanie Klein, Her world and her work*. (London: Hodder and Stoughton).

Hermes, G., Tretiakova, M., McClintock, M. (2009) 'Social isolation dysregulates endocrine and behavioral stress while increasing malignant burden of spontaneous mammary tumors', *Proceedings of the National Academy of Sciences of the United States of America*, 106, (52), 22393–8.

Hinshelwood, R. D. (1986) 'The Psychotherapist's role in a large psychiatric institution', *Psychoanalytic Psychotherapy*, 2, (3), 207–15.

Hinshelwood, R. D. (1989) *A Dictionary of Kleinian Thought*. (London: Karnac).

Holmes, J. (2001) *The Search for the Secure Base*. (London: Brunner-Routledge).

Klein, M. (1937) 'Love, Guilt and Reparation' in *Love, Guilt and Reparation and other works 1921–1945*. (London: Virago). 1993.

Klein, M. (1946) 'Note on Some Schizoid Mechanisms' in *Love, Guilt and Reparation and other works 1921–1945*. (London: Virago). 1993.

Klein, M. (1963) 'On the Sense of Loneliness' in *Envy and Gratitude and other works 1946 –1963*. (London: Virago). 1993.

Lawrence, M. (2008) *The Anorexic Mind*. (London: Karnac).

Likierman, M. (2001) *Melanie Klein: Her Work in Context*. (London: Continuum).

MIND (2004) *How to...Cope with Loneliness* by Meakins, E and Gorman, J. (London: National Association for Mental Health).

Minne, C. (2008) 'The dreaded and dreading patient and therapist' in Gordon, J & Kirtchuk, G. (eds) *Psychic Assaults and Frightened Clinicians*. (London: Karnac).

Mitrani, J. (2001) *Ordinary People and Extraordinary Protections*. (Sussex: Brunner-Routledge).

Oxford English Dictionary (1969) 4th edition. (Oxford: Oxford University Press).

Quinodoz, J-M. (1993) 'The Taming of Solitude' in *Separation Anxiety in Psychoanalysis*. (London: Routledge).

Quinodoz, J-M. (1996) 'The sense of solitude in the psychoanalytic encounter', *International Journal of Psychoanalysis*, 77, 481–496.

Rey, H. (1994) 'Universals of Psychoanalysis' in *The Treatment of Psychotic and Borderline States*. (London: Free Association Books).

Scanlon, C. and Adlam, J. (2008) 'Refusal, social exclusion and the cycle of rejection: a cynical analysis?', *Critical Social Policy*, 28, (4), 529–49.

Scanlon, C. and Adlam, J (2011) 'Defacing the currency? A group-analytic appreciation of homelessness, dangerousness, disorder and other inarticulate speech of the heart', *Group Analysis*, 44, (2), 131–48.

Searles, H. (1959) 'The effort to drive the other person crazy' in *Collected Papers on Schizophrenia*. (London: Hogarth).

Segal, H. (1997) 'Termination: Sweating it out' in *Psychoanalysis, Literature and War Papers 1972–1995*. (London: Routledge).

Storr, A. (1989) *Solitude*. (London: Fontana).

Stubley, J. (2009) 'Mourning and migration', *Psychodynamic Practice*, 15, (2), 113–27.

Victor, C. Scambler, S. and Bond, J. (2009) *The Social World of Older People: Understanding Loneliness and Social Isolation in later life*. (Berkshire: Open University Press).

Weegmann, M. and Cohen, R. (2002) *The Psychodynamics of Addiction*. (London: Whurr).

Winnicott, D. W. (1947) 'Hate in the Countertransference' in *Through Paediatrics to Psychoanalysis*. (London: Karnac). 1984.

Winnicott, D. W. (1951) 'Transitional Objects and Transitional Phenomena' in *Through Paediatrics to Psychoanalysis*. (London: Karnac). 1984.

Winnicott, D. W. (1958) 'The Capacity to be Alone' in *The Maturational Process & the Facilitating Environment*. (London: Karnac). 1990.

Winnicott, D. W. (1960) 'Ego Distortion in terms of the True and False Self' in *The Maturational Process & the Facilitating Environment*. (London: Karnac). 1990.

Winnicott, D. W. (1963) 'Communicating and Not Communicating Leading to a Study of Certain Opposites' in *The Maturational Process & the Facilitating Environment*. (London: Karnac). 1990.

9
Living with Mortality

Lynsey Hotchkies and Neil Hudson

To know that you do not know is the best.
The Way of Lao Tzu (Tao-te ching) (Wing-Tsit Chan, 1963)

Introduction

Our experience of working as psychotherapists has led us to believe that therapeutic practice requires an understanding of our being in its broadest sense and
to start from the point that 'to know that you do not know is the best' (Wing-Tsit
Chan, 1963) is important in any exploration. Ontology (from the Greek ontos,
meaning 'existence') is the study of being which includes exploring our attitudes, values and prejudices in relation to ourselves, others and society. This
exploration inevitably must also include our relationship with our own death.
It is arguable that if we fail to acknowledge and explore this painful subject
with our clients then we are not fully engaging with life and what it means to be
alive. Living and mortality are two words that in practice cannot be separated,
their meanings are tautologous. Many writers have described as fundamental
to the nature of being (i.e., living) the fact that we are mortal and we are going
to die. Mortality is not the same as death: mortality means the life of a mortal
being, that is, we are subject to death. Death is the biological process of dying
at the end of our lives; those few precious seconds or possibly minutes when
biology fails as described by Kellehear (2007). We all have to face the limitations
and fragility of life and in this sense we are no different from the clients with
whom we work. Sometimes as psychotherapists we can spend many clinical
hours exploring clients' lives and relationships but avoid mortality because it is
so difficult to grasp and hold in mind.

This chapter is personal and anecdotal because no matter how hard we try to
engage with the topic objectively, we have observed, in our work with both clients and running a workshop entitled 'Living with Mortality', that we can only
really relate to our mortality subjectively. Each of us is an individual with our
own personal experience. Mortality is beyond the reach of scientific enquiry
because such a scientific enquiry would require an objective perspective

(Nagel, 1974). However, an exploration of death, dying and mortality is inherently valuable even though it is unlikely to lead to an answer. A dialogue with living with mortality may help us make sense of our lives in the here and now and who we are and what is important to us can become clarified. Surely as psychotherapists we all hope that through working with us, clients will be able to lead deeper and richer lives, making the most of the limited time available.

We will begin this chapter by discussing the avoidance of mortality whilst at the same time recognising the ubiquitous presence of representations of death in our culture through news, art, poems, films etc. As Yalom writes, 'Death...itches all the time; it is always with us, scratching at some inner door, whirring softly, barely audibly, just under the membrane of consciousness. Hidden and disguised, leaking out in a variety of symptoms, it is the wellspring of many of our worries, stresses, and conflicts' (Yalom, 2008: 9).

Often we deny our mortality and live our lives as if those final few precious seconds will never come. Through exploring how fear may govern this experience and the possible reasons for these 'worries, stresses, and conflicts', we will argue it is only in facing our mortality that we can fully engage with life (Freud, 1915; Levine, 1998). Many resist the idea that death creates a structure for our life, but as Martel writes in his novel *Life of Pi* 'Only death consistently excites your emotions, whether contemplating it when life is safe and stale or fleeing it when life is threatened and precious' (Martel, 2003: 217).

Avoiding Mortality

To engage with our mortality means grappling with the reality that you are going to die. This conscious awareness, of your own death, is often brief and quickly goes; one moment we feel we have grasped something significant and then it is gone. However, without this awareness it is not possible to fully explore mortality and what it means to each person's life. Each time this awareness shatters our daily reality, it is as if it has never been experienced before. Charles du Bos describes 'le réveil mortel' (quoted in Barnes, 2008): 'It is like being in an unfamiliar hotel room, where the alarm clock has been left on the previous occupant's setting, and at some ungodly hour you are suddenly pitched from sleep into darkness, panic and a vicious awareness that this is a rented world' (Barnes, 2008: 23).

This shock of awareness, when it breaks through into our consciousness, is even more surprising given that we are surrounded by images of death (see below). Why is it so difficult to engage with this subject especially when a dialogue is fundamental to an exploration of our lives and its meaning? It could be argued that this proliferation of images serves to reinforce our avoidance because despite this milieu in which we find ourselves, we rarely contemplate our personal mortality or that of our loved ones.

Take a moment to look at a newspaper and observe for yourself the number of times death is mentioned. Watch the daily news and popular films and video games. According to the US National Institute of Mental Health, by the time the average American reaches age 16, he or she has seen 18,000 murders on television (Kearl, 1995, cited in Durkin, 2003). For example, the film of J.R.R. Tolkein's *Lord of the Rings: Return of the King* (2003), one of the most popular films of 2003, has 836 deaths.

At the same time, death is denied all the time both at the individual level and the cultural level. We use euphemisms to talk about death, for example, 'passed on', 'bite the dust', 'an awfully big adventure', 'kicked the bucket', 'shuffled off this mortal coil' or 'pushing up the daisies'. There is a social taboo against talking openly about death and we may avoid the dying and their relatives. When we have told friends and family about running our workshops on mortality, they respond with comments about how depressing and morbid that must be to spend a day on this topic. This is the complete opposite of our experience: in fact, participants tend to leave energised and enthusiastic about their lives.

When we stop to reflect on mortality most of us can agree that we are living in a culture where there is a denial of death (Becker, 1997) and in which we prioritise beauty, youth, wealth and consumerism. We purchase this through cosmetic surgery, fashionable diets, expensive creams and lotions and whatever we can come up with to extend our lives and evade death. The precedence of youth and sexual attraction over wisdom and maturity leads to a custom of putting our elderly in homes, so that we neither actively participate in the care of the dying, nor witness the realities of death. There are very few sensitive portrayals of real death in the media and if there is there is often a public outcry.

Have we eradicated death from our lives? Are we being sold it back through the media either as a fantasy that only happens to other people or as something clean and easy? Berridge writes:

> There is a disparity between our emotional expressiveness and interest in news story victims and celebrity deaths, where it is fashionable to be seen to feel other people's pain and our awkwardness and denial with death in our midst...we should be wary of death by proxy and between human interest and humanity, we should mind the gap. (Berridge, 2011: x)

There can also be a real sense of being cushioned from death, largely as a result of the conquest of infectious diseases.[1] Real death is often hidden away in hospitals and medicalised. Advances in medical science lead us to an expectation that doctors will fix us – things can be treated – no one is allowed to be ill. Illness is seen as a weakness; death is the ultimate failure. Over medicalisation is stripping the necessary thoughtfulness (process) surrounding mortality and replacing it with shame and catastrophe. This brings us into contact with our feelings of lack of control and entitlement.

We might contrast this with *Artes moriendi*, or the art of dying well, which was a carefully cultivated seventeenth-century practice in response to the gruesome scenes of death in daily life. People contemplated their death and aimed to have a 'good' death, at home, surrounded by family and friends. They sensed the coming of death and prepared for it. They saw death as part of life and were surrounded by it, often in crude and distressing ways (e.g., plague, illnesses, etc). In modern industrial society where medical technology has reduced infant mortality, deadly infections and epidemic disease death has become less visible. Seventeenth-century people did not enjoy the luxury of denying death (Olsen, 2002).

However, an awareness of our own mortality often cannot be tolerated, so it is no wonder that many people cushion themselves and are shocked when it impacts on them directly. As previously stated, at the same time we are surrounded by mortality, death and dying in culture. Does this proliferation in culture help or hinder our ability to fully engage with death and thus life? In our view, it does not help, rather it serves to reinforce the avoidance. Durkin (2003) reviews this fascination with death in popular culture, including portrayals of death, dying, and the dead on television, in cinema, in music, and in products of the print media, as well as in recreational attractions, games and jokes. He argues that as death is a traumatic and anxiety provoking experience the proliferation of representations of it in popular culture makes it safe.

Fear of Mortality

Underlying this avoidance, we would argue is fear: fear of death, the great unknown. The fear of facing our mortality is really the fear of facing our own death. As these feelings are an unbearable experience we leave them to the poets, musicians, artists, filmmakers and writers. Shakespeare's famous stanza from *Measure For Measure* sums up this fear

> Death is a fearful thing...
> Ay, but to die, and go we know not where,
> To lie in cold obstruction, and to rot,
> This sensible warm motion to become
> A kneaded clod; and the delighted spirit
> To bathe in fiery floods, or to reside
> In thrilling region of thick-ribbed ice,
> To be imprisoned in the viewless winds
> And blown with restless violence round about
> The pendent world... or to be worse than worst
> Of those that lawless and uncertain thoughts
> Imagine howling – 'tis too horrible...

The weariest and most loathed worldly life
That age, ache, penury and imprisonment
Can lay on nature – is a paradise
To what we fear of death
 (Shakespeare, Measure for Measure, Act 3 Scene 1. (Craig, 1914))

Fear of death is pervasive but often hidden in other symptoms. Without the psychotherapist having actively engaged with this subject themselves, it can easily be missed in clinical work. Death is associated with shame, failure and a lack of control. Because we are also impotent in the face of death, there is little that we can do other than be 'with' our clients and help them to unlock the fear. Unless the psychotherapist has experienced the utter terror themselves, it creates a blind spot that the client will not be able to explore either.

For example, a 36-year-old client who came to see one of us for therapy presented with anxiety and depression relating to her relationship and her inability to commit. Even though she professed a desire for a family and children, over the course of the sessions it became apparent that the client was in fact paralysed in an adolescent phase wishing to continue a lifestyle of drugs, sex and partying. It became clear that she was struggling with an unconscious fear of aging and her own mortality. She behaved as if there was no time limit on her life and that she did not have to take responsibility for her contradictory decisions and actions.

There have been several studies into fears about death. One example is that conducted by The Life Awareness Centre (2010). Their research shows that the top four most common fears are: the fear of permanent loss of identity; the fear of loss of control; the fear that there is nothing after death; the fear of physical pain at our time of death. We would argue that people are also frightened of losing their identity, their character and characteristics. 'Loss of identity is the crux of contemporary anxiety about death' (Berridge, 2001: 46). For Freud (1918), 'in the unconscious every one of us is convinced of his own immortality' (304).

Craib (2003) writes about the fears he experienced when he was diagnosed with a brain and lung tumour. At the moment of diagnosis he experienced an abject terror, an intense anxiety for which words were just not adequate. For Craib this terror cannot be recalled later, in the same way that is it is difficult to recall moments of physical pain in their full intensity. He found very little written on the fear that he and many others experience with regard to long-term illness diagnosis. His fear provoked a strong reaction to get as far away from it as possible. Craib thinks that acknowledging this fear is more important and humbling than what he describes as the more arrogant, all knowing explanations of Heidegger and Nietzsche (Craib, 2003: 9). Craib argues that the intellectualising approach of the philosophers is of no help when faced with the reality of the fear. It is much better to face the fear and everything that comes with it than to hide behind the distancing of the philosophers.

A client with Crohn's disease, with whom one of us worked over a number of years, was hospitalised on multiple occasions to have operations including reducing the bowel itself. Each removal of a portion of the bowel brought the client closer to the time when there would be no more bowel left to remove. Every hospital visit seemed to produce more and more fear for both the client and, in the countertransference, the psychotherapist. In the countertransference, the psychotherapist felt frightened, powerless and impotent. But for the client, who, as Craib above suggests, in life found few who could tolerate these unbearable feelings, there was an increasing need for the presence of a psychotherapist to tolerate and explore the feelings without explaining or intellectualising.

Facing the fear of death is something we can do in the consulting room with our clients but, as stated above, only if we have allowed the terror and fear to break into our own awareness temporarily. The client does not need to 'stand alone' but we can stand together to bear the unbearable fear with them as much as is possible. Socrates famously promoted the idea that we should practice dying every day. In this practice, we learn how to live and (may) be able to face death with more awareness. Phowa is a meditation practice in Buddhism which facilitates the transference of the consciousness of the dying. None of us know how to die. Flaubert said, 'everything must be learned from reading to dying. But we don't get much practice at the latter' (quoted in Barnes, 2008: 98). If we do not face the fear, our actual death may be doubly painful as (1) we are dying and (2) we are fearful. However, we acknowledge that people disagree with this position. 'Do not go gentle into that good night, Old age should burn and rage at close of day; Rage, rage against the dying of the light' (Thomas, 1952).

Barnes (2008) argues that we should be death fearing but not death avoiding. We should not let the fear of death creep up on us unexpectedly. We have to make the fear familiar. We are used to thinking about death by ourselves, and yet, death is the one reality we all have in common. The consulting room can provide a safe space to explore and become familiar with our fear. As psychotherapists this is something we can all learn to experience with our clients once we have explored it for ourselves. We would argue that we bring freshness to our thinking when we are able to contemplate death. Fear can open the senses, making things clearer.

For example, a client presented with anxiety about her baby not sleeping and not eating enough food. The client thought that her baby was ill but the doctors had told her that the baby was not ill and would grow out of the difficulties it had with food, even though there had been serious problems when the child was first born. In one session, the client's fears that the baby would die broke through in a powerful expression of impotence. She told a story of how, alone, without the support of the baby's father, she had had to plan the infant's funeral, when the baby was born. She described the tiny coffin she had bought and the clothes she had planned to bury him in. It seemed that the only work that could be done with these very powerful feelings was to allow them space in the room to be expressed with another present. After this turning point, the client was able to engage in a dialogue with the psychotherapist about her fears and anxieties rather than projecting them into the baby.

In thinking about this client and this therapy, it was helpful to return to Bion's seminal work on thinking and containment. Bion experienced death first hand, as a teenager, during the First World War. Souter (2009) links Bion's wartime experiences with his theories of thinking, linking and containment. Bion relates in several books (e.g., Bion, 1982; 1997) his terrible experience on the Amiens-Roye road on 8th August 1918. As described by Souter, 'Sweeting [a young soldier] and his brother accompany Bion into battle; the brother is killed, and Sweeting and Bion take cover in a shell crater. Bion becomes aware that the boy's chest has been ripped off and his left lung has gone. Clouds of steam emerge from the terrible void in the boy's side as he drives Bion to despair with his regressed questions ... The ghastly outcome is that, after many terrible hours, Sweeting is forced to walk to casualty to die, as the stretcher-bearers are full up' (Souter, 2009: 801). Bion wrote several accounts of this traumatic incident, most of which differ as to Bion's responses to the boy, including his own uncontrollable vomiting. In his famous papers on thinking (Bion, 1967), Bion describes how the infant needs the mother to accept his feelings and return them to the baby in a 'digestible' form. For Bion, at this point in his life, he could only vomit out Sweeting's pleas. Bion develops, in his papers of the 1950s and 1960s, the idea that 'thinking' can only take place when two minds are linked.

We would argue that it is only with another that we can really think about, or reflect on our own mortality rather than 'vomit' it out uncontrollably.

Facing Mortality

Yalom states that we cannot leave death to the dying (Yalom, 1980). It is there from the beginning. Montaigne asked 'Why do you fear your last day? It contributes no more to your death than each of the others. The last step does not cause the fatigue, but reveals it' (Montaigne, 1958: 67).

Handbooks on death and how to die are proliferating as described in James Wolcott's article 'Final-Exit Strategies' in the March 2009 edition of *Vanity Fair* with the subtitle 'It's the Grim Reaper as life coach'. Wolcott argues that the ageing baby-boomers 'have turned death into a teaching moment, motivational tool and sales pitch' (Wolcott, 2009: 92). Is this sudden interest another example of the denial of death – or death being sold back to us as a commodity? 'As if death weren't exacting enough (lights out, party's over, stop tape), we now have the burden of attaining wisdom and bequeathing it to others before we go, providing a gallant example at the exit ramp to a round of glistening tears' (Wolcott, 2009: 92). We are faced with an overwhelming fear of death and attempt to control it by manuals on how to die rather than engaging fully in life and how to live it.

The fact of our own death is always going to be a paradoxical kind of loss (at once ours and not ours). According to Phillips, 'It is suffering which makes us human – nothing else in nature seems quite so grief-stricken, or impressed by its own dismay' (Phillips, 1999: 15). He argues that we are stuck in perpetual mourning, mired in disappointment and regret. Refusal to mourn is refusal to live. Mourning is the necessary suffering that makes more life possible. 'Loss not as the acknowledgement that creates pleasure, but as the addiction that kills it' (Phillips, 1999: 28). If we accept that the denial is so strong then facing our mortality is a difficult task requiring much courage.

We have been surprised by how popular the workshops that we have run on the topic of Living with Mortality have been. Whilst participants express anxiety and fear at the beginning of the day and indeed, the days are powerful and often painful, participants almost always leave excited and inspired, keen to engage more fully with their lives and their relationships. In spending time facing their own mortality they are able to engage more creatively with their lives.

In our opinion it would be useful in the consulting room to think about Heidegger's idea that there are two fundamental modes of existing in the world: (1) a state of forgetfulness of being or (2) a state of mindfulness of being (Heidegger, 1962: 210–224). 'When one lives in a state of *forgetfulness of being*, one lives in the world of things and immerses oneself in the everyday diversions of life. ... One surrenders oneself to the everyday world, to a concern about the *way* things are' (Yalom, 1980: 30–31). This is the everyday mode of existence.

In the *state of mindfulness of being*, we might speculate not about the *way* things are but *that* they are. When in this state, we are continually aware of 'being':

> not only mindful of the fragility of being but mindful, too, of one's respon-
> sibility for one's own being ... Heidegger refers to forgetfulness of being as
> "inauthentic" – a mode in which one is unaware of one's authorship of one's
> life and world, in which one "flees", "falls" and is tranquillised ... Since it is
> only in this ontological mode that one is in touch with one's self-creation it is
> only here that one can grasp the power to change oneself. (Yalom, 1980: 31)

We think that this is a powerful observation, and may be useful when thinking about those clients who, despite insight, remain stuck, and unable to face their limitations and the limitations of life. Such awareness can put the individual in touch with their own capacity to be creative within the confines of life and mortality.

When one enters this state one exists 'authentically': with a mindfulness and awareness of being. We may become fully self-aware and are then able to

embrace our possibilities and limits. We face absolute freedom and nothing-
ness; but are confronted with anxiety in the face of them:

> To place both feet on the ground at last. To live with mercy and awareness
> in the midst of the consequences of love, or the lack thereof. To explore this
> ground, the ground of being, out of which this impermanent body and ever-
> changing mind originate. (Levine, 1998: 10)

Living with Mortality

As we have discussed it is difficult to acknowledge or talk openly about mortality,
so in many ways it can be useful that we are surrounded by death and mortality
in popular culture because it is a sanitised, safe expression of what we struggle
to experience directly. It can make us feel alive. For Freud the transience of life
augments our joy in it and he commented, 'Limitation in the possibility of an
enjoyment raises the value of the enjoyment' (Freud, 1916: 304).

Cousins (1992: 33) also makes an important point in the comment that, 'the
tragedy of life is not death but what we let die inside us while we live'. Following
on from this comment, we would suggest that the more disconnected we are
from our own mortality, the more of life we are letting slip through our fingers.
Our fears do not stop death, they stop life (Kubler-Ross and Kessler, 2000).

Imagine life without death. Life loses its intensity. Life shrinks. As Muriel
Spark comments:

> If I had my life over again I should form the habit of nightly composing
> myself to thoughts of death. I would practise, as it were, the remembrance
> of death. There is no other practice which so intensifies life. Death, when
> it approaches, ought not to take one by surprise. It should be part of the
> full expectancy of life. Without an ever-present sense of death life is insipid.
> (Spark, 2010: 150–151)

It could be said that once we face our mortality we are then forced to explore the
question of meaning and purpose. What is it all about? What is the point if we
are going to die? Would we prefer to give up and just die? We become 'a being
without a reasonable reason for being…..' (Barnes, 2008: 65). In our experience,
this can be a difficult view to accept: the view that death has a positive contribution to life. Again, provoked by fear many see death as something painful to be
suffered, or at best a failure.

If we are to consider that death is not just an unbearable end, but it is an
endpoint which structures and gives meaning to our life, then we must face
the challenge of how to live. With the fear felt, death faced, mortality grasped,
is the next day really different? The reality is that for many they return to their

family, friends, work etc., but with a different state of awareness. Who I am is not defined by what I do, but rather by the way I do it. The changes can be subtle and are reflected in a presence of attentiveness.

In thinking about our death it is possible to clear the decks, sort out priorities and remember that time is limited. Moving forwards with clarity around feelings and identity, finding the courage to prioritise and make clear choices. Each moment can be a reflection of purpose and meaning. Thinking about death can provoke ideas of life and stimulate a way of living and being in the world.

Conclusion

In our opinion, it is in acknowledging fear that you are put in touch with your own inner drama, fears, powerful feelings, contradictions and the horrors of death. Experiencing these feelings puts you in touch with the very essence of what it means to be a human being, regardless of gender, race, class or culture: the endless search for purpose, curiosity, the struggle with isolation, and the inevitable fear of death, etc. Only then is it possible to connect intimately with others, which can be a powerful position for a therapist to take in the consulting room with clients:

> What is crucial is *how one relates to* whatever one may be relating to. ... If, for example, one's emotional reality or truth is despair, what is most important is not *that* one may be in despair, but one's attitude *toward* one's despair. Through one's basic attentiveness one's despair can declare itself and tell its story. One enters profound dialogue with it. If one stays with this process, an evolution even in the quality of despair may begin to be perceived, since despair itself is never uniform. (Eigen, 1981: 428)

What it means to the individual to live with their mortality is not something which we, as therapists, can answer. Carl Rogers, in the *Gloria* films (Shostrom et. al, 1965), in response to clients demanding answers from him said, 'I feel this is the kind of very private thing that I couldn't possibly answer for you, but I will try to help you work toward your own answer'. Here, Rogers is emphasising the importance of acknowledging that we do not 'know' and the importance of working towards a new 'knowledge.' When we sit with our not knowing we can feel uncomfortable but this is necessary in order to illuminate our dilemma:

> We are the mortal creatures who, because we are self-aware, know that we are mortal. A denial of death at any level is a denial of one's basic nature and begets an increasingly pervasive restriction of awareness and experience. The integration of the *idea* of death saves us; rather than sentences us to

existences of terror or bleak pessimism, it acts as a catalyst to plunge us into more authentic life modes, and it enhances our pleasure in the living of life. (Yalom, 1980: 32–33)

We do not pretend to have special knowledge of death but we will all die. Perhaps the real value in life is discovering something about that death before we get to the end. Facing our mortality means facing our fears of death and dying. By not doing that we are not living in reality and we miss out on how an awareness of our own mortality may inspire us. We may find ourselves encouraged to discover something new about our lives and ourselves, we may learn how to fully engage with life. We may be rewarded with a deeper connection with ourselves and others. As practitioners we are trying to help our clients live their lives more fully, and that includes facing their fear of death. How can we help our clients do that if we are not able to engage with that process ourselves? The expansion of ourselves, gained by living with mortality, far outweighs the fleeting yet intolerable, experience of our fears.

Note

1. Child Mortality: 1850: 300 in 1000 die before age 15; 1900: 230 in 1000; 1950: 40 in 1000; 1999: 0.523 in 1000 (cited in Berridge, 2001 p19).

References

Barnes, J. (2008) *Nothing to be Frightened of.* (London: Jonathan Cape).

Becker, E. (1997) *The Denial of Death.* (New York: Simon & Schuster Ltd).

Berridge, K. (2001) *Vigor Mortis – The End of the Death Taboo.* (London: Profile Books Limited).

Bion, W. R. (1967) *Second Thoughts.* (London: Karnac). 1984.

Bion, W. R. (1982) *The long weekend: 1897–1919 (Part of a Life)* Bion F., (ed.). (Abingdon: Fleetwood).

Bion, W. R. (1997) *War Memoirs 1917–1919.* Bion F., (ed.). (London: Karnac).

Cousins, N. (1991) *The Celebration of Life: A Dialogue on Hope, Spirit, and the Immortality of the Soul.* (University of Minnesota: Bantam Books).

Craib, I. (2003) 'Fear, death and sociology', *Mortality: Promoting the interdisciplinary study of death and dying.* 8, (3), 285–95.

Craig, W. J. (ed) (1914) *The Complete Works of William Shakespeare.* (London: Magpie Books). 1992.

Durkin, K. (2003) 'Death, Dying and the Dead in Popular Culture' in *The Handbook of Death and Dying.* C. Bryant (ed.). (New York: Sage Publications).

Eigen, M. (1981) 'The area of faith in Winnicott, Lacan and Bion', *International Journal of Psychoanalysis.* 62, 413–33.

Freud, S. (1916 [1915]) 'On Transience' in *SE.XIV.* (London: Hogarth Press). 1957.

Freud, S. (1918) 'Thoughts for the Times on War and Death' in *SE.XIV*. (London: Hogarth Press). 1953.

Heidegger, M. (1962) *Being and Time*. (New York: Sharper & Row).

Kellehear, A. (2007) *A Social History of Dying*. (New York: Cambridge University Press).

Kubler-Ross, E. and Kessler, D. (2000) *Life Lessons: Two Experts on Death and Dying Teach Us about the Mysteries of Life and Living*. (New York: Scribner Book Company).

Levine, S (1998) *A Year to Live: How to Live This Year As If It Were Your Last*. (London: Three Rivers Press).

Lord of the Rings: Return of the King (2003) [Extended Version] Jackson, P. (Director). Movie Body Counts. http://www.moviebodycounts.com/LotR_Return_of_King.htm 17th December 2011.

Martel, Y. (2003) *Life of Pi*. (New York: Mariner Books).

Montaigne, M. de, (1958) *The Complete Essays of Montaigne*. Frame, D. M. (trans.). (Stanford: Stanford University Press).

Nagel, T. (1974) 'What is it like to be a bat?', *The Philosophical Review* LXXXIII, 4, 435–50.

Olsen, J. (2002) *Bathsheba's Breast; Women, Cancer and History Johns*. (Baltimore: Hopkins University Press).

Phillips, A. (1999) *Darwin's Worms*. (London: Faber and Faber).

Shostrom, E. L., Rogers, C. R., Perls, F. S., Ellis, A., Psychological Films, inc., Concord Video & Film Council Ltd., and Inc Graves Medical Audiovisual Library. (1965) *Three Approaches to Psychotherapy – Gloria I* (Suffolk, Ispwich: Concord Video & Film Council). 1970.

Souter, K. M. (2009) 'The war memoirs: some origins of thought of WR Bion', *International Journal of Psycho-Analysis*, 90, 795–808.

Spark, M. (2010) *Memento Mori*. (London: Virago Press).

The Life Awareness Centre. (2010) *Research On Our Fear Of Death*. http://www.lifea-warenesscenter.com/Reasrearch1.html 17th December 2011.

Thomas, D. (1952) *Collected Poems 1934–1952*. (London: Dent). 1984.

Yalom, I. (1980) *Existential Psychotherapy*. (New York: Basic Books).

Yalom, I. (2008) *Staring at the Sun: Overcoming Our Terror of Death*. (San Francisco: Jossey-Bass/Wiley Books).

Wing-Tsit Chan, L. (1963) *The Way of Lao Tzu (Tao-te ching)*. (Indianapolis: Bobbs-Merrill Comp).

Wolcott, J. (2009) 'Final exit strategies', *Vanity Fair*, March 2009, 182–4.

Part III

The Personal, Social and Cultural

In Part III, the authors consider wider issues that may be brought to the therapist and which are influenced by, and impact on, social and cultural dimensions of being.

This section starts with a chapter by John Stewart which reflects on ideas related to the personal and the self and how such concepts help the therapist consider the nature of the self. The following two chapters by Juliet Newbigin and Brid Greally enter into, and explore, debates within the profession around diversity and sexuality. Written from related but different perspectives, they challenge the reader to consider these issues in relation to their own perceptions as well as in terms of the issues that clients bring to therapy.

The final three chapters bring in wider aspects of an individual's sense of self and sense of being. Mary Thomas in Chapter 13 examines issues of artistic creativity in relation to psychotherapy. David M. Black explores the significance of religion in relation to our sense of self and our values and the final chapter by Lesley Murdin, 'Time and Rites of Passage', examines the life cycle in relation to our experience of time and the stages, transitions and rites of passage that occur within it and which may be paralleled within the therapeutic relationship.

Overall the chapters aim to challenge and broaden our perspectives on the many dimensions of being that are brought into the consulting room by clients and therapists and which influence and impact on our work as clinicians. Taking being into account requires constantly struggling to consider the person, including ourselves, as a whole.

10

An Exploration into the Nature of the Self

John Stewart

Introduction

We can be taken by surprise by that which has seemed familiar. Psychotherapists are accomplished at giving thought to the interchange between internal process and external reality in their work with clients, but they can be less comfortable when they are asked to personally reflect on what it is to be a self. In my former role as a seminar leader in Ontology at WPF Therapy, I found that it was very useful for students to reflect, in a seminar, on the following questions as a backdrop to their identity as therapists. Who are you? How do you define the 'self'? What are the boundaries – both physical and intellectual – of your essential selves? Do you feel you have an 'essential self'?

My interest in exploring questions about the philosophical self grew out of my own attempts, as someone who had not been a student of philosophy, to contemplate the concept of self. In this chapter, I set out a brief developmental outline of the philosophical notion of the self and its evolution through the development of Western thought, a tradition from which psychoanalytic theories emerged.

The purpose of this chapter then is to think about what it means to be a self and to outline the ways in which the development of the notion of self in Western thought provides a context for the development of psychoanalytic and psychotherapeutic thinking.

Reflections on the Concept of Self

The concept of self refers to both personal experience and the conceptualisation of that experience. The notion of implicit and explicit senses of self helps to clarify the distinction between being a self and the capacity to think about self. The concept of the unconscious relates to aspects of the self of which we are

121

unaware but which have the potential to be utilised by the explicit self if they become conscious.

When tying my shoe laces, I automatically draw on past experience in order to respond to immediate stimuli. I am, in the moment, engaged in purposeful activity that does not pause for contemplation or have an awareness of total body image. I am being a self in a way that is implicit but not conscious. It is open to question whether this is much different from that of our ancient antecedents who first evolved as modern man from higher forms of animal life. As Colman comments, 'Any creature whether human or not, who is experiencing consciousness without self reflexive awareness cannot know that they are experiencing it...We make a mistaken equation between being conscious and knowing we are conscious' (Colman, 2008: 352). He goes on to reflect that 'we might say that all living creatures *are* selves but only human beings are capable of *having* a self' (Colman, 2008: 357).

Modern humans have an evolutionary advantage that distinguishes them from other species, such as the great apes or our evolutionary ancestors, that enables them to think in a reflexive manner. This could be called an explicit sense of self. It implies the capacity to think about thinking, to be consciously aware, and to do so – to reflect on the existence of self within time and space – is a state of knowledge of one's consciousness. It also implies a capacity to think symbolically, principally in the use of language, which enables the individual to communicate the result of their self-reflection to others. While an implicit sense of self is a vital and a constant component of our psychological functioning, it is self in this explicit sense that is the subject of this chapter.

Self is an inclusive term for the totality of function that brings together the physical and the mental – the body and the mind. The concept of the mind describes the mental processes within a single self, including the capacity to be self-aware. Self is a construct uniquely private to an individual and therefore not known to others. The existence of other minds can only be inferred by observing human behaviour, by the acceptance of the self that others report to us and on the evidence given by our experience of our own self.

The physiological processes of the body support the nervous system and the complex brain functions that give rise to thinking. If the body dies or the brain stops functioning then what we call mind ceases to exist. The exact nature of the relationship between body and mind is, however, a controversial one that has exercised philosophers down the centuries.

The notion of person is a much more public one than that of mind but it contributes to the definition of self. Bodily characteristics determine our recognition of other people. We identify others and are ourselves identified through inherited features such as skin pigmentation, hair colour, eye colour, bodily dimensions such as shape and height, left or right handedness, and occasionally some familial similarities. Personal identification in a forensic sense can be determined by factors such as DNA profiles, finger prints or patterns in the iris.

In a more general sense, we define ourselves and are, therefore, consciously defined by others using terms that describe where we come from, what we do for a living, and our role in our personal relationships and families. How we describe ourselves to others is integral to our sense of self. A difficulty with identifying people by their physical attributes is that they change over time both in appearance and physical capability. A photograph, for instance, captures an image at a given point in time so that the photographic image of a young baby will be very different from that of the same person in their declining years. In more socially mobile societies relatively few people know an individual over their whole life span. Perhaps all we can say is that we locate the other within a range of a few years and in the context of an ongoing acquaintance. We rely on other factors, such as oral and written narratives and the capacity to remember past events and remembered behaviour, to establish continuity in our perception of other people's identity.

The reciprocal feedback given by a sense of mutual recognition forms the basis for self in the interactions of infancy and subsequent maturational processes. However, reciprocity becomes problematic when brain function is severely impaired by illness or injury. Others may recognise the physical attributes of a person but find that their behaviour is altered so as to leave the impression that this is not the same person they knew before. This can be particularly acute when the ability to recognise personal identity is lost in the victim and can cause the acquaintance to grieve the loss of being recognised. Science, philosophy and theology are still locked in great debate as to the point at which a self ceases to exist in patients with severe brain impairment.

Up to this point I have considered self in an individual context but the importance of wider cultural influences on the explicit sense of self cannot be underestimated. A thinking self seeks meaning from the conceptual framework of the society in which it exists and validation and self esteem through social structures. In his paper 'The Location of Cultural Experience', Winnicott (1971) argues that we have to find and internalise the body of knowledge contained in our culture in order to make it our own. Historically this was often through an oral tradition whereas we now experience culture through written language, art, media and the vast and rich tapestries of cultural expression. In addition all societies and kinship groups evolve social conventions that define a moral code to establish what it is to be an ethically virtuous member of the group or, if conventions are broken, what behaviour risks public censure. On occasions, individuals may act against social norms in order to preserve the integrity of self. Charles Taylor (1992) addresses the need to attain feelings of esteem and personal validation as components of self in his volume, *Sources of the Self*.

A mixture of awe, helplessness and despair has prompted humans to try to discover a sense of meaning for self in the vastness of the universe, to find reason in the hand of fate and the vicissitudes of life and death. I would call this a cosmic sense of self. In the face of this perplexity, humans have sought and collated the wisdom of shamans, sages and priests to mediate the intentions of the supernatural forces or deities that are woven into their mythologies. The written forms of these understandings are accorded the status of sacred scripts based on the divine revelations they are said to contain.

Religious truths are held as a matter of belief and as such are not subject to the burden of proof required by a scientific hypothesis, but they can have a powerful effect on the notion of self. Many people hold, for religious or other reasons, a belief in an existence that lies beyond death and, in some cases, before birth. It transcends the travails of life in the form of an eternal sense of self – the soul. This could be seen as a projection of a known state of self onto an unknown state of existence, which is given names such as heaven or paradise. This is philosophically and psychologically problematic in that we are left with a notion of a disembodied something with no tangible vehicle for recognition or expression. This notion of self, however, allows for a spiritual dimension to human life that offers believers a vision of something that transcends the limits of material existence.

Historical Views of the Self

The philosophical concepts that are debated in the wider social context have a bearing on what is considered to be true through the process of reasoning and the principle of logical deduction. An example of this is the notion of self and the relation of the body to the mind, an enduring philosophical discussion in which philosophy can both conflict and interface with the presuppositions of religion. Both of these branches of human thought have had an important influence on the history of European culture, itself firmly rooted in the culture of Ancient Greece, where a particular notion of self evolved. The study of psychoanalytic theory is enhanced by an understanding of this philosophical heritage, some broad highlights of which I now wish to outline.

Plato followed the innovative thinking of Socrates in turning away from Greek religious mythology to a belief in the power of reason that enables us to recollect what is already known in the form of eternal and pre-existing forms. He held that reality existed in the mind and that the truly rational person had an immortal soul that transcended death (Plato, 2003). The mind was of more importance than the body. His follower Aristotle adopted a stance that took the contrary view that reality existed in the essence or soul of the material world. Body predominates over mind. In short, these two great thinkers laid the basis for 'the two philosophical traditions that have occupied western intellectual tradition for the past 2500 years. Rationalism – knowledge is *a priori* (comes before experience) and Empiricism – knowledge is *a posteriori* (comes after experience)' (Kreis, 2009: 1).

Christianity marked the rise of the second major influence on western intellectual development. The early Christians modified the roots of their Jewish heritage to form a belief in an after-life, open only to believers and based on the resurrection of the body. When Jesus did not return as they expected, the early Christians further modified their beliefs, turning to notions of the immortality of the soul which had been prevalent in Græco-Roman civilisation since Plato.

The collapse of the Western Roman Empire and the Græco-Roman world in the fifth century marked the beginning of the medieval period which occasioned a retreat into a very fixed world view. Theologians such as Augustine consolidated the Christian belief system, making a distinction between the spiritual purity of the soul and the carnality of the body, seen as existing in a state of original sin. The cosmological context of the sense of self was also rigidly defined, as set out by Ptolemy (90–168AD). If the earth was the centre of the universe then the God-given status of humans as rulers of the earth gave them a pivotal role in the universe (Crowe, 2001). The writings of Aristotle resurfaced in Europe around 1200 AD, having been preserved by Arab scholars, and were used defensively by the church. Thomas Aquinas (1274) founded the scholastic school of thinking that adapted Aristotle's logical formulations to deductively prove the existence of God.

The Christian Church resisted the innovative thinking prompted by Aristotelian thinking, but around 1300 AD, the onset of the European Renaissance prompted an intellectual exploration in the natural sciences and the arts that, in effect, subverted many of the previously accepted truths about the nature of the world. Copernicus (1473–1543) was a mathematician and astronomer who challenged Ptolemy's geocentric model of the universe by proposing that it revolved around the sun (Crowe, 2001). This represented a seismic shift in the way the order of the universe was understood. It posed a huge challenge to the Christian Church, and, in fact, a hundred years later Galileo would be tried for heresy for advancing such ideas.

Over the next 200 years, the tide of innovation and discovery continued in Europe. The incremental effect of these changes paved the way for a revolution in philosophical thinking, in the works of Descartes (1596–1650). A French philosopher, mathematician and scientist, he rejected the scholastic method of arguing the way to the truth using Aristotelian logic, and his books were banned by the Pope in 1643. He was convinced that the truth could be discovered through the sceptical method of doubting everything until he could discover that which was true without doubt. He came to the conclusion that the only indubitable truth was that he was a thinking being, as expressed in the phrase 'I think therefore I am' (cogito ergo sum). His insistence that the essence of the self was comprised in the very act of thinking lay more in the tradition of Plato. However, Descartes' (1637) views on the nature of the self are referred to as Cartesian dualism. He followed the reasoning that if the body was a recognisable thing then the mind was also something in its own right. A significant problem for body/mind dualism is to explain the way in which the body relates to the mind.

In England, a different philosophy of mind was developing that fell more in the tradition of Aristotle. The stage this was set by Francis Bacon (1561–1626) who challenged the deductive reasoning of scholasticism (Bacon 2008), arguing for a system that used reason to study the natural world based on observation. Sir Isaac Newton (1642–1727) argued that the universe and the motions of the planets are based on understandable and rational natural laws, including that of gravitation (Newton 1687), which challenged the notion of the divine ordering of the universe, one of the last pillars of the medieval world view.

A contemporary of Newton, John Locke (1632–1704), applied a similar approach to the philosophy of mind. He set out the empiricist approach to the notion of the self, arguing that we have neither innate knowledge nor an immaterial soul and that at birth the mind is a blank slate on which experience writes. All knowledge comes from experience and consists of the simple knowledge gained from sensation or the complex knowledge gained through reflection. He defined a person as 'a thinking intelligent being that can consider itself as itself, the same thinking thing in different times and places' (Locke, 1690: 448). Consciousness is the bedrock of personal identity.

David Hume (1711–1776) accepted Locke's empiricist ideas but disagreed about the continuity of the person in our conscious awareness, arguing that the concept of the self is not supported by the senses. Thoughts are 'nothing but a bundle or collection of different perceptions, which succeed each other with inconceivable rapidity and in a perpetual flux and movement' (Hume, 2000: 164). Hume was concerned about the notion of causality and argued that the future cannot be inferred from the past because any attempt to do so is dependent on custom and habit. Life is a sequence of experiences.

The disagreement between rationalism and empiricism was addressed by the highly influential European philosopher Immanuel Kant (1724–1804), who argued in his work for a synthesis of the two approaches (Kant, 1787). He was vexed by Hume's assertions that the self existed in the moment without continuity, and agreed with Locke that knowledge was *a posteriori*, with experience being both dependent and based on sensation. He took issue, however, with the empiricist view that we do not have innate knowledge and held the position that aspects of the mind have an *a priori* basis that cannot be learned through experience. However, in arguing for an inborn knowledge of moral and logical precepts which provides a framework through which we order and categorize sensations, he is not postulating a mind furnished with ideas as envisaged by Plato (2003). According to Kant, the self has both *a posteriori* and *a priori* characteristics.

In the eighteenth century, the idea of the contract between the citizen and the state developed in the strongly rational philosophy of the Enlightenment. This was played out in the excesses of the French Revolution (1789–1799) and also contributed to the formation of the American Constitution (1779), including the Bill of Rights. The right of the citizen to challenge the state when their self-expression was unfairly denied was enshrined in law. The rights of the peoples colonized, and in some cases enslaved, by European powers, however, were not considered.

The social, economic and political upheavals of ninteenth century Europe threw up very significant challenges to the underlying assumptions about the philosophical sense of self. Against the background of poor social conditions, brought about by the industrial revolution, Karl Marx argued that individuals realize their potential through productive labour in *Capital: The Critique of Political Economy* (Marx, 1876). Marx was a rationalist thinker who argued that work that is inadequately rewarded becomes meaningless and alienates the worker from their sense of self identity, and that conflict is the path to the realisation of self in an unjust society.

Charles Darwin (1993) published *The Origin of the Species* in 1859, in which he advanced the hypothesis that all forms of life have evolved through natural selection, challenging the prevalent anthropocentric world view of a uniquely created human species. This was a disturbing concept for many people, where an inflated image of the self was confronted by the humbling notion that humans were merely one species of many, and demanded considerable psychological maturity in both intellectual and theological terms.

Some Reflections from Psychoanalytic Perspectives

The notion of self as a rational state of being that prevailed by the nineteenth century was profoundly shaken by the emergence of the psychoanalytic assertion that human behaviour was influenced by unconscious aspects of the mind. The notion, proposed by Freud, that human behaviour was driven by sexual drives that began in infancy scandalised many people and challenged traditional beliefs about the sinfulness of sex and the innocence of children (Freud, 1905; 1906/08).

While Freud and Jung were drawn together by a common passion for the notion of the unconscious, it is not surprising that they were unable to sustain their collaboration. Two highly intelligent and strong minded men of differing temperament and interests, their theoretical development reflects the split in Western thought between Empiricists, such as Aristotle, Locke and Hume, and the Rationalists, such as Plato and Descartes.

Freud was a neurologist who became increasingly interested in working with the neuroses of his patients and the unconscious motivations for their behaviour. An admirer of Darwin, he was an empiricist determined to establish a scientific basis for his theory, central to which was the primacy of the sexual drive in human behaviour. It was ironic that in taking this stance he effectively opened a gap between psychoanalysis and science. Freud regarded the unconscious mind and the content of dreams respectively as a repository and as disguised representations of repressed sexuality. Like Marx, he dismissed religion as wishful thinking.

Jung was a psychiatrist whose notion of the unconscious and his approach to dreams was a more purposeful one than that of Freud, and this contributed to their dispute. While Jung accepted the empirical need for clinical observation and scientific method, he also sought meaning in a more rationalist understanding of the self. He was influenced by Kant's (1787) idea of *a priori* knowledge and his theory of archetypes was, in some ways, foreshadowed by Plato's theory of forms. Jung was also interested in the role of spirituality in the human sense of self, while for Freud religious belief was an illusion.

Self was a term that Freud seldom used as it possibly was too general and non-scientific, unlike the ego, which held a specific meaning for him, although the term 'ego' was introduced by Freud's English translators. Freud held the view that the emergence of ego functioning to manage the impact of primitive drives marked the beginning of the infant as an individual and also thought that 'the ego is that part of the id which has been modified by the direct influence of the external world' (Freud, 1923: 24). Rycroft (1985) considered that: 'The self refers to the subject as he experiences himself while the ego refers to his personality as a structure about which impersonal generalizations can be made' (149). Prior to this, Jung had placed the notion of self at the very heart of his theories:

> Since Jung viewed the self as both the centre and the totality of the psyche, it has a strong claim to be regarded as the central concept of his whole psychology. The self is the process towards which the process of individuation strives. It represents psychic wholeness and the process by which self division may be healed. (Colman, 2006: 153)

Jung regarded self as present from the very beginning of life, present in archetypal potentials that are *a priori* in nature but devoid of the content that will be furnished by experience and known through images that arise in the mind. He envisaged it as having a purposeful or teleological nature and regarded the expression of the self and the search for wholeness, through the process of individuation, as the defining purpose of the human being: 'The self, like the unconscious, is an *a priori* existent out of which the ego evolves. It is, so to speak, an unconscious prefiguration of the ego. It is not I who create myself, rather I happen to myself' (Jung, 1942/54: para 391). But Jung also commented that 'the self can appear in all shapes from the highest to the lowest' (Jung, 1951: para 356).

Winnicott credits Jungian psychology with keeping the notion of self in focus but in his 'Review of Memories, Dreams, Reflections' (Winnicott, 1964) he makes some very interesting observations about the differences between Freud and Jung that raise pertinent points about the notion of self:

What must be remembered, I think, is that Jung spent his life looking for his own self, which he never really found since he remained to some extent split (except in so far as this split was healed in his work on his autobiography).

In his old age he appears to have.... lived by his True Self, and in this way he found a self that he could call his own. ... The fact remains that the search for the self and a way of feeling real, and of living from the true rather than from the false self, is a task that ... belongs to a large proportion of the human race. Nevertheless it must also be recognised that for many this problem is *not* the main one; their infantile experiences took them satisfactorily through the early stages, so that a solution was found in infancy to this essential human problem. Generally, the problems of life are not about the search of self, but about the full and satisfying use of the self that is a unit and is well grounded. (Winnicott, 1964: 491)

Conditions That Promote the Development of the Self

Winnicott's notion of self as a well-grounded unit formed in the early stages of development would, I think, be an acceptable basis for most psychoanalytic schools of thought, including developmental Jungians, to look at the essential conditions that promote the development of self. I would list these as follows:

1. The presence of a core and implicit sense of self that is programmed genetically to initiate contact with adult caregivers. These are responding thinking selves that appropriately meet the infant's needs in a reciprocal manner that enables a sense of basic trust to develop.
2. The coalescing of a functioning self for which the term ego is generally accepted but defined in a variety of ways. The ego establishes a sense of identity through an awareness of me/not me, it develops a sense of will through the ability to accept or turn away, to say yes or no, and it achieves the capacity to hold ambivalent feelings in relation to significant others. The latter achievement balances the destructive and constructive impulses to hate and to love through the capacity to assuage guilt by making reparation. This is a position that underpins the development of our sense of morality.
3. The forming of the moral framework as in Freud's concept of the super ego. The developing infant needs to learn a sense of right and wrong that is reinforced by parental approval. This leads to the making of moral judgements of that which is good or bad and to the accepting of responsibility or apportioning blame for behaviour.
4. The fourth essential element of the developing self comes with the dawning realisation of the full impact of sexuality. 'My parents make babies and they

made me.' An understanding of the genital basis for gender differentiation is complicated by the need to understand the more complex notions of masculinity and femininity and the way in which these are played out in relationships. Freud famously described this as the Oedipus conflict but some current thinkers question the way in which his underlying assumptions present an unbalanced view of the gender roles that establish a template for sexual roles in adult life (See Chapter 12 by Brid Greally).

5. The grasping of the existential reality of human mortality is the last essential component of the unitary self. The notion of time begins to make sense and a remembered awareness of continuity over time develops. From the pain of enduring temporary separation emerges the shocking realisation that parental figures will die inducing a fear that this could happen at any time.

These essential elements of an awareness of self are hopefully in place by the time the child reaches the latency stage. They will be employed and reemployed as the individual adjusts emotionally to the physical maturation of a body (including the brain) that is genetically and hormonally programmed to grow in size and capability. Although the idea of the unconscious is defined differently in psychoanalytic schools of thought, it would be generally accepted that the capacity to engage in a process that allows the unconscious aspects of mental functioning to become more conscious is one that enhances self.

The split that developed when Freud turned away from the science of neurology and turned his attention to psychoanalysis has been somewhat reversed, over the past two decades, by the research of neuro-biologists such as Alan Schore (2001; 2003), who links brain function to psychoanalytic thinking. He argues that the potential of the brain is realised through input from the external environment that stimulates neurons to form pathways. These neural pathways form linear patterns that relate to specific functions such as speech and they also form complex pathways linked to the limbic system that excite the whole brain including its decision-making centre, the prefrontal cortex. Caregivers who protect the infant from external impingement regulate an infant's emotional affect enabling neural pathways to form. Poorly regulated infants develop default positions that may lead to a lack of self esteem, poor social skills and dysfunctional behaviour in later life. Bowlby (1971) described these as a poor internal working model linked to insecure patterns of attachment. Fonagy (2004) combined the psychoanalytic model with insights of neuro-biology and attachment theory to promote the capacity to mentalize as fundamental to the development of the self.

Ryle (1949) argued against the dualist philosophy of mind as formulated by Descartes as 'a ghost in the machine' (Ryle, 1949: 15/16). He made the case that dualism commits a 'category mistake' that attempts to equate a physical entity with a metaphorical concept. Mind is essentially a metaphor.

In his recent publication *The Ego Trick* (Baggini, 2011) the philosopher Julian Baggini engages in a comprehensive discussion of the notion of self. He reaches the conclusion that self is what we do rather than what we are. He links the notion of a bundle of thoughts with Hume's idea that life consists of a rapid succession of events that we experience as if it were a self: 'The ego trick should be seen in this way. There is no single thing that comprises the self, but we need to function as though there were' (Baggini, 2011: 120). He argues that there is no fixed entity or 'pearl' that can be isolated as mind or soul, a position that has some similarities with the Buddhist view of the self. He rejects the dualism of Descartes but is left holding the paradoxical position that 'we are no more than, but more than just, matter'. He adds, 'But no matter how good technology gets, there is always a difference between observing a brain event and experiencing a mental event' (Baggini, 2011: 124). In other words, you can 'wire up' the brain to observe the excitation of neurons but the actual experience of self is a strictly personal process.

What are the implications of Baggini's position on the self for psychoanalytic thinking? He accepts the notion of the unconscious aspects of self: 'The unconscious matters because of its influence on the conscious, not in its own right' (Baggini, 2011: 130). If self is viewed as something we experience in the moment, as a uniquely integrated psycho-somatic process that draws upon past experience to maintain a sense of continuity then Baggini's thesis about the 'ego trick' is compatible with psychoanalytic theory.

Clinical Considerations

Clinicians work with a variety of clients some of whom are beset by an overwhelming loss of self and sense of meaninglessness, a fragile sense of self or the distress of confronting a false self organisation. This may involve a therapeutic regression to the point of failure in the establishment of a grounded sense of self, described by Balint (1968) as a basic fault. For other clients this may involve the need to achieve a point of basic trust from which they can progress, as there is little to which they can regress or, as Winnicott (1976) put it, to move towards the integration of the ego and the development of a true self.

Therapists of all persuasions have to work with the notions of the self that are prevalent in society. Within a multi-cultured community, therapists will encounter a range of perspectives on the concept of self and soul that will impact on the client's experience of self. Belief systems, cultural, political as well as religious, can be thought of as existing on a horizontal axis. There is at the same time a vertical axis cutting across this spectrum that ranges from a fundamentalist mind-set at one polarity to a more open and liberal attitude to perceived truth at the other. Clinicians can be confronted with rigid psychological defences expressed in the form of dogmatically driven and persecutory attitudes towards the self and others. In time clients may be able to move from such a rigid position towards developing a more benign attitude which enables them to realise a more expansive sense of self.

My experience of clients who are facing their own mortality (see also Chapter 9) is that they very often express a vague belief, prevalent in modern society, in an after-life devoid of substantial content. This may be a defence against the pain of separation and loss. Campbell and Hale (1991) record a prevailing fantasy in suicidal clients of some sort of blissful life after death that denies the reality that the death extinguishes existence. Other clients may have a more sanguine attitude to their mortality and will face the thought of the self being extinguished, the point at which the brain ceases to function, with equanimity.

Conclusion

I began by setting out a double purpose. In the first place I referred to questions posed to students in ontology seminars: Who are you? How do define your sense of self and self value? In thinking about these questions, I made a suggestion that the notions of an implicit and explicit self differentiate between being a self and being aware of being a self that could be reflective and therefore have a capacity to think about thinking. I commented on the issue of self as body and mind, discussed self and identity and looked at the wider cultural context that contributes to a sense of self.

Particular reference was made to the philosophical evolution of the concept of self and ways in which this was reflected in the development of psychoanalytic thought and the controversy between Freud and Jung.

I then set out some of the elements essential to the development of what Winnicott called a well-grounded sense of self. In setting out these elements I was attempting to draw on themes that are common to a range of psychoanalytic theoretical approaches.

I then briefly discussed some recent philosophical thinking about the notion of self and concluded by looking at some of the ways in which the experience of self might arise in clinical work and the significance of this.

What the exploration in this chapter identifies is that the nature of the self is 'both discovered and created' (Colman, 2006: 169).). Baggini argues that we do not 'have' a self – self is what we do and this doing creates an illusion, based on a sequence of events that enables us to think about being a self (Baggini, 2011: 144–153). Colman comments on the relational aspect of self: 'No one can come to "have a self" except through first being endowed with one in the mind of others' (Colman, 2008: 359). Self is difficult to define, no more so than in the philosophical debate about the relationship of 'mind' and 'body', terms that refer to different categories of experience. The importance of the notion of self, across a range of psychoanalytic theory, is that it holds together the clinical concepts of psyche and soma as integral to a uniquely human process.

Acknowledgement

With thanks to Ben Stewart for help in editing the text.

References

Aquinas, T. (1274) *The Suma Theologica*. Online Edition. Copyrights. Kevin Knight. 2008. http://www.newadvent.org/summa/ 28.01.2012.

Bacon, F. (2008) *Francis Bacon. The Major Works*. (Oxford: Oxford University Press).

Baggini, J. (2011) *The Ego Trick*. (Granta Books: London).

Balint, M. (1968) *The Basic Fault*. (London: Routledge).

Bowlby, J. (1971) *Attachment and Loss*. (London: Penguin Books).

Campbell D. and Hale, R. (1991) 'Suicidal Acts' in *The Textbook of Psychotherapy in Psychiatric Practice*. Holmes, J (ed.) (London: Churchill Langston).

Colman, W. (2006) 'The Self' in *The Handbook of Jungian Psychology*. Papadopoulos, R.K. (ed.) (London and New York: Routledge).

Colman, W. (2008) 'On being, knowing and having a self', *Journal of Analytical Psychology*, 53, 351–366.

Crowe, M, J. (2001) *Theories of the World from Antiquity to the Copernican Revolution*. (Mineola, NY: Dover Publications, Inc).

Darwin, C. (1993) *The Origin of Species*. (New York: Random House Inc). First published 1859.

Descartes, R. (1637) *Discourse on Method and the Meditations*. (London: Penguin Books). 1968.

Fonagy, P. et al. (2004) *Review of Affect Regulation, Mentalisation and the Development of the Self*. (New York: Other Press New York).

Freud, S. (1905) *The Three Essays on Sexuality*. SE.VII. (London: Hogarth Press). 1961.

Freud, S. (1906/08) *Jensen's 'Gradiva' and Other Works*. SE.IX. (London: Hogarth Press). 1959.

Freud, S. (1923) *The Ego and the Id: On Metapsychology*. SE. XIX. (London: Hogarth Press). 1961.

Hume D. (2000) 'On Personal Identity, Book 1 Part 4 Section 6' in *A Treatise on Human Nature*. (Oxford: Oxford Philosophical Texts).

Jung, C.G. (1942/54) 'Transformation Symbolism in the Mass' in *CW.11*. (London; Routledge). 1991.

Jung, C. G. (1951) *Aion. CW, 9 Part 11*. (London: Routledge). 1989.

Kant, I. (1787) *Critique of Pure Reason*. Cambridge Edition of the Works of Immanuel Kant. (Cambridge: Cambridge University Press). 1999.

Kreis, S. (2009) Lecture 8. Greek Thought: Socrates, Plato and Aristotle. *The History Guide. Lectures on Ancient and Medieval European History*. http://www.historyguide.org/ancient/lecture8b.html 29.01.2012.

Locke, J. (1690) *An Essay Concerning Human Understanding*. (Oxford: Oxford University Press). 1975.

Marx, K. (1876) *Capital: The Critique of Political Economy*. Fowkes, B. (trans.) (London: Penguin Books). 1990.

Newton, I. (1687) *The Principia: Mathematical Principles of Natural Philosophy*. (California: University of California Press). 1999.

Plato. (2003) *The Republic Book V*. (London: Penguin Book).

Rycroft, C. (1985) *A Critical Dictionary of Psychoanalysis* (London: Penguin).

Ryle, G. (1949) *The Concept of Mind*. (London: Penguin).

Schore, A. (2001) 'Minds in the making: attachment, the self organising brain, and developmentally-orientated psychoanalytical psychotherapy', *British Journal of Psychotherapy*, 17, (3), 297–328.

Schore, A. (2003) *Affect Regulation and the Repair of the Self*. (New York: Norton New York).

Taylor, C. (1992) *Sources of Self: The making of the Modern Identity*. (Cambridge Massachusetts: Harvard University Press).

Winnicott, D.W. (1964) 'Review of Memories, Dreams, Reflections' in *Psychoanalytic Explorations*. (London: Karnac). 1989.

Winnicott, D. W. (1971) 'The Location of Cultural Experience' in *Playing and Reality*. (London: Tavistock Publications).

Winnicott, D. W. (1976) 'Ego Integration in Child Development' in *The Maturational Processes and the Facilitating Environment*. (London: The Hogarth Press).

11

The Diversity Agenda in the Consulting Room

Juliet Newbigin

Introduction

While, like all modern institutions, psychoanalytic training bodies subscribe to an Equal Opportunities policy, it has, in the past, not had much impact on the way that psychotherapists working with individuals are trained. However, the Equality Act now requires organisations that sponsor psychoanalytic therapy in the UK to look seriously at the way that stereotyping assumptions may affect interactions in the consulting room and to consider how to incorporate this awareness into their theory and practice.

These concerns are usually defined as the impact of difference or 'diversity', but what is being referred to is, of course, not just any difference – brown eyes or blue, left- or right-handedness, for example. The apparently innocent word 'diversity' is being used to flag up distinctions which are involved with power, inequalities and prejudice. This can lead to accusations of 'political correctness', a term sometimes heard to imply an over-zealous policing of the inadvertent assumptions that spontaneous speech can betray. These concerns originated in the identity politics of the 1960s and 1970s, when thinking of this kind became a mainstream preoccupation. At that time, the political focus turned towards an examination of prejudice and the manner in which oppressive attitudes could be internalised and played out in individual relationships, as well as in institutional settings. The women's movement, the campaigns against racism and pressure groups for gay liberation drew attention to the balance of power in relationships, and the damaging impact of discrimination on the individual's feeling of self-worth. Identifying oneself as a member of an oppressed group fuelled a new attitude of assertiveness. For some, this was an empowering time – women had the confidence to speak and write about their lives from the perspective of their gender, and it became possible to voice the experience of 'being black' or 'being disabled' or 'being gay', drawing attention to what it felt like to be the object of thoughtlessly discriminatory treatment, or at the receiving end of others' unexamined prejudices. This 'consciousness-raising' informed the development of new intellectual disciplines such as cultural studies and postcolonial history, which incorporated an awareness of how the social dynamics of power and subjugation are unconsciously internalised in an individual's way of understanding and valuing themselves.

This awareness depends on recognition of the psychological potency of social categories. And identifying oneself in terms of category distinctions can produce polarised thinking. When a group attempts to discuss the impact of these distinctions, righteous indignation fuelled by a sense of victimhood often stifles creative exchange. Thinking about social categories inevitably leads to generalising judgements, and in place of understanding, a culture of paranoid splitting can develop, in which blaming accusations are met by resistance or paralysing guilt.

Psychoanalytic trainings in individual psychotherapy have tended to remain apart from this discussion, claiming that their focus is the internal world and that the unconscious does not recognise social categories. An individual is unique, the argument runs, and therefore every encounter in the consulting room raises its own 'issues of diversity'. Some have said that it is impossible to consider a single aspect of identity, such as ethnicity, without splitting it off from the client as a whole psycho-social being.

Identity and Subjectivity

However, if we take seriously the fact that these collective categories affect the way we see ourselves and others, we are bound to take account of 'psycho-social' factors in our therapeutic practice and attempt to incorporate this thinking into training without presenting it in a split-off way. A superficial approach would simply encourage therapists to tiptoe around areas of sensitivity that have arisen in the wake of anti-discriminatory social policy.

In this chapter I shall attempt to answer the challenge that this poses. At the heart of the discussion about differences which divide us, there are important issues for psychoanalytic theory. However, they are slippery and confusing and, because of their disruptive nature, they create anxiety and it may be more comfortable to lose sight of them. Nevertheless, the consequences of ignoring them can cause serious distortions in clinical thinking.

How has it happened that psychoanalytic theory has largely relegated the psycho-social aspects of our identity to 'external world experience' that can be disregarded in the consulting room? I suggest that this is the result of an ambiguity at the heart of the psychoanalytic project. Freud presented psychoanalysis as the scientific study of enduring structures in the human mind, which included the individual's experience as an embodied self – 'the ego is first and foremost a bodily ego' he wrote in 1923 (Freud, 1923: 26). Although later he showed interest in how human beings functioned together at the level of wider society, he described the development of the personality either in individual or evolutionary terms. He writes from the stance of the open-minded scientist, often revising his theories, and he returned to many ideas again and again, sometimes with changes of emphasis which allowed him to hold together areas of thought that contain contradictions. One of these contradictions was present in his account of mental life, describing human consciousness from two aspects, one objective, in essentialist terms, and the other subjective, from the perspective of individual internal experience.

This is an inescapable but crucial ambiguity which we must keep in mind, and the confusion to which it gives rise is evident in Freud's theory of the development of those foundational human categories – female and male sexual identities. Schafer has pointed out that, influenced by Darwin's evolutionary biology, Freud regarded reproduction as the goal of mature sexual development, seeing the individual as 'the carrier of the reproductive organs and substances designed to guarantee the survival of the species' (Schafer, 1997: 244). The child became aware of his or her psychic constitution in the family setting, described by Freud as that of the liberal, bourgeois Viennese, like his own and most of his clients. Being a man of his time, he placed the nuclear family in this form at the apex of the 'civilised' world.

However, at the heart of this apparently objective and universalising theory, Freud placed an irreducibly subjective element. His view of the sexual drive, or instinct as Strachey translates it – the *libido* – although inevitably embodied, was never simply biological: 'the concept of instinct is thus one of those lying on the frontier between the mental and the physical.....An instinct is without quality, and, so far as mental life is concerned, is only to be regarded as a measure of the demand made upon the mind for work' (Freud, 1905: 168). The inevitable recognition of anatomical difference was a crucial moment in the small child's evolving sense of self, and the meaning the child made of it was subjective, understood in terms of his or her evolving body awareness and the potential pleasures to be had from it.

As Juliet Mitchell puts it,

> The psychoanalytic concept of sexuality...can never be equated with genitality, nor is it the simple expression of a biological drive. It is always psycho-sexuality, a system of conscious and unconscious human fantasies involving a range of excitations and activities that produce pleasure beyond the satisfaction of any basic physiological need. ... Only with great difficulty and then never perfectly does it move from being a drive with many component parts...to being what is normally understood as sexuality, something which *appears* to be a unified instinct in which genitality predominates. (Mitchell and Rose, 1982: 2)

Although Freud viewed the Oedipus complex which brought the child to an awareness of sexual identity as an evolutionary and inevitable aspect of all human development, he also attempted to explain the shock of that moment, on being confronted with difference, from the point of view of the individual's subjective experience. He understood this as an initiation, through which the individual was introduced to the human collective. Gender is the first social category we come to recognise.

Freud always admitted he was in ambiguous territory. He found the terms masculine and feminine,

> ..among the most confused that occur in science. It is possible to distinguish at least three uses. 'Masculine' and 'feminine' are used sometimes in the sense of activity and passivity, sometimes in a biological, and sometimes, again, in a sociological sense. (Freud, 1905: 219 footnote)

Dana Breen (1993), in her helpful introduction to *The Gender Conundrum*, points out that the German words that Freud uses convey the ambiguity of any attempt to make generalised statements about gender distinction. He speaks of how '"masculinity" and "femininity" are always tending to "fade away" – the verb "Verblassen" – and "vanish" – "Verflüchtigen" – into activity and passivity' (Breen, 1993: 4–5). This is no trivial matter, as these states are intimately bound up with assertiveness and processes of individuation. Breen sees this as arising from the fact that, although sexual identity is a universal aspect of our experience, psychoanalysis does not illuminate the objective fact of sexual identity, but rather its meaning for the individual. At the end of his life, Freud continued to write in 'Analysis Terminable and Interminable' of 'the great riddle of sex' (Freud, 1937: 252). Breen herself uses the term 'slippage' and ends her introduction by saying:

> Ultimately it is, from a psychoanalytic perspective, the underlying phantasy that determines whether an act is masculine or feminine. But the phantasy takes the body as its foundation and incorporates bodily characteristics and sensations. Understanding masculinity and femininity means understanding that interplay, means tolerating the out-of-focusness. (Breen, 1993: 38)

But what do we understand, in practice, by this 'slippage' and 'out-of-focusness'?

The controversial implications of Freud's theory of gender identity are well known and have been much discussed. Partly through his self-analysis he arrived at the Oedipal story of a small boy's discovery of genital excitement, and his desire for physical possession of his mother to consummate their passionate exclusive relationship. But his observation of women's genital difference awakens his fear of castration, which becomes grounds for terror when he encounters his father's prohibition against incest. The repression of this traumatic confrontation initiates the formation of the super-ego and thereafter submission to other authority figures who oversee the boy's education and induction into conventions of social behaviour.

As women analysts emphasised the impact of the child's earlier relationship with the mother, Freud became aware that the little girl's Oedipal experience differed from the boy's. Conjecturing how her anatomy would affect her social destiny, Freud specifically noted that his own capacity to understand might be limited by his subjectivity. Speaking of 'the riddle of femininity' he said: 'Nor will you have escaped worrying over this problem – those of you who are men; to those of you who are women this will not apply – you are yourselves the problem' (Freud, 1933: 113). Unable to understand the essential experience of women, he restricted himself to describing how a little girl 'comes to be'. From his masculine perspective, he took for granted that if the little pre-Oedipal girl believed she had everything necessary to satisfy her mother, this must mean that she saw herself as 'a little man'. This 'phallo-centric' picture, with its consequent stress on the woman's Oedipal experience of disappointment and penis-envy, provoked intense argument from the outset. In Chapter 12, Brid Greally explores how far-reaching its consequences have been and argues for an alternative view.

However, what I wish to emphasise here is the importance of Freud's attempt to conceptualise the little girl's discovery of her femininity, and the way in which it illuminated the subjective experience of gender difference, and our difficulty in escaping from the binary terms in which it first appears to us. Breen, Mitchell and Rose all argue that Freud's version, although contentious, manages to convey the paradoxical element in the experience of sexual identity. Although it is seen from a perspective which assumes that a woman's primary developmental task involves internalising an evaluation of her bodily function and feminine role in phallo-centric terms, the transformation she must undergo demonstrates the complex and shifting meanings that she is required to find in her anatomy and her desire in a cultural context that has privileged patriarchy. If femininity is a 'riddle' it must be the case that masculinity is too. Gender identity is something that can be ascribed anatomically, defined by the physical fact of sexual difference. Or it can be thought of in a sociological sense, arising from the divergent social roles and respective spheres of authority that follow in a given society from biological differences. Attempts to generalise take place within a shifting realm of social expectations, phantasies and stereotypes. This is what 'slippage' means. Gender is the primary area in which we discover that we can never be completely free of subjective bias in understanding the other. Women analysts recognised the partisan nature of Freud's account and argued that woman's desire for the penis was itself a defence against a more primal fear of the omnipotent mother (for example, Chasseguet-Smirgel, 1981). But this simply replaced a phallo-centric position with one which gave primacy to the archaic imago of the mother. The truth of the matter is that there can be no final objective standpoint from which to describe the essential difference that distinguishes a woman's embodied experience from that of a man.

Judith Butler (1990: 82) points out that thinking about gender leads to confusion because we are always losing sight of the subjective aspect of this binary distinction between 'masculinity' and 'femininity'. Even when we seek to resolve it by recourse to the idea of inherent 'bisexuality', we find ourselves inevitably confusing 'masculinity' with activity and 'femininity' with passivity. We end up with a picture of conflicting stereotypical heterosexual identities, coexisting in the individual. What is foreclosed is the capacity to imagine a desire that does not follow this template, as Greally explores in Chapter 12. Butler points out that, although Freud was aware of this 'riddle', the confusion is embedded in his theory. Her argument sheds light on the troubled position that psychoanalysis has always taken towards non-heterosexual identities. Recognising our confusion in this area illuminates the difficulties faced by individuals whose sexual orientation or gender identity do not fit into what society has regarded as 'normal' heterosexuality (Butler, 1990: 93).

Subjectivity, Group Identity and Prejudice

Is this 'slippage' that occurs when we try to think about the categories of 'masculinity' and 'femininity' an inevitable feature of our subjective awareness? Is our difficulty in keeping it in mind only a conceptual one, or are there emotional factors at work?

Psychoanalytic theory presumes that the Oedipal awakening brings to an end the omnipotent period of infancy. Prior to this stage of development, all things seemed possible. The French psychoanalyst, Bela Grunberger (1989: 168), has suggested that, entering the Oedipal stage, both boys and girls have to face the inadequacy of their genitals, whether it be as a result of castration anxiety or penis envy. It is the awareness of immaturity that deals the fatal blow to infantile omnipotence, and initiates a realisation of generational, as well as sexual difference. Juliet Mitchell, in her work on siblings, echoes this and suggests that this moment of awareness demands a recasting of the ego-ideal – the ability to let go of a fantasy of uniqueness and recognise the place of a sibling, who is like me, and yet not me (Mitchell, 2003: 52–53). On the other side of the Oedipal divide, lies a new accommodation to reality, coloured by an inevitable melancholy recognition of an external world that is not of our own making. We enter the social world, and embark on the process of becoming a 'subject', exploring our unfolding sense of an identity which is experienced both intrapsychically and interpersonally. The word 'subject', with its implication of accountability, carries within it, as Judith Butler points out, the notion of submission (Butler, 1997). From this point onwards, as Freud puts it, our ego is 'a poor creature owing service to three masters'

(Freud, 1923: 56); we are always managing conflict between the pressure of our libidinal wishes, the demands of the super-ego and the requirements of the external world.

Becoming a subject brings us to an awareness of social categories. Freud's study of groups focussed on the manner in which the individual ego could become submerged in a group, or 'transfer' authority onto the person of the group leader, as demonstrated in the church or the army (Freud, 1921: 93–99). Psychotherapists in anglophone countries who work with individuals have tended to leave the social world to group therapists, focusing on the universalising aspect of Freud's work. The 'negative capability' required, in listening to unconscious communication in the therapeutic relationship, has seemed at odds with concerns about the external social world and stereotypes.

However, group psychoanalysts such as Foulkes have thought about group dynamics as a crucial means of binding primitive, existential anxiety. Foulkes said that the three ingredients of human personality formation – our evolutionary constitution, the contribution of our personal history and our ongoing social experience – 'are all the time linked up with one another and in a state of interaction' (Foulkes, 1948: 14). Anton Obholzer adds that we have a life-long need to deal with primitive anxiety that we play out in our social experience:

> It is clear that the earliest relationships have as their task the containing of the child's anxiety and the fostering of a sense of self: the development of a psychological 'skin'. In the earliest stages this serves both as a physical boundary for a sense of self and also as a psychological one. Thus a sense of self, of belonging to a family, a group, an institution, a nation, are all various layers of skin to foster a sense of identity, security and belonging. (Obholzer, 1989: 32)

These preconscious assumptions about where we belong, this social 'skin' which Obholzer describes, take the form of internal fantasy of group membership, and the Oedipus complex can be thought of as the threshold of this awareness. As Foulkes suggests, our sense of identity is in an ongoing state of negotiation, and we discover this in the powerful internal impact of changes in social status, the traumatic sense of injury and insecurity that can be aroused by losing one's job, or by the loss of one's language and cultural context, as a result of migration.

Psychotherapy reveals how fragile our sense of identity is and how we regress in the presence of anxiety to more primitive ways of thinking. Experiences which appear to alienate us from the other disturb our wish for a world that is predictable and under our control. Faced with the other's visible difference, we find ourselves shifting, almost without realising it, into a generalising state of mind, where we find that we have placed them in a different category from ourselves. Tan points out that this process involves a retreat from reality. It is an attempt 'to control and dominate the object that is felt to be different and separate' as a defence against paranoid anxiety (Tan, 1993: 33). It is this process which gives rise to a stereotypical way of viewing the other – we somehow know what to expect from 'a person like that'. Thus social categories not only underpin our sense of identity but also reassure us in our dealings with the external world. Collective prejudice is built on the projective action of category distinction, where the disparagement involved in diminishing the other's full humanity has become so entrenched in the collective mind that it begins to assume the concreteness of accepted fact. Young-Bruehl, speaking of racism, spells out this process further. She suggests that racist generalisations,

> manifested in slurs, acts of discrimination, attacks, are followed by prejudices – not necessarily the same ones – manifested in rationalisations, self-serving descriptions, denials, commentaries, often ones designed to discredit the victims' truthfulness or belittle their pain. Prejudices have histories, and the second stage commonly involves a reference to history ... (Young-Bruehl, 1996: 5)

This process of category assignment is used for narcissistic reassurance to elevate our sense of superiority and power at the expense of others. One need only think of the way in which advertising appeals to our weakness in this area, suggesting that certain commodities – a new car, for instance – can influence the status we are accorded. In today's more mobile society, where the way we see ourselves is less dependent on stable communities or defined regional and class identities, this is a potent mechanism. It is therefore inevitable that when a therapist and a client meet for the first time, each of them is taking in cues about the other's identity, assigning categories which create fantasies about who the other person is. Some of these will be shared, and form part of the work of therapy, but categories associated with prejudice feel more dangerous to explore because of the highly charged feelings they arouse. Therapists have sometimes tended to fall back on their authority in the consulting room to steer away from these difficult areas, I would suggest, because anxiety can threaten to pull the therapist's thinking 'out of focus'. Although we may not be actively prejudiced ourselves, it is a mechanism that we all understand. When faced with a client or therapist who may have been the object of prejudice and who we fear will assume that we will share such views, we become wary. In our minds, the presence of the difference that separates us may come to dominate the encounter. Although it may feel dangerous territory to enter, it is potentially an area of intersubjective discovery, and it is only when these issues can be explored from both sides of the divide that we can begin to dispel the defensive assumptions and suspicion that they arouse.

Clinical Implications

A disabled psychotherapist, Rhoda Olkin, describes how it feels to be categorised by her disability:

> When people hear I had polio (in 1954), they are often confused – isn't there a polio vaccine to prevent things like this (i.e., people like me) from happening?... In fact, the Salk vaccine was not out on clinical trials and widely available until 1955. People often look visibly relieved to hear this; why? Because it provides an explanation for my misfortune; it relieves anyone of fault....The world is put right again. People prefer to have explanations for bad events, and if that bad event happened to another person, they prefer explanations that exempt themselves from the possibility of the bad event happening to them. (Olkin, 1999: 58–59)

Olkin is describing the emotional current of relief that she senses in her questioners when they can safely feel themselves to be members of one group, protected by the polio vaccine, and assign her – who has suffered the 'misfortune' of polio – to another. Their relief communicates itself to Olkin as rejection. They have identified her with her disability, and, as such, she is now an object, from which, in a phobic manner, they seek to distance themselves. Olkin, on the receiving end, conveys in her ironic aside that she can feel this: 'things like this (i.e., people like me)'. It is a vivid example of how our paranoid response to the unsettling fact of another's disability can lead us instinctively to employ primitive projective defences of which we are barely aware, but which are vividly experienced by the disabled person, as an attack on their status as a human being.

Unless we are prepared to examine this area of our subjective phantasy, we will remain unconscious of the way that our stereotypical view is experienced by the receiver of our projection. Fakhry Davids (1992) in his paper, 'The Cutting Edge of Racism: An Object Relations View', states that the impact of the racist projection is not only an attack on 'the truth that the black is an ordinary person' but also contains by implication, a controlling effect so that the black person is 'at every turn... confronted by the practical operation of powerful stereotypes that push (that individual) into acting, thinking and feeling in particular ways' (Davids, 1992: 19–20). In Davids' view, this tendency to react in a categorising way is universal. He also says: 'the internal racist is just a fact of life. It has to be lived with and cannot be subject to the idealised demand that it disappear... at best one could hope that awareness and acceptance of the internal racist will help one to be less dominated by it' (Davids, 1992: 27).

However, rather than explore the possible complication that an internal racist organisation can contribute to a cross-cultural therapeutic encounter,

individual psychotherapy has tended to adopt the position that we are all basically the same. Morgan (1998) describes this as 'colour blindness', which can
have important clinical consequences. Farhad Dalal describes an encounter
with his white supervisor, who took this position, saying he was 'not usually
aware of the person's "race" or colour in a session'. Dalal describes how he, as
a black therapist, felt about this response:

> Why might I be more sensitive than my supervisor on this matter? An inter-
> nalist interpretation is bound to look for the cause inside me. Thus it might
> be suggested that I am overly sensitive or have a chip on my shoulder. In
> effect this is an interpretation of paranoia in which I am projecting some
> internal difficulty into the territory of black and white, which is now thought
> of as a vehicle for this latent difficulty. Another possibility is as follows. The
> white, by virtue of their colour, is in the mainstream and near the centre,
> whilst the black is marginalised and nearer to the edge. The closer one is to
> the edge, with the resultant danger of going over, the more one is aware of
> the circumstances that put one there – colour. Meanwhile, those at the centre
> have a vested interest (often unconscious) in maintaining the status quo by
> blanking out the colour dynamic altogether: if it does not exist in the first
> place, it cannot be changed. (Dalal, 2002: 219)

When his supervisor – an authority figure for Dalal – argues that the unconscious is colour blind, this places the entire burden of the experience of racial
difference with Dalal, implying that his subjective experience of himself as
black and his supervisor as white is his problem, and even his pathology. In
order to argue against this, he must assert the importance of the psycho-social
perspective that his supervisor does not acknowledge. If he shows his feelings,
he might 'go over' the edge and might appear simply angry, to have 'a chip
on his shoulder'. Challenging the supervisor, who speaks with authority and
seems clear and calm, becomes difficult for the supervisee who is full of strong
feeling. To take it up would evoke anxieties of a paranoid nature: 'If I think
there's a problem, does it mean that it's *my* problem?'

While women analysts have from the outset taken up the disparagement
implied by Freud's theory of female psycho-sexual development, in other areas
where there has been no community of opposition to point out the value-laden
slant of an apparently objective description, the stereo-typical assumption it
contains remains unchallenged. Psychoanalytic psychotherapy trainings have
attracted some candidates from culturally diverse backgrounds, but remain
predominately white.

This has also been true of psychoanalytic theories of homosexuality, both
male and female. The profession came to reject Freud's liberal stance that
homosexuality should not be a barrier to acceptance for analytic training.
Although Freud argued that we have all made a homosexual object choice in

our unconscious, a profession which excluded self-identified homosexual candidates had no way of examining this statement in its full complexity. Instead psychoanalysis subsequently took the socially accepted path, and located the problem defensively in the non-heterosexual other, concluding that an individual whose desires were different had failed in a fundamental way to adjust to a 'normal' identity as a man or woman. Homosexuality was seen as the consequence of a failure to negotiate the Oedipal stage, a developmental arrest at a narcissistic stage of relating. Non-heterosexual desires were defined as evidence of an identity disorder, a 'borderline' condition. Since the decriminalisation of male homosexuality in Britain in 1967, and the declassification of homosexuality as pathological in the DSM II in 1973, the theoretical assumptions that underpinned this diagnosis have remained hard to dismantle. This has perpetuated a problematic attitude that has left the gay, lesbian, bi-sexual and transgendered community with a suspicion of psychoanalytically oriented psychotherapy. Only recently have therapists begun to recognise their own heterosexist bias and the impact homophobia has had on the internal world of their clients.

Now that the pathologising definition has been removed, psychoanalysis can find itself in a theoretical vacuum when confronting alternative sexual orientation. Instead the therapist can adopt an attitude of 'neutrality', or resort to distinctions between 'healthy' and 'unhealthy' homosexuality. The psychoanalyst Martin Frommer (1995) points out that, unless the heterosexual therapist is willing to confront his or her countertransference feelings towards clients whose orientation is different from the therapist's own, assuming an apparently neutral stance may mask a resistance to a fuller, more emotionally engaged enquiry. Focusing on a male therapeutic dyad, Frommer says:

> As psychoanalysts we bring our gendered selves, and all that implies, to the process of understanding the other. Our gendered and gendering selves lead the way to and often guide the assumptions we make about the other and how their sexuality inhabits their psyches in ways different from ours. Whatever it means for a man to sexually desire and love another man, currently, our culture has infused same-sex desire with meanings that have the potential to evoke powerful counter-transference reaction. Presently homosexual desire goes to the core of a man's socially constructed self and therefore puts one's total self on the line. (Frommer 1995: 73)

A heterosexual therapist's failure to be aware of this may lead him or her to replicate the response that the gay or lesbian client may have experienced from a heterosexual parent, whose detachment could be felt to convey a lack of understanding and acceptance. It is almost inevitable that both client and therapist will have internalised the same culturally conditioned assumption of the 'normality' of heterosexuality.

These ambiguities will challenge our profession increasingly, as medicine makes further inroads into what were hitherto regarded as 'natural' biological processes. Already we are trying to grapple with the experience of couples undergoing IVF and conceiving children through donor insemination or the use of surrogates. Such families may involve heterosexual or homosexual couples, or single parents. In addition there are the issues raised by the recognition and treatment of Atypical Gender Identity Organisation (Di Ceglie, 2009). We cannot simply avoid these areas by making the assumption that such individuals undergoing treatment are motivated by a search for something that is, as some might argue, 'perverse' or 'psychotic'. Although we may wish to assume a settled correspondence between sexuality and gender identity, this will always elude us.

Dealing with differences and their tendency to throw our view of the other 'out-of-focus' provokes fundamental anxiety in all of us – client and therapist alike. As therapists, we may feel that our internal authority is hard won and we do not want to be confronted with humiliating evidence of our capacity to become confused. When an awareness of difference intrudes, it can bring about a disorientating shift in the preoccupation of the therapeutic dyad, from a shared focus on the client's internal reality, into an interpersonal experience which reminds the therapist of the projective processes that are potentially active, and underlying paranoid anxiety. In these moments of uncertainty the therapist can lose confidence in his or her neutral stance on which internal authority is based. It is understandable, therefore, that therapists attempt to side-step this issue by denying that the external difference is of significance in the consulting room.

Difference – A Wider Perspective

Here I have addressed only a few of the most obvious, embodied differences – gender, sexual orientation, ethnicity and disability. But there are other important areas – age, social class, religious affiliation, for example. These are all characteristics which trigger anxiety in the encounter and an impulse to retreat to a categorising way of perceiving the other without necessarily being aware that this has happened. As therapists, if we are to tolerate our own 'out of focus' reactions, we must make a theoretical adjustment. Although we need to be responsible for providing containment in the therapeutic setting, allowing it to be a space for the client to use us in the transference, through projection and enactment, we must also be willing to interrogate our countertransference open-mindedly. Sometimes we may find that we are harbouring some assumptions of our own about the client that we have failed to notice. In her paper, 'Frozen Harmonies', Morgan (2010: 39) suggests that there may be times when we use transference interpretation as a defence against immersing ourselves in the more confusing immediacy of the session. 'This rather aloof position allows us to act as if we can distance ourselves from the terror of being exposed to the other, and to affect, and be affected in a way which is outside our awareness, never mind our control, and which we may never fully understand' (Morgan, 2010: 39). In the United States a shift in this direction has been led by the interpersonal and relational analysts. Benjamin says:

> The intersubjective dimension....refers to experience *between and within* individuals, rather than just *within*. It refers to a sense of self and other that evolves through the consciousness that separate minds can share the same feelings and intentions, through mutual recognition. (Benjamin, 1990: 125)

Conclusion

So to return to the question at the beginning of this chapter – how to confront difference in our perception of the other, without splitting it off from recognition of their whole psycho-social being – we may have to acknowledge that it is not possible. Indeed, as therapists, we may have to admit that this splitting is a natural tendency to which we are all prone, which produces preconceptions and misunderstandings of which we may be only vaguely and defensively aware. Often the misunderstandings that arise from unacknowledged stereotyping occur to us only afterwards, or they may be painfully brought home to us by the other's response. I have argued that being aware of this dimension, and prepared to explore it in the therapeutic relationship, has the potential to bring the work alive. Rather than trying to side-step this confusing area that can make us feel painfully deskilled, we should embrace it as a reminder of how fluid our sense of our own identity actually is. This is one of the original insights of psychoanalysis, but it is also one that it is hard to remain open to. I believe that psychotherapy offers the most fertile method we have for illuminating the phantasy life that we generate as embodied individuals in a diverse social world. I am arguing for a stance which recognises that, although we aspire to a state of reflective understanding of our clients, we can never be wholly objective. If we are alert to this dimension, and aware of the impact that it can have on our relationship, the therapist and client together may turn it to creative effect.

References

Benjamin, J. (1990) *The Bonds of Love: Psychoanalysis, Feminism and the Problem of Domination*. (London: Virago Press).

Breen, D. (ed.) (1993) 'Introduction', *The Gender Conundrum: Contemporary Psychoanalytic Perspectives on Femininity and Masculinity*. (The New Library of Psychoanalysis. London: Routledge).

Butler, J. (1990) *Gender Trouble*. (New York: Routledge).

Butler, J. (1997) *The Psychic Life of Power: Theories in Subjection*. (Stanford CA: Stanford University Press).

Chasseguet-Smirgel, J. (1981) *Female Sexuality*. (London: Virago).

Dalal, F. (2002) *Race, Colour and the Processes of Racialization: New Perspectives from Group Analysis, Psychoanalysis and Sociology*. (Hove and New York: Brunner-Routledge).

Davids, F. (1992) 'The cutting edge of racism: an object relations view', *Bulletin of the British Psychoanalytical Society*, 28, 19–29.

Di Ceglie, D. (2009) *A Stranger in My Own Body*. (London: Karnac).

Foulkes, S. H. (1948) *Introduction to Group-Analytic Psychotherapy*. (London: Karnac). 1983.

Freud, S. (1905) *The Three Essays on Sexuality*. *SE. VII*. (London: Hogarth Press). 1961.

Freud, S. (1921) 'Group Psychology and the Analysis of the Ego' in *SE.XVIII*. (London: Hogarth Press).

Freud, S. (1923) *The Ego and the Id*. *SE.XIX*. (London: Hogarth Press).

Freud, S. (1933) 'Femininity' in *New Introductory Lectures on Psychoanalysis*, SE.XXII. (London: Hogarth Press).

Freud, S. (1937) 'Analysis Terminable and Interminable' in *SE.XXIII*. (London: Hogarth Press).

Frommer, M. S. (1995) 'Countertransference Obscurity in the Psychoanalytic Treatment of Homosexual Patients', in *Disorienting Sexuality: Psychoanalytic Reappraisals of Sexual Identities*. Domenici, T. and Lesser, R.C. (eds) (New York: Routledge).

Grunberger, B. (1989) *New Essays on Narcissism*. (London: Free Association Books).

Mitchell, J. (2003) *Siblings: Sex and Violence*. (Cambridge: Polity).

Mitchell, J. and Rose, J. (eds.) (1982) *Feminine Sexuality: Jacques Lacan and the Ecole Freudienne*. (London: Macmillan Press Ltd).

Morgan, H. (1998) 'Between fear and blindness: the white therapist and the black Patient', *Journal of the British Association of Psychotherapists*, 34, 48–61.

Morgan, H. (2010) 'Frozen harmonies: petrified places in the analytic field', *British Journal of Psychotherapy*, 26, (1), 33–49.

Obholzer, A. (1989) 'The Comfort of Groups' in *The Nuclear Mentality: A Psychosocial Analysis of the Arms Race*. Barnett L. & Lee I. (eds) (London: Pluto Press).

Olkin, R. (1999) *What Psychotherapists Should Know About Disability*. (New York: Guilford Press).

Schafer, R. (1997) 'The Evolution of My Views on Nonnormative Sexual Practices' in *Tradition and Change in Psychoanalysis*. (London: Karnac).

Tan, R. (1993) 'Racism and similarity: paranoid-schizoid structures', *British Journal of Psychotherapy*, 10, (1), 33–43.

Young-Bruehl, E. (1996) *The Anatomy of Prejudices*. (Mass. USA: Harvard University Press).

12

Sexuality and Therapeutic Practice

Brid Greally

Sexual difference is one of the major philosophical issues, if not the issue, of our age.
(Irigaray, 1993: 7)

Introduction

Many people dismiss Freud's (1905b) discovery of the importance of sexuality to our psychic health and claim that society is no longer suffering from the repression of sexuality. Instead, writers such as Walter (2010) are concerned about the hyper-sexualisation of culture, as the advertising, fashion and entertainment industry are increasingly saturated with sexual imagery. The French psychoanalyst Irigaray (1993) claims that we still do not yet fully understand the implications of Freud's theory of sexuality and comments that 'sexual difference is one of the major philosophical issues, if not the issue, of our age' (Irigaray, 1993: 7). She calls for a therapeutic practice where the body is implicated in modes of existence and lived experience and which would elaborate how sex, death and power are folded into each other. The originality of her work lies in how she revisits the nature-nurture debate; rather than putting forward a psychotherapeutic practice where nature is sublimated by culture, she understands the body as the ground of the mode of being which generates a paradoxical tension of being constituting, as well as constituted, in a way which is active and open ended. Her interrogation of sexuality links the repression of embodiment, to the promulgation of a psychoanalytic discourse which claims neutrality but is based on what she calls the 'male imaginary'. This male imaginary serves to cover over the fact that both men and women are 'of a woman born', a debt which it seeks to repress resulting in detrimental consequences for the lived experiences of both men and women. In her book (1993) entitled *The Ethics of Sexual Difference*, she writes of psychoanalysis as an ethic of self-exploration and self-actualisation which links ethics and the erotic and she argues for the installation of a way of thinking about sexual difference which would allow for the possibility of flourishing lives for both women and men and the possibility of sharing a world. She is particularly concerned about the psychic cost to women and she claims that 'women are not allowed a full humanity that transcends itself in a way different from that of men' (Irigaray, 2008: xiii). I believe that much of psychoanalytic practice is in danger of lagging behind the more progressive aspects of contemporary society which Newbigin outlines succinctly in Chapter 11. I will attempt to address some of these issues by using threads of Irigaray's work in dialogue with others to pose the possibility of a progressive psychoanalysis. Such a practice is conditioned on open institutions which allow for new questions and new listeners and allow us to hear the prophetic in our clients' dilemmas and how they may have a particular ability to instantiate the unarticulated suffering of our time.

Irigaray insists that a self-reflective psychoanalysis needs to be able to situate itself historically, accept its limitations and articulate a subjectivity which is both embedded and embodied within history and culture. Psychoanalytic practice grew out of and is a response to Western culture which she diagnoses as being preoccupied with occluding the debt to the mother's body. She interrogates the subsequent symbolic matricide and misogyny with its failure to allow subjectivity to mothers and to all women through her. Western culture of the twenty-first century, which prioritises mastery, reason and economic accumulation, results in psychoanalysts being asked to bear witness to: a crisis of love and self-orientation, an instrumental relationship to the body, a weakening in the capacity to remember and intolerance for the ability to bear loss and mourning. Rather than providing the conditions for life, contemporary Western culture can exacerbate a deadly jouissance which appears as self-loathing and nihilism. Irigaray (1993) alerts us to the danger of a therapeutic response to this which resorts to a nostalgic search for the lost object of certainty, a resorting to definite identities and solid foundations which, in turn, excludes and colonise others.

However, Western culture can also be understood as bringing new freedoms for both women and men including: democracy, reproductive and sexual rights, and the right to a personal life (Weeks, 2007). These new freedoms, some hard won by feminist and gay activism campaigns and some caught in the tailwind of the drive towards global capitalism, allow for new possibilities, and generate new questions and new contradictions. In modern times, sexuality has continued to be a central preoccupation of Western culture with its promise of the freedom for sexual self-expression and its link to the project of a search for identity. With the help of Irigaray, I will enquire as to whether psychoanalysis is able to analyse the effects of the symbolic matricide and misogyny of Western culture or whether it perpetuates it in a non-critical manner, creating clinical impasses. I will seek to diagnose the extent of misogyny in some aspects of Freud's (1909) and Lacan's (1966) theory of the Oedipus complex and the pre-Oedipal theory of the British School of Object Relations. I will question whether these approaches are able to deconstruct the deadening effects of normative presumptions in relation to masculinity and femininity and whether a clinical space can be protected for the unfolding of the transference for both women and men.

Misogyny: The Symptom of Psychoanalysis

Since its instigation, psychoanalytic practice and its role in society have been in question and its future continues to be uncertain. Currently, there is a concern that the institutionalisation and regulation of psychoanalysis is strangling the emergence of a progressive contemporary practice. In Britain training societies have become institutionalised around Schools of Thought relating to major figures such as Klein, Lacan and Winnicott which raises concerns about the freedoms necessary for intellectual and clinical dissent and creativity. Attempts to regulate psychoanalysis threaten to compound the problem and fail to allow an open structure which would allow for the possibility of unforeseen change or new questions (Parker and Revelli, 2008). The historian Zaretsky (2005) in his social history of psychoanalysis queries the role of psychoanalysis in contemporary life:

> One century after its founding psychoanalysis presents us with a paradox. Almost instantly recognised as a great force for human emancipation, it played a central role in the modernism of the 1920's, the English and American welfare state of the 1940s and 1950s, the radical upheavals of the 1960s and the feminist and gay liberation of the 1970s. Yet it is simultaneously a fount of antipolitical, antifeminist and homophobic prejudice, a degraded profession, a pseudo science whose survival is very much in doubt. (Zaretsky, 2005: 3)

Fortunately, in contrast to psychoanalytic clinical trainings, new thinking in relation to psychoanalysis has taken place in gender studies and cultural studies departments of some universities (Frosh, 2010). Paradoxically, it would seem that these university departments, despite being subjected to the logic of capitalism and the commodification of knowledge, have escaped the worst excesses of psychoanalytic tribalism. They have been able to create a critical space for the possibility of dialogue and the emergence of new controversies. These debates in feminism, queer theory and post-colonial theory, have been generated by some threads of the work of Irigaray and others.[1] They present a powerful challenge to psychoanalytic practice to address its own misogyny and 'sexual indifference' and to develop a contemporary practice which allows for an understanding of sexuality in a way which addresses the differing clinical implications of working through for men and women.

Irigaray's (1985) first major psychoanalytic publication, entitled *Speculum of the Other Woman*, a retrospective study, beginning with Freudian thought and ending with the philosophy of Plato, highlights how misogyny gets reproduced throughout Western thought. She seeks to deconstruct and transform Western thought, using the insights gleaned from psychoanalysis, of the formative role of the maternal function which it simultaneously seeks to repress. This 'inoperable potential' is occluded when psychoanalytic discourse is based on the premise of one sex, the male sex which is achieved through the erasure of the generative mother, and of the subjectivity of all women through her. She claims that it fails to pose any question of the 'riddle of masculinity'; instead the male is taken as the universal subject of humanity, the 'man of reason': 'all Western discourse presents a certain isomorphism with the masculine sex: the privilege of unity, form of the self, of the visible, of the specularisable, of the erection' (Irigaray, 1985: 64). This male imaginary erases the feminine, represses embodiment and projects and imagines the future as if it were an extension of the present. In a deconstructive and utopian exercise she asks us to imagine a different sexuality that is based more on the morphology of the woman's body. She puts forward a corporeal approach to language; with her metaphor of the 'two lips' she wants to highlight what may be the specificity of women's sexuality and how it is conditioned on women having a voice. In contrast to Freud's focus on passivity, she wants to stress the possibility of multiplicity, fluidity and excessiveness of women's sexuality. Likewise with her use of pregnancy as a metaphor she wants to put forward a sexual difference that neither negates nor assimilates the other. With her use of the feminine metaphors of pregnancy, and the two lips she aims to highlight the possibility 'of being two' that is not returned to the one and the same but where the other is recognised as other. She wants to pose the possibility of a non-traumatic encounter with the other.

Irigaray situates psychoanalysis as an extension of the male imagery of the Judaeo-Christian tradition in so far as it reinforces the father–son relationship and puts it forward as the paradigm of love. The resolution of the Oedipus complex as outlined by both Freud and Lacan requires a renunciation of the incestuous mother and an installation of paternal protection from her and her dangerous desires for her son and from his desires for her. The incestuous mother is anti-social and socialisation requires the intervention of the father and becomes associated with the fear of castration. Freud (1909) wrote about how the boy comes to realise that the mother does not have a penis which he then understands in terms of punishment. The fear of this punishment installs his conscience, helps him identify with his father and protects him from a castrated and castrating mother. Lacan's (1966) post-structuralist theory claims a return to a non-biological reading of Freud. It elaborates the structuring effects of language and the connection to the 'name of the father'; a paternal metaphor which acts as a third term which separates the child, both boy and girl, from the mother. The son must renounce his first love, his mother, and identification with her is blocked. In exchange he can have everything else as he identifies with his father and gains access to language, symbolization and the promise of power over women. Under patriarchy, this third term, the prohibiting father of Freud and the paternal metaphor of Lacan protect the subject from psychosis and install the stabilisation of sexual identity by allowing a position within the Symbolic. Irigaray's work could be understood as making the opposite argument, as she highlights how these theories rely on biology where the male body is given higher value as it is linked to the civilising role of the paternal metaphor and where an acknowledgement to the debt to the maternal is foreclosed. Rather than shoring up the (patriarchal) Symbolic she wants to imagine that there is an alternative which does not lead to psychosis.

Klein's (1928) contribution to the Great Debate of the 1920s (Grosskurth, 1986) which was ignited by Horney's (1926) challenge to Freud's theory of penis envy, gave central place to oral sadism as the aetiological cause of difficulties in working through pre-Oedipal conflicts. These difficulties, including all sexual difficulties, were due to an inability to have mature genital heterosexual relations. Her theory relies on a biological view of reproductive sexuality, and fixations are interpreted in terms of the sadistic destructiveness of oral, anal and genital attacks and psychopathology is understood as deviations from a teleological unfolding of a biological trajectory. Some contemporary Kleinian theorists (Waddell, 1999) have grafted on a form of developmental psychology so that oral sadism and other forms of destructiveness are interpreted as a response to a maternal deprivation which cause developmental fixations.

Whilst the Great Debate was an international affair the Controversial Discussions (King and Steiner, 1992) was a London based conflict in 1945 over the hegemonic control of psychoanalysis. It concluded with the gentlemen's agreement of three major schools of thought. The Independent tradition emerged from this conflict by demarcating their work from that of both Klein and Anna Freud. The concept of 'the good enough mother' (Winnicott, 1971), however, has become a central concept for the three schools. It has become an ideal which can be understood as a variation of the Christian virgin mother who is not allowed to be also a woman with something to say and her own story to tell. The 'good enough mother' is theorised as the object of instinctual gratification without any sexuality or voice of her own (Baraister, 2009). In so far as psychoanalysis is unable to theorise the sexual specificity of women and in so far as it fails to take account that mother is a woman who speaks, it limits its clinical effectiveness for both men and women. Irigaray comments, 'It is indispensable that the child, girl or boy, have a representation of the sexes... But in the traditional conception of the family in fact, he or she doesn't have this. Because if the mother is uniquely mother, the child has no image of women and thus of sexual difference' (Irigaray, 1981: 62). Rose (2002) writing on the work of the Bollas notes the loss of the role of fantasy within the Object Relations tradition and how it has been replaced with 'mother blaming', where maternal deprivation is understood as the cause of all structural and contingent trauma, and where the effects of symbolic matricide and misogyny are reconfigured as environmental failure. In this double manoeuvre, the effects of misogyny are hidden whilst, simultaneously, mothers are blamed for all pathology.

Although Irigaray does not engage directly with Object Relations theory, her work highlights how psychoanalysis generally can become implicated in sexism and heterosexism rather than being a resource to analyse the psychic consequences of misogyny in Western thought. She is concerned that in the work of Freud and Lacan the mother is theorised as incestuous and engulfing and in the theories of Object Relations she is simultaneously engulfing and depriving. Rather than focussing on a repressed sexuality she wants to focus on the ethics of sexual difference, an ethics which rethinks the relationship between nature and culture and which does not conflate misogynistic assumptions under the rubric of reproductive sexuality based on biology. I understand her work as helping us to find a way between the Scylla of the desexualisation of Object Relations and the Charybdis of the phallicization of Lacan and his followers or what Oliver (1998) has described as the abjection of the maternal body and the abstraction of the father's body, respectively.

Irigaray claims that we have not yet been able to elaborate a psychoanalytic trajectory which allows for sexual difference. She wants to imagine a different future and an aesthetic of a new mode of living, of eroticism and social relations. She wants to theorise a mother who is also woman and who is involved in socialisation. Although her criticisms of psychoanalysis are profound, she valorises the concept of the unconscious and how the 'feminine' survives and escapes misogyny and enables us to think about that which is other, strange, different and un-masterable. She also helps us to think about the necessity for open democratic training institutions which allow for new possibilities and new questions as to the possibility of women becoming subjects and of men having access to a less defensive, embodied subjectivity.

Clinical Issues: Men and Women

Even though we learn from Freud (1905b) of the extent of psychic work involved in the achievement of sexual difference, and even though psychoanalysis is part of expansive debates within gender and cultural studies departments of universities, questions of sexual difference are presumed as already given in some psychoanalytic training organisations (O'Connor and Ryan, 1993). Some have strict requirements and go into some detail in inspecting and prescribing the sex of training patients, the sex of the training therapist and the sex of training supervisors. Irigaray helps us to think about how resorting to such essentialist ideas of what it is to be a man or woman closes down pivotal psychic work. In these organisations the therapist takes up the position of 'the one who knows' and refuses to acknowledge that the lived situation of man and woman is a process of becoming and cannot be known in advance. This procedure, which ensures more employment and influence for male supervisors, could be understood as reinforcing misogyny and an example of male bonding which can reproduce symbolic matricide and male privilege at an institutional as well as a theoretical level. Irigaray calls for a practice which allows for an understanding of masculinity and femininity which facilitates an ongoing openness to change and which allows for new possibilities rather than a returning to the same.

Also, Irigaray helps us to think how despite the privileges afforded men there is something brutalising in the construction of masculinity. Even though the psychoanalytic theory of the Oedipus complex describes the son's access to masculinity as conditioned on access to power over women which is connected to the heroic and other phallic ideals, men also suffer under patriarchy. She helps us think about the troubling statistics of the very high rates of men in prison, and how men are both the major perpetrators of violence as well as being the main victims. Men also tend to be the main perpetrators of sex crimes. Patriarchy encourages a particular type of masculinist thinking based on a defensive detachment from mother's body generating a simultaneous detachment from their own bodies.

> In the system of production that we know, including sexual production, men have distanced themselves from their bodies. They have used their sex, their language, their technique, in order to get further and further in the construction of a world which is more and more distant from their relation to the corporeal. But they are corporeal. It is necessary therefore for them to reassure themselves that someone [a woman] is indeed the guardian of their body for them. (Irigaray, 1981: 64)

Irigaray writes about how psychoanalysis does not question the place of men or the construction of masculinity, but instead it collusively covers over the cost of the normative fiction of masculinity. It settles for the fiction of men and boys as that which is opposed to the maternal as masculinity is considered of higher value and status. Masculinity then becomes a dominant value which aspires to define truth and reality. In so far as psychoanalysis is saturated with the male imaginary it becomes non-perspectival and fails to address the entanglement of male sexuality and violence.

Shere Hite (2006) set out to address the silence around men's sexuality and in a series of published works she claims to have interviewed over 7000 men. Taking the theory of the Oedipus complex as her starting point she wants to listen to men's experience of 'becoming man'. Many of the men interviewed spoke of their adolescence as being an especially traumatic period. She concludes that young adolescent boys find themselves in a double bind in the first painful initiation rites of becoming a man. The boy becomes subject to a kind of psychic violence which requires him to reject his first formative love for his mother and to break any identification with her. This traumatic break with his first love is neither acknowledged nor mourned. Instead denial is often reinforced by peer pressure manifested as taunting and bullying in relation to feminisation.

Some adolescent boys focus on localized pleasures relating to the penis and erections and resort to an instrumental relationship to their sexuality in order to resolve questions relating to masculinity. Identification with the prohibiting father takes on defensiveness against the relation with mother and with mother's body and can result in disidentifying with their own vulnerability and emotional continuity. This defensive masculinity and masculine pleasure becomes structured around detachment, voyeurism and objectification which turns women into a part-object whilst also insisting that a woman make him complete even though he simultaneously denies any dependency on her. Thomas (2008) understands the increase in online pornography as resulting from congruence between the normative dominant fiction of male sexuality and pornography. He concludes that this not only leaves men ignorant of women's sexuality but that they can become locked into a relationship to their own sexuality which is often driven by a compulsive search for impossible mastery and domination.

Natasha Walter's (2010) latest book, *Living Dolls: The Return of Sexism* has become a bestseller. It highlights the current phenomenon of the prevalence of raunchiness among young girls and the commodification of 'girl power'. She claims that in contrast to Victorian times when women's sexuality was hidden, pornography and prostitution are now taking central stage. She describes how adolescent girls frequently watch and aspire to star in semi-pornographic pop videos and how university students supplement their income through involvement with the escort business. At times, Walter seems to blame this on feminism, when in the 1970s it facilitated, for the first time, an articulation of the possibility of women's sexual pleasure. The first wave of feminism with its focus on suffrage was criticised for its normative and puritanical approach to women's sexuality. The possibility of women's sexual pleasure became an important site of resisting the psychic consequences of women's domination for the second wave. However, feminism since the publication of Simone de Beauvoir's (1945) book entitled, *The Second Sex*, has continued to question women's complicity with their own oppression. Whilst previously it was understood that women had access only to self-denial now a different kind of enjoyment became possible: a revelling in the enjoyment and power of objectification. However, Irigaray claims that objectification, despite claims of empowerment, can betray women's desire in order to become not the same as men but to become his other, to become the other of the same. Woman becomes the mirror which reassures man of his existence, her enjoyment is restricted to becoming the object of his enjoyment whilst her subjectivity is being erased. She becomes the opposite sex.

Irigaray claims that under patriarchy women cannot find a way to 'tell her story of the economy of her libido' and how this state of dereliction can lead to destructiveness, which can either have a masochistic element in relation to phallic power and/or an aggressivity towards other women. The 'erasure of the feminine' generates difficulties pertaining to the mother-daughter relationship generating collapsed separations, and primitive anxieties of being engulfed and taken over. This can lead women to break any filiations to the mother or other women and to seek psychic protection in a flight to the patriarchal and objectification, or to a desexualised maternity:

> The world [of women] seems very like that of certain primitive societies that have no official sacrifice, no recognised rites, and no indigenous jurisprudence. Revenge is taken outside of law or rights and in the form of private attacks, whether concerted or not. [...] Real murders occur as well as (if the two can be separated) cultural murders, murders of the spirit, the affections, the intelligence, that women perpetuate among themselves. Woman needs to develop words, images and symbols to express her inter-subjective relationship with her mother, and then with other women, if she is to enter into a non-destructive relation with men. (Irigaray, 1993: 196)

Phallocratic thinking, including both passive and active objectification of women and men, leaves a remainder which is often described as the 'monster mother' who is without form or lack and who affects both men and women albeit differently. Men, through identification with their fathers, can continue to externalise the threatening omnipotent mother onto other women. Women, on the other hand, lack a mediation which interferes with both the mother-daughter relationship and with women's relationship with their own bodies. The girls, like the boys, lose their relationship with their mother but critically they also lose their auto-eroticism. In the boy it is replaced by higher order identification with father. This is understood within a dominant fiction where the boys receive narcissistic compensation due to their more powerful status in relation to women and due to the unacknowledged emotional mirroring supplied by women. Under patriarchy this compensation is denied to women leaving them enthralled of being an attractive object and/or overburdening their relationship with their child.

Irigaray wants to theorise an intervention at the level of the Symbolic. She deconstructs how Lacan's (1966) theory of the Symbolic attempts to erase the debt to the generative mother and afford women a place only if they act as an envelope and container for male demands both in terms of emotional and physical care and in terms of desire. If the Symbolic hinders women's ability to deconstruct their oppression then they are unable to own their own aggression, and this can generate a type of compulsive caring and reparation, examples of which we can find in the dynamics of on-going domestic violence. If the only place given to women is that of the maternal then they will be trapped in a rivalrous relationship with all other women. If women do not have relationships with men and other women which are more reciprocal and more mutual then they are walled up in the place of the container which is both objectifying and reifying.

The Clinical Implications: Transference and Working Through

Although Freud (Breuer and Freud, 1895) took the radical step of listening to women he went on to position the psychoanalytic cure in the tradition of the Enlightenment: as a journey of male transcendence. Femininity came to stand in for all, including nature, death and the irrational that needed to be transcended. 'Working through' and other the processes of psychic change required the freeing of desire from the traces of 'the family romance' and a move to a higher order of thinking and relating through a journey of separation and individuation. In order to achieve this, Freud and Lacan gave central place to the identification with the prohibiting father and the paternal metaphor, whilst Klein and Winnicott focussed on the development of the capacity for reparation and concern.

As Freud (1905a) explored the role of authority within the Enlightenment tradition he discovered the importance of transference and how it is the necessary condition for working through to take place as it allows for something new. Although many training institutions are prescriptive in relation to the sex of patients, analysts and supervisors, they simultaneously prescribe working mainly with the maternal transference. Phillips (1993) regrets the loss of the neutral space for the emergence of the transference within the Object Relations tradition. He claims that 'It is integral to the psychoanalytic process that the analyst cannot know beforehand which sex he is going to be' (108).

Some feminists, such as Gilligan (1982), have sought to recuperate the maternal as a paradigm for a new ethic which could be understood as aligned to the trajectory of analysis in the Object Relations tradition. She highlights women's greater capacity for reparation and concern. Women do not have to disidentify with their mothers and consequently they have a greater capacity for an ethic which is more relational and concerned with the particular, whilst men are more able to engage in promoting the abstract universal concept of justice. Lee Bartky (1990) describes the phenomena of the attraction and pleasure of caring for women:

An apparent reversal has taken place: The man, her superior in the hierarchy of gender, now appears before the woman as the weaker before the stronger, the patient before the nurse. A source within the woman has been tapped and she feels flowing outward from herself a great power of healing and making whole. She imagines herself to be a great reservoir of restorative power'. (115)

She goes on to claim that, in contrast, awareness and analysis of oppression seems abstract and irrelevant. She concludes that love and care can be one of the pivotal points where women perpetuate their own oppression through an excess of fusion, possessiveness and masochism. Frosh (1994), writing as a male therapist, is mindful of working within a patriarchal culture and how in the work with male clients there can be an expectation of collusion, of male bonding, as men seek recognition from other men and disown any mutuality in their relationships with women, especially when they are dependent on women to take care of their emotional needs.

Freud's (1905a) theories of sexuality, which both open and at times close off unconscious dynamics, highlight how there is an inherently traumatic aspect to sexuality rather than there being normative lines of development. As well as theorising loss, lack and the fractal nature of sexuality Irigaray also wants psychoanalysis to take on board the joyful as well as the traumatic moments in the encounter with the other. Taking wonder as the first of the passions, where one is able to be taken by surprise and moved at the wonder of the other, she focuses on the possibility of the ecstatic capacity between the sexes. She (Irigaray, 2008: iv–xx) wants to appropriate transcendence and divinity for relations between the sexes, a transcendence, then, which not only stays beyond and outside ourselves and to which we ought to submit our desire, but rather what the desire for the different other can awaken in ourselves.

Irigaray helps us to think of the possibility of 'working through' conflicts arising from the ecstatic excess of desire and the dispossession of the encounter with the incalculable other which can be both a mixture of trauma and wonder. In contrast to the Enlightenment project she draws hope from the failure of patriarchal reason to completely dominate the body and she wants to put forward feminine jouissance as a strategy to reimagine and to resignify sexual difference.

Conclusion

I have turned to the work of Irigaray out of concern with the sexism and heterosexism which persists within much of psychoanalysis and the clinical impasses which this generates. Irigaray helps us to interrogate how psychoanalytic practice's uncritical embrace of an understanding of the trajectory of individuation as conditional on occlusion of the mother can create a fantasy of matricide, leading to a haunting of the monstrous mother as the castrating and/or engulfing mother. I have sought to outline how this can lead to clinical problems such as: mother blaming and the loss of unconscious fantasy, reductive thinking in relation to cause and effect, the reification of the maternal transference[2] and the shoring up of a patriarchal Symbolic. This can limit the clinical effectiveness of psychoanalysis to address the double binds which men and women encounter in living in a patriarchal culture.

Irigaray helps us to think new questions and to break with binary thinking and hetero-normativity which closes off the path to difference and otherness. Her early work focuses on a deconstructive and subversive strategy to highlight the misogyny underlying much of psychoanalytic theory. She goes on to take feminine jouissance as the site of posing utopian futural possibilities and ideals where women are more able to talk and love each other. Her later work looks to the differences between men and women in both their traumatic and ecstatic moments which can allow for the 'not yet' and provide a mediation for the possibility of community. Even though much of her work is addressed at the level of culture, I have used some of her work to prompt us to think about the possibility of a progressive psychoanalytic practice and how this requires new ways of thinking and theorising and new ways of organisation. Her work alerts us to the necessity of breaking free from schools of thought so that the therapist is able to allow for critique and what we have not yet imagined or understood. She helps us to listen to that which is 'not yet' and beyond representation so that we may be able to hear the un-articulated and the prophetic in the suffering of our clients. Such a utopian disposition would help us to hear other differences, including differences among women, and those pertaining to class, race and sexual orientation.

Notes

1. The academic reception of Irigaray's work by feminists has generated lively and at times agonistic debates. I will draw on a reading of Irigaray as a post-*structuralist* writer as in Whitford (1991), Chanter (1995), Huntingdon (1998), and Oliver (2004).
2. See also Caldwell (2005), Harding (2001) and Mann (1999) on this issue.

References

Baraister, L. (2009) 'Maternal Encounter' in *The Ethics of Interruption*. (Routledge: London and New York).
Breuer, J. and Freud, S. (1895) *Studies on Hysteria*. SE.II. (London: Hogarth).
Caldwell, L. (ed.) (2005) *Sex & Sexuality, Winnicottian Perspectives*. (London: Karnac).
Chanter, T. (1990) *Ethics of Eros; Irigaray's Rewriting of the Philosophers*. (New York: Routledge).

De Beauvoir, S. (1949) *The Second Sex*. Cape, J (trans.) (Paris: Gallimard Press). 1953.

Freud, S. (1905a) 'Fragment of Analysis of a Case of Hysteria' in *SE.VII*. (London: Hogarth Press).

Freud, S. (1905b) 'Three Essays on the Theory of Sexuality' in *SE.VII*. (London: Hogarth Press).

Freud, S. (1909) 'Analysis of a Phobia in a Five-Year-Old Boy' in *SE.X*. (London: Hogarth Press).

Frosh, S. (1994) *Sexual Difference, Masculinity and Psychoanalysis*. (London and New York: Routeledge).

Frosh, S. (2010) *Psychoanlaysis Outside the Clinic: Intervention in Psychosocial Studies*. (London: Palgrave Macmillan).

Gilligan, C. (1982) *In a Different Voice: Psychological Theory and Women's Development*. (Harvard: University Press).

Grosskurth, P. (1986) *Melanie Klein: Her Work and Her World*. (New York: Knopf).

Harding, C. (ed.) (2001) *Sexuality: Psychoanalytic Perspectives*. (London: Routeledge).

Hite, S. (2006) *Oedipus Revisited: Sexual Behaviour in the Human Male Today*. (London: Arcadia Books).

Horney, K. (1926) 'The Flight from womanhood: the masculinity complex in women, as viewed by men and women', *International Journal of Psychoanalysis*, 7, 324–39.

Irigaray, L. (1981) 'And the one doesn't stir without the other', *Signs*, 7, (1), 60–7.

Irigaray, L. (1985) *Speculum of the Other Woman*. (New York: Cornell University Press).

Irigaray, L. (1993) *The Ethics of Sexual Difference*. Burke, C. (trans.) (London: Athlone Press).

Irigaray, L. (2008) *Sharing the World*. (London & New York: Continuum Press).

King, P. and Steiner, R. (1992) *The Freud-Klein Controversies 1941–1945*. (London: Routledge).

Klein, M. (1928) 'Early stages of the Oedipus complex', *International Journal of Psychoanalysis*, 5, 313–31.

Lacan, J. (1966) *Ecrits*. (Paris: Editions du Seuil).

Lee Bartky, S. (1990) *Feminity and Domination, Studies in the Phenomenology of Oppression*. (London and New York: Routledge).

Mann, D. (ed.) (1999) *Erotic Transference & Countertransference*. (London: Routeledge).

O'Connor, N. and Ryan, J. (1993) *Mistaken Identities: Lesbianism and Psychoanalysis*. (London: Virago).

Oliver, K. (1998) *Subjectivity without Subjects: From Abject Fathers to Desiring Mothers*. (Lanham, MD: Rowman & Littlefield).

Oliver, K. (2004) *The Colonization of Psychic Space: A Psychoanalytic Social Theory of Oppression*. (Minneapolis: University of Minnesota Press).

Parker, I. and Revelli, S. (2008) *Psychoanalytic Practice and State Regulation*. (London: Karnac Books).

Phillips, A. (1993) *On Kissing Tickling and Being Bored*. (London: Faber & Faber).

Rose, J. (2002) 'Of Knowledge & Mothers: On the Work of Christopher Bollas' in *The Vitality of Objects: Exploring the Work of Christopher Bollas*. Scalia, J. (ed.) (London: Continuum).

Thomas, C. (2008) *Masculinity, Psychoanalysis, Straight Queer Theory*. (Basingstoke: Palgrave Macmillan).

Waddell, M. (1999) *Inside Lives: Psychoanalysis and Growth of the Personality*. (London: Routledge).

Walter, N. (2010) *Living dolls: The Return of Sexism.* (London: Virago Press).

Weeks, J. (2007) *The World We Have Won; The Remaking of Erotic and Intimate Life.* (London: Routledge).

Whitford, M. (1991) *Luce Irigaray: Philosophy in the Feminine.* (New York: Routledge).

Winnicott, D. W. (1971) 'Mirror Role of Mother and Family in Child Development', in *Playing and Reality.* (London: Tavistock Press). Methuen 1982.

Zaretsky, E. (2005) *Secrets of the Soul: A Social and Cultural History of Psychoanalysis.* (London and New York: Vintage Press).

13

The Artist's Fear of the Psychotherapist

Mary Thomas

Do not look too hard for meaning here. I am not an historian. I am an artist.
(Grayson Perry, 2011)

The artist Grayson Perry's plea that we should not 'look too hard for meaning' is one of the first written statements that greeted the visitor on entering his (November 2011) exhibition at the British Museum, The Tomb of the Unknown Craftsman. Yet, paradoxically, the exhibition is all about a search for meaning, from Perry's selection of objects from the vast collections of the British Museum that have some meaning for him, to the creation of new meanings when he placed selected objects from the museum next to his own creations. Perry says that he is more interested in creating imaginary worlds and telling stories and that the British Museum has provided much inspiration and insight into other cultural and historical worlds, as it has for many people. But is not telling, or hearing, or viewing stories in part a search for meaning? Arguably one of the features of good art, writing or storytelling, is that there can be multiple meanings, and that the experience that the viewer or reader brings to bear is important. I wondered if what Grayson Perry was voicing in his plea not to 'look too hard for meaning here' was a fear of the stripping of the mystery or complexity of the artwork, or the art-making process.

When Will Self (2009) states that 'the writer of fiction requires a certain willed ignorance of the symbolic cogs of the imagination and traumatic winding gear of the unconscious', and that the novelist 'fears the psychoanalyst as both an enemy and a usurper', he seems to be echoing Grayson Perry's, and many other artists' and writers' fears that analysing what might unconsciously drive the artist or writer or musician to create will inevitably lead to a lessening or withering of the creative drive, or a stripping bare of a mysterious, possibly neurotic, process that is better left alone, like sleeping dogs, or unexamined, even by those creative individuals whose search for meaning and truth usually leaves no stone unturned. Is creativity the stone that cannot be turned, or the sleeping dog that must be allowed to lie? Is there an oedipal origin to these anxieties, or a warning that we should not pry too much into the parents' sexuality as if they should be allowed to just get on with it in the privacy of the bedroom, without interruption, because if they are interrupted in their intercourse, the new baby/art work/novel would never be conceived?

Leave Some Stones Unturned

The fear of the stripping out of the complexity or mystery of the creative process seems to lie at the heart of many artists' fear of engaging in psychotherapy. I would argue that this fear is based on a misunderstanding of what psychotherapy is about, and is based on an assumption that it is a process of stripping away complexity of meaning rather than a process that might potentially enhance or enable a more creative engagement with one's life.

Paradoxically, many people come into psychotherapy with the demand that the therapist should simplify their life – they want answers, now, and if answers are not supplied quickly enough they may leave. However, on the whole, many people who enter therapy with the conscious aim of finding a simple answer come to engage more with their unconscious need to find a relationship where they can be engaged with, in all their complexity. Many people who seek out psychotherapy have not had sufficient experience of being engaged with as a complex individual as infants because of narcissistic or absent parenting, and a longing to be recognised as a complex individual can persist for a life time, sometimes feeding in to a stereotype of the artistic personality, where the artist may be tolerated as a 'difficult' or 'misunderstood' person as a friend/lover/sibling on the strength of the power of their art. This is part of the romance of the artist – the outsider, the maverick, the one who lives on the edge, the risk taker and the one who lives to excess. One thinks of Jimi Hendrix, Janis Joplin and a whole generation of rock musicians whose use of alcohol and drugs was seen as contributing to the power of their art in terms of the range of emotional highs and lows they articulated in their music.

The artist is the one who goes to the brink and then comes back to tell the rest of us what it is like, if they live to tell the tale. And if they do not live, if they die a premature death, optimally if there is a degree of uncertainty as to whether it was by accident or suicide, then the romance is enhanced. A book about the life of Vincent Van Gogh (Naifeh and White Smith, 2011) claims that Van Gogh was killed in a freak shooting accident, where two schoolboys had accidentally shot him when playing around with their new air rifles. This calls into question the myth and romance of his suicide. Not that Van Gogh was not a tortured soul, as his writing attests, but all those art historical interpretations about his last painting, the symbolism of the crows over the wheat field, may be more part of the tortured artist myth-making machine than a correct assessment of Van Gogh's state of mind when he painted his last painting.

The idea that artists are repositories of the projections of the rest of society is not a new one. We need to hear those reports of how tough it is living on the edge – we may be stimulated by it, challenged by it, but we do not have to risk putting our necks on the line. Is this why we have a love/hate relationship with the current incumbents of the maverick artist role, Grayson Perry and Tracey Emin? Both artists, Perry, who describes himself as a transvestite potter, and Emin, whose work is preoccupied with her sexuality, her body, sexual relationships, loneliness, vulnerability, one could say the difficulty of living a life, seem to court publicity and notoriety. Emin especially attracts a lot of negative attention from the British press. The journalist Melanie McGrath describes how she had to work through all her assumptions and projections about Tracey Emin the celebrity in order to be able to ponder the question, 'I don't know whether Tracey Emin is a great artist', McGrath had to get past all the knee-jerk responses and condemnation from the art establishment to examine her own responses to Emin's work, and found that it was 'comfortingly dangerous':

> At its best, Emin's art presents the world in ways you have always known about but never admitted, or you have never wanted to admit, or never perhaps to that moment articulated. If it's any good, art does this. It acts as the key to an unopened cupboard in some remote corner of your heart, a cupboard you once filled then locked so far distant the memory of it is like a mist. Once the cupboard is open you can't close it again. (McGrath, 1997)

The Suffering Artist

There is a widely held belief that the suffering, illness, melancholia or angst of the artist is what drives their creativity and that without it the creative urge would wane or burn less fiercely. I remember visiting an artists' studio event which was held in a number of private houses in an affluent suburb of London, where the impressive interior decor seemed as much part of the display as the artwork, and agreeing with my artist friend that the work was not edgy enough, that there had not been enough suffering or hardship in its conception or creation, and that a certain complacency showed in the work. Of course there were a number of assumptions here. What if I had seen the same artworks in a more grungy setting, say a new East London gallery operating on a shoestring? But the influence of the setting apart, what this exchange with my friend reminded me of was how ingrained this connection between suffering, hardship, illness and creativity is.

Strong links have been identified between creativity and mood disorders, particularly manic depressive disorder. In her study of manic depressive illness and the artistic temperament, Kay Redfield Jamison (1994) summarised many studies of mood disorder rates in writers, poets and artists. One study of 300,000 people with schizophrenia, bipolar disorder or unipolar disorder and their relatives found a significant over representation of bipolar disorder in creative professionals. Jamison conducted a survey of 47 eminent British artists and writers in 1989 (Jamison, 1989) and was especially interested in the role of moods in the creative process:

> When asked about the importance of very intense moods in the development and execution of their work, 9 out of 10 stated that such moods were integral and necessary, or very important. (Jamison, 1994: 79)

Many artists and writers have articulated how crucial they believe the connection is between their mental anguish and their art, and how suffering and pain are part and parcel of creative production:

> But seriously I wonder whether for a person like myself whose most intense moments were those of depression a cure that destroys the depression may not destroy the intensity – a desperate remedy. (Edward Thomas, in Storr, 1997: 123)

The poet John Berryman, who was manic depressive and eventually committed suicide, as his father and aunt had done before him, described the role of ordeal in his work:

> The artist is extremely lucky who is presented with the worst possible ordeal which will not actually kill him. ..... Beethoven's deafness, Goya's deafness, Milton's blindness. ..... I hope to be nearly crucified. (Jamison, 1994: 115)

Edgar Allen Poe wondered whether,

> ...all that is profound-does not spring from disease of thought–from *moods* of mind exalted at the expense of the general intellect. (Jamison, 1994: 116)

Van Gogh wrote:

> The more I am spent, ill, a broken pitcher, by so much more am I an artist – a creative artist. .....this green shoot springing from the roots of the old felled trunk, these are such abstract things that a kind of melancholy remains within us when we think that one could have created life at less cost than creating art. (Jamison, 1994: 117)

Then the question that arises is what would fuel the creativity of the artist who was cured of his/her anguish? Nathaniel Hawthorn comments:

The world owes all its onward impulses to men ill at ease. The happy man inevitably confines himself within ancient limits. (Jamison, 1994: 124–125)

Paradoxically, and in contrast to the view that suffering is a prerequisite for creative production, many artists and writers have articulated the relief from mental anguish and pain that their work can bring them:

Writing is a form of therapy. Sometimes I wonder how all those who do not write, compose or paint can manage to escape the madness, the melancholia, the panic fear which is inherent in the human situation. (Greene, 1980: 285)

Truth to feeling is the important thing and that is why I don't see how analysis could make anyone a worse poet. Poetry is about telling the truth. The poet and the psychoanalyst are both seekers after the truth. (Cope, 2011)

The Compulsive Element in Creativity

Another aspect of the artist's fear of psychotherapy is perhaps centred on the extent to which the compulsive element is seen as essential to the creative process. If one questions too hard what is driving your creative process is there a danger that you may end up with a creative block, staring at the blank page or canvas, too afraid to make a mark on it? After all, is not 'going with the flow', not thinking too hard, essential to the creative process? Inspiration is all important for artists but can sometimes be elusive or fickle. If we question our Muse will it disappear? Better to just harness that restless energy and carry on creating.

David Hockney, often referred to as Britain's greatest living artist, is still driven by a restless energy and spirit of exploration that has led him to use new technology, including an ipad, alongside more traditional brushes, to paint very different subject matter from that of his early artistic career. He recently had a major exhibition at the Royal Academy in London, at the age of 74, and shows no sign of slowing down, or running out of ideas. The level of drive, energy and purpose that Hockney shows can evoke admiration and envy in others, but is not this a sign of a healthy engagement with life and an openness to discovery, rather than a sign of a compulsive need to make things?

Where is the dividing line between creative drive and energy and a more obsessive compulsive disorder? Artists may be characterised as more chaotic, disorganised or spontaneous than most but, conversely need a high degree of drive, single mindedness and determination to produce their work. The desire or need of the artist to make art can often seem to have a compulsive edge, especially to non-artists, but does it need to be analysed or pathologised?

The South African artist, William Kentridge, described drawing for him as 'a medium in which one can think'. Kentridge articulates something of the restless energy and compulsive element in making art:

> The ideas are not the driving force in drawing, nor is meaning. The need to make an image is the driving force. It isn't like a writer who has a story they have to tell, and so they write a novel. It isn't as if I have an image the world has to see. Rather I have a need to be making marks on paper. Drawing isn't a decision; it is a need. (Berning, 2009)

Creative Blocks

In contrast to the fear that some artists have, that entering psychotherapy or psychoanalysis may subject their creative drive to too great a scrutiny and result in a weakening of their creativity, many artists come to psychotherapy because they want help with creative blocks – a shrinking, withering or drying up of the creative juices has already occurred.

Storr (1991) explored the role of creativity in various personality types, including the schizoid and the manic depressive. Whereas the schizoid person may withdraw from people because they fear the destructive influence of unpredictable relationships and fear being swallowed up by others, the person with a manic-depressive temperament fears withdrawal of the love or approval of others. Their self-esteem is dependent on a good relation with the other and if an artist finds that approval can be won through their artistic productions then the work, rather than the person, becomes the focus of self-esteem. This can lead to the artwork becoming so overloaded with the need for approval that it can become too much of a life or death situation for the artist, and the work cannot be completed:

> If the whole of one's self esteem comes to be bound up in the production of a particular work, it is too dangerous to risk its exposure, and it may, therefore, be put off by means of one excuse after the other. More commonly, it becomes impossible to proceed at all, although the reason for the block is generally unconscious. (Storr, 1991: 108)

Storr also observes that hostility and resentment towards parents who have, either in reality or fantasy, deprived the depressive of love, may be a feature of the repressed aggression that can drive some artists, where the artwork may function as a safer outlet than a direct confrontation with another person.

Many psychoanalytic writers have written of the inherent destructiveness and aggression in creativity and the need for something old to be destroyed before something new can be created. Melanie Klein's belief that part of the compulsion to create is to make reparation for what has been destroyed places aggression and destructiveness at the heart of creativity. The artist's creative block can result from a difficulty in coming to terms with his or her destructiveness or aggression, or from a fear that the discovery of the aggression could lead to a withdrawal of love and approval. This is partly why the artist lives on such a precarious tightrope. It's as if there is an optimum level of aggression, enough to supply the drive and energy to create something new, but not so much that it results in a creative block where nothing new can be produced.

Psychotherapists on Artists

Where does the artist's suspicion of the psychotherapist originate from? Storr (1991) describes the ambivalence of Sigmund Freud, the founder of psychoanalysis, whose statements on artists range from denigration to adulation:

> An artist is once more in rudiments an introvert, not far removed from neurosis. He is oppressed by excessively powerful instinctual needs. He desires to win honour, power, wealth, fame, and the love of women; but he lacks the means for achieving these satisfactions. Consequently, like any other unsatisfied man, he turns away from reality and transfers all his interest, and his libido too, to the wishful constructions of his life of phantasy, whence the path might lead to neurosis. (Freud, 1917: 376)

Works of art were derived from primitive sexual and aggressive instinctive impulses for which they were substitutes, that is, art was a form of sublimation and wish-fulfilment. The artist has found a socially acceptable way of 'showing off', exhibiting their work as a substitute for their bodies, especially the genitals. It's interesting to think of Grayson Perry here, who could be seen as 'showing off' both in his work, and in his transvestite alter ego, Claire, who accepted the Turner Prize for him at the award ceremony. Also, is that our objection to Tracey Emin and her courting of celebrity status, that she 'shows off' too much and does not convey any shame about this? Or that she exhibits how she lives the high life and does not seem to feel guilty about showing that she enjoys her success and her wealth, challenging the stereotype of the poor starving artist in the garret.

At other times, Freud showed that he valued highly the contribution of creative individuals:

> But creative writers are valuable allies and their evidence is to be praised highly, for they are apt to know a whole host of things between heaven and earth of which our philosophy has not yet let us dream. In their knowledge

of the mind they are far in advance of everyday people, for they draw upon sources which we have not yet opened up for science. (Freud, 1907: 8)

Freud was clearly interested in the artistic personality and wrote studies of Leonardo da Vinci, Michelangelo's Moses, as well as papers on Ibsen, Shakespeare and Dostoyevsky, but he thought that psychoanalysis could not explain creativity, and stated, 'Before the problem of the creative artist analysis must, alas, lay down its arms' (Freud, 1928: 177). The allusion to weaponry here is interesting; it seems that there is a note of defeat, as if Freud has been trying to solve the riddle of creativity through scientific understanding and yet it refuses to give up its secrets.

Subsequent generations of psychotherapeutic thinkers developed very different understandings of the nature of creativity. To summarise, and at the risk of over simplifying, Melanie Klein and her followers saw creativity as an attempt to restore lost and damaged internal objects, that is, the damage that the infant believes it has done to the parent in fantasy.

The artist Louise Bourgeois described her work as a form of restoration:

> The restoration of the tapestries functioned on a psychological level as well. By this I mean that things that have broken down or have been ripped apart can be joined and mended. My art is a form of restoration in terms of my feelings to myself and others.
>
> My works are portraits of a relationship, and the most important one was my mother. Now, how these feelings for her are brought into my interaction with other people, and how these feelings for her feed into my work is both complex and mysterious. I'm still trying to understand the mechanism. (Cooke, 2007)

Hanna Segal (1952) believed that depressive position anxieties, where the infant is struggling with recognising their loved objects (parents) as whole and other people as having an independent existence outside of their omnipotent control, were at the root of all later sublimation and creativity. The infant struggles with feelings of guilt and loss, and his/her capacity to mourn, and to repair and restore the lost loved objects outside and within the ego, and this forms the basis of the growth and development of a healthy ego and engagement with life. Segal agrees with Marcel Proust, that an artist is compelled to create by his need to recover his lost past. She asserts what she believes is present in the unconscious of all artists:

> ....That all creation is really a re-creation of a once loved and once whole, but now lost and ruined object, a ruined internal world and self. It is when the world within us is destroyed, when it is dead and loveless, when our loved ones are in fragments, and we ourselves in helpless despair – it is then that

we must re-create our world anew, re-assemble the pieces, infuse life into dead fragments, re-create life. (Segal, 1952: 199)

In the same paper, Segal states that it is the inability to acknowledge and over-come depressive anxiety that leads to creative blocks, and presents case studies to support her argument. The clients she described all suffered from sexual difficulties as well as creative blocks and this leads her to assert that there is a genital aspect of artistic creation:

Creating a work of art is a psychic equivalent of pro-creation. It is a genital bisexual activity necessitating a good identification with the father who gives, and the mother who receives and bears the child. The ability to deal with the depressive position, however, is the pre-condition of both genital and artistic maturity. (Segal, 1952: 200)

I think it's interesting to return to Grayson Perry in the light of Hanna Segal's comments on bisexual identifications and creativity. On the face of it, Perry might seem to personify bisexuality. There is the blokey, motorbike-riding, heterosexual Essex man. And there is his alter ego, Claire, a little girl with a sticking-out dress and a bow in her hair, who has evolved over time from an earlier version of Claire who looked more like an ordinary adult woman (Jones, 2006). Perry observed that people were more comfortable with him being dressed as a child than as a woman because it's less ambiguous: 'I'm a bloke in a ridiculous frock and that's nice and clear' (Barber, 2006).

Perry did have 6 years of psychotherapy which according to Parker (2006) has made him more relaxed about his transvestism, but does not mention if it helped him attain his artistic success. He thinks that the fear that a lot of creative people have that therapy would rob them of their creativity is misplaced: 'It's more like someone coming in and tidying up your toolshed – they're not taking the tools away, they're just tidying them up. I think people mistakenly get their chaos muddled up with their creativity. Provided you know what your issues are, they're not going to go away' (Barber, 2006). Perry is ambivalent about whether therapy helped his creativity: 'I think in many ways I am not doing a better job of it now [exploring his issues in his artwork]. I think I did a pretty good job of it then' [before therapy] (Barber, 2006).

His interviewer poses the question whether there was a danger that, now that Perry is so happy and well-adjusted, and so adored by the art establishment, that his work might become bland? 'No, because kinky sex is always my unpal-atable stain' (2006). Does this mean that he thinks he can preserve his artistic integrity because there is a fundamental aspect of him that remains beyond the pale, on the margins, inhabiting a psychic retreat that ensures he will never be swallowed whole by the art establishment, no matter how much artistic success he achieves? Perry thinks he might be able to change the mood of his work now that he has explored a lot of his 'issues' in his autobiography:

> One of my ambitions is to make happy art. I think the idea that you have to be suffering and angst-ridden to make art can go out of the window along with the one about therapy ruining your creativity. Often artists or critics, when they want to bolster the seriousness of the art, say, 'Oh, it's about mortality!' But I go, what about natality, what about positiveness? That's a serious subject – it's a serious business being alive. Happiness is not given it's due, but it's just as profound an issue as, We're all going to die. (Barber, 2006)

More Artist Friendly Psychotherapists?

A later generation of psychoanalytic writers, notably D.W. Winnicott and Marion Milner developed a different understanding of art and creativity and argued that art was not just about sublimation of forbidden drives and restoration of lost and damaged internal objects but was about the artist engaging in a dynamic encounter with the external world, inner world and outer interacting and bringing into existence something new, the artwork (Hagman, 2010: 20–21).

Winnicott devoted a lot of thinking to the importance of creativity in human development and developed a theory of the significance of transitional space and transitional objects, which was based on his observation and understanding of mothers and their babies interacting with each other. He proposed a notion of primary creativity which depends on the existence of a transitional space between mother and baby, where the baby can grapple with the me and not me-ness of the breast (mother), and where the paradox of 'The baby creates the object, but the object was there waiting to be created' (Winnicott, 1971: 104) can be tolerated:

> Winnicott's view of the intermediate, or transitional, space is of a realm of experience in between mother and baby (or between artist and artwork), where the paradox of inside/outside, me/not me, fantasy/external reality could be tolerated and played with. His assertion that the baby should not be challenged as to whether the baby created the object (mother) or found her, echoes the descriptions of artists who talk of not merely having imposed their ideas on the material but of having responded to and expressed something that they found already there in the material they were working with. Michelangelo conceived of his sculpture of David as being imprisoned in the block of marble, and he was going to set him free. (Thomas, 2005: 116–117)

Marion Milner, who was for a time a patient of Winnicott, devoted most of her life and professional career to the study of creativity and the interplay between internal and external reality, subjectivity and objectivity. She did this through exploring her own internal processes through doodling and image making. She was particularly interested in allowing herself to be open to seemingly irrational and unexpected feelings in order to break through the creative blocks that rational and logical thought imposed. Her book, *On Not Being Able to Paint* (Milner, 1950), is a detailed and illuminating study of her drawings, thought associations to her doodles, and her thinking about the creative process, creative blocks and living creatively. In the foreword to the second edition of *On Not Being Able to Paint*, Anna Freud compares Milner's attempts to rid herself of the obstacles which prevent her painting, her fight for artistic expression, with the battle for free association and the uncovering of the unconscious mind which is the core of psychotherapeutic work:

> The amateur painter, who first puts pencil or brush to paper, seems to be in much the same mood as the client during his initial period on the analytic couch. Both ventures, the analytic as well as the creative one, seem to demand similar external and internal conditions. There is the same need for 'circumstances in which it is safe to be absent-minded' (i.e. for conscious logic and reason to be absent from one's mind)......There is, above all, the same terror of the unknown. (Freud, A., in Milner, 1950: xiii)

Psychotherapists and Artists – Compatible Bedfellows?

Winnicott and Milner paved the way for subsequent psychotherapeutic writers and thinkers who have moved away from the more classic psychoanalytic conceptualising of artistic production as defensive and pathological to a view of creativity as a complex and fundamental aspect of psychological and emotional growth and development. Both psychotherapeutic and artistic endeavours are essentially truth-seeking and meaning-making activities, and perhaps there is now a greater sense of mutual interest and interplay between the two disciplines. After all, many psychotherapists look at, collect and display art in their consulting rooms (as Freud also did), and some of them also make art, and many artists are in psychotherapy.

However, creativity remains a complex and mysterious phenomenon, and creative or artistic production can be a conflict ridden and painful process, as I found again in the process of writing this chapter. I struggled to resist being distracted by all the external demands of my life and my other creative activities in order to prioritise this creative project. I was heartened to read that even Marion Milner who spent a lifetime studying creativity and creative blocks complained to a friend when she was struggling to write an extra chapter for a new edition of *On Not Being Able to Paint*, 'But it's nearly killing me writing it (when I really want to paint)'. (Milner, 1950/2010: xliii)

I think it's important to distinguish between the psychotherapeutic understanding of creativity in the sense of the provision of transitional space and the mother's recognition of the child's subjectivity as a prerequisite for the psychological development and good mental health of the individual, and creative and artistic production which relies on an energy or compulsion that drives it and that may always remain partly obscured. Winnicott (1963) wrote of a core of the self which would (and should) always remain unknowable, perhaps this is the wellspring of the imagination, the creative Muse, the stone that should remain unturned.

Conclusion

The artist's fear of the psychotherapist seems to be based on a persecutory fantasy that a psychotherapeutic exploration of the meaning of the difficulties in life which brought the client to find help, which are often connected to a sense of creative blockage, meaninglessness and a feeling of 'Is this all there is?', would leave the client feeling stripped bare, too closely scrutinised, left with no hiding place. The reality is that for many people, including many artists and writers, psychotherapy can offer a more benign relationship which can facilitate and nurture growth and creativity.

Adam Phillips, in his foreword to Marion Milner's book, *The Hands of the Living God* (Milner, 1969), which describes her psychoanalysis of a schizophrenic client in which the exploration of the drawings of the client played a central part, articulates something important about the growth enhancing potential of psychotherapeutic work:

> The aim of psychoanalysis is to sustain the uncertainty that makes growth possible. The only knowledge worth having is not the knowledge born of experience but the knowledge that gives birth to experience. ... it is inevitable Milner adds, that we love and hate the unknown. ....she is saying that the unconscious is an artist and that the conscious mind is a scientist, and that the analyst is a kind of third party, a referee, a mediator, a translator, the person who speaks up for collaboration when only antagonism is on the cards. (Philips in Milner, 1969/2011: xxiii)

Acknowledgement

During the course of writing this chapter, I conducted a mini-survey with a group of artists. I put to them the main questions posed in this chapter. Most disagreed that an artist would fear engaging in psychotherapy whilst acknowledging that they recognised the potential threat to creative output.

With many thanks to my colleagues and friends at Morley College Printmaking Department for their generosity – a true hub of creativity.

References

Barber, L. (2006) *Pot Luck*. Interview with Grayson Perry. (London: The Observer Newspaper). 08.01.2006.

Berning, D. (2009) *Drawing Supplement*. Interview with Wiliam Kentridge (London: Sunday Observer). 19.09.2009.

Cooke, R. (2007) *My Art is a Form of Restoration*. (London: The Observer Newspaper). 14.10.2007.

Cope, W. (2011) Notes on *'The Creative Mind – What can Artists Learn from Psychotherapy, and What can Psychotherapy Learn from Artists?'* An event at the National Portrait Gallery in conjunction with WPF Therapy. London, 14.10.2011.

Freud, S. (1907) 'Delusions and Dreams' in *SE.IX*. (London: Hogarth). 1959.

Freud, S. (1917) 'The Paths to the Formation of Symptoms' in *SE.XVI*. (London: Hogarth Press). 1963.

Freud, S. (1928) 'Dostoevsky and Parricide' in *SE.XXI*. (London: Hogarth Press). 1961.

Greene, G. (1980) *Ways of Escape*. (New York: Simon & Schuster).

Hagman, G. (2010) *The Artist's Mind*. (Hove/New York: Routledge).

Jamison, K. R. (1989) 'Mood disorders and patterns of creativity in British writers and artists', *Psychiatry: Interpersonal and Biological Processes*, 52, (2), 125–34.

Jamison, K. R. (1994) *Touched with Fire: Manic Depressive Illness and the Artistic Temperament*. (New York: Schuster & Schuster).

Jones, W. (2006) *Grayson Perry, Portrait of the Artist as a Young Girl*. (London: Vintage). 2007.

McGrath, M. (1997) 'Tracey Emin: I Need Art Like I Need God' in *Something's Wrong*. Article on Tracey Emin. (London: Tate Magazine). Issue 1. http://www.tate.org.uk/magazine/issue1/something.htm. 30.01.2012.

Milner, M. (1950) *On Not Being Able to Paint*. (London: Heinemann [Reprint Routledge]) 2010.

Milner, M. (1969) *The Hands of the Living God*. (London: The Hogarth Press [Reprint Routledge]). 2011.

Naifeh, S. and White Smith, G. (2011) *Van Gogh: The Life*. (New York: Random House).

Segal, H. (1952) 'A psycho-analytical approach to aesthetics', *The International Journal of Psycho-Analysis*, 33, 196–207.

Self, W. (2009) *Incidents Along the Road*. (London: Guardian Newspaper). 07.02.2009.

Storr, A. (1991) *The Dynamics of Creation*. (London: Penguin Books).

Storr, A. (1997) *Solitude*. (London: Harper Collins).

Thomas, M. (2005) 'Through the Looking Glass: Creativity in Supervision' in *Supervision and the Analytic Attitude*. Driver C. & Martin E. (eds.) (London: Whurr).

Winnicott, D. W. (1963) 'Communicating and Not Communicating Leading to a Study of Certain Opposites' in *The Maturational Process and the Facilitating Environment*. (London: Karnac). 1990.

Winnicott, D. W. (1971) *Playing and Reality*. (Harmondsworth, Middlesex, England: Penguin Books). 1980.

14

Religions in Relation to Values

David M. Black

Introduction

It's an interesting fact about Freud that he took particular pleasure in his friendships with imaginative men. Fliess, Jung and Ferenczi, none of them quite conforming to the orthodoxies of contemporary scientific thought, attracted a warmth from Freud that important but more conventional figures, such as Karl Abraham or Ernest Jones, did not. It's easy to think that Freud's adventurous temperament welcomed the freedom that these less-orthodox people allowed him. Perhaps too they allowed him to project some of his own unorthodox tendencies and maintain more firmly his resolutely 'scientific' stance.

One such imaginative figure was Romain Rolland, the French writer who in 1915 won the Nobel Prize for literature (Werman, 1977). To celebrate Rolland's 60th birthday, Freud published a letter to him beginning: 'Unforgettable one! By what troubles and sufferings must you have fought your way up to such a height of humanity as yours!' (1926: 279). Ten years later, Freud again wrote an honorific letter to this 'apostle of the love of mankind' (279). It became the attractive short paper entitled 'A Disturbance of Memory on the Acropolis', written, says Freud, 'to give expression to my admiration for your love of the truth, for your courage in your beliefs and for your affection and good will towards humanity' (Freud, 1936: 239).

At the beginning of *Civilization and its Discontents*, Freud also speaks of Rolland admiringly. He is 'one of the exceptional few' whose 'greatness rests on attributes and achievements which are completely foreign to the aims and ideals of the multitude' (Freud 1930: 64). They were rather foreign too, one might think, to the aims and ideals of Freud. Rolland was a follower of the Hindu Vedantic teacher Sri Ramakrishna (1836–86), who played an important part in the revival of Indian self-confidence during the nineteenth century. Later Western disciples included Aldous Huxley and Christopher Isherwood, and Ramakrishna's movement still survives, though somewhat eclipsed in recent years. Ecstatic, virtually illiterate and an inspiring teacher, Ramakrishna was vividly memorialised by his disciple, Mahendranath Gupta ('M'), who during the 1880s recorded Ramakrishna's life and many verbatim conversations. Ramakrishna's teaching is a dazzling mixture of traditional Indian tales, teasing asides, profound insights and sudden interruptions as he goes off into enraptured trance. He comes across as gentle, enchanting and dominant. 'To read through these conversations', wrote Aldous Huxley, 'in which mystical doctrine alternates with an unfamiliar kind of humour, and where discussion of the oddest aspects of Hindu mythology give place to the most profound and subtle utterances about the nature of Ultimate Reality, is in itself a liberal education in humility, tolerance and suspense of judgment' ('M', 1969: vi).

Vedantic Hinduism is a mystical teaching of the oneness of all things, extremely sophisticated in its philosophical statements but capable of quite simple popular exposition. In ecstasy, the devotee becomes one with the ultimate deity, whose attributes include consciousness. 'Some say this state of mind is a disease,' said Ramakrishna, referring to his *samadhi* (rapturous meditative state), 'I say to them, "How can one become unconscious by thinking of Him whose Consciousness has made the whole world conscious?"' (195).

It was Romain Rolland who used the phrase 'oceanic feeling' to describe the essential experience of religion, which he felt Freud had failed to understand in *The Future of an Illusion* (1927). He was speaking out of this Hindu philosophical and experiential background. And when Freud delighted in honouring Rolland for his courage and love of truth, it was the vision of the Hindu Vedanta on which Rolland was standing.

Nevertheless, despite Freud's extravagant admiration, he gave short shrift to his friend's 'oceanic feeling'. He cannot discover it in himself, said Freud, though he is willing to believe it exists. It may perhaps 'seek something like the restoration of limitless narcissism' (Freud, 1930: 72). Freud had no doubt that in reality the origin of the religious attitude goes back to infantile helplessness and the longing for a father. 'There may be something further behind that, but for the present it is wrapped in obscurity' (72).

We, listeners to this curious dialogue, are left with a sense that something has gone missing. Freud sincerely admired the values he saw in Rolland, and yet, when Rolland attempted to state the foundation of his values, Freud sent him packing. 'The restoration of limitless narcissism' is clearly not a goal to be respected, yet Freud was unmistakably admiring *something*. I shall argue in this paper that Freud, like many recent scientific thinkers, forcefully led the argument off along a false trail. Because he misperceived, essentially, what a religion is, Freud felt he had refuted 'religion' when in fact what he had shown was certain ways in which religions are often misused. This is a pity, because his admiration for Rolland's values was in touch with something genuinely important.

The Psychoanalytic Critique of Religion

Freud's argument may be summarised briefly. Adult human beings, and especially 'our wretched, ignorant and downtrodden ancestors' (Freud, 1927: 33), are helpless in many situations in life. This causes them, like children, to long for a protecting father who will calm their fears; this wish is fulfilled by the fantasy of an all-powerful God. Similarly, we have to make extremely consequential decisions, with no guarantee of our rightness in doing so. A set of absolute commandments allays our anxiety about right and wrong. Our fear and sorrow in relation to death, both our own and that of others, is consoled by the illusion of an afterlife – additionally gratifying if we can also believe that for our hated enemies the afterlife will be an experience of horrible suffering. With so many advantages, says Freud mordantly, no wonder religion has been so successful.

What sort of thing is Freud conceiving a religion to be, when he employs such arguments? Essentially, he conceives religion to be a science-like thing, making factual claims about the world. (We would not believe, he says, 'that whales bear young instead of laying eggs, if it were not capable of better proof than this' (27).) Religion, therefore, can be refuted by pointing out the absence of observational evidence supporting it. It can then be treated as a structure of wish-fulfilling phantasies, susceptible to psychoanalytic interpretation. In a revealing if ironic passage, Freud praised the 'creationists' in Dayton, Tennessee, who prosecuted a science teacher for contradicting Genesis. These religious people showed 'consistency', he said (38). In fact, what they showed was Freud's own attitude to religion: a belief that the statements of religion are strictly comparable to those of science.

In some ways, Freud's arguments are rather disappointing. He confines himself to very superficial observation of religious beliefs and behaviour, makes no enquiry into the depths of actual religious experience, and even as a psychoanalyst his thought lacks the vigour and cutting edge we would usually expect of him. Nietzsche's account of the rise of Christianity as the revenge of the slaves on the masters in the Roman Empire (dating from the 1880s) is both more original and in a sense more truly 'psychoanalytic' than Freud's rather conventional picture.

Nevertheless, Freud expressed clearly enough the grounds for the widespread retreat from religion by scientific thinkers that has occurred in the past 150 years, inseparably connected with Darwinism and the rise of physicalist and developmental modes of explanation. To realise how widely human beliefs and behaviour had varied over time, how often religions had been responsible for appalling consequences including wars, cruelty and many sorts of abuse and oppression and how continuous contemporary religion was with the superstitious past, resulted understandably in a widespread turning to science as the one rational form that knowledge could take. Psychoanalysis, courageously acknowledging that the conscious mind itself was built on an unconscious, non-rational infrastructure, still held tenaciously (at that time) to a rational and scientific viewpoint above the battle. There was a paradox here that would not be satisfactory for long.

However, the idealisation of Freud by the first generations of psychoanalysts caused the repudiation of religion to become part of psychoanalytic orthodoxy. Analysts such as Ernest Jones prided themselves on their rejection of it. Melanie Klein, close to death, emphasised that she wanted her funeral to be 'totally non-religious in character' (Grosskurth, 1985: 461). To be religious in any way was tantamount to being neurotic in public. I have sketched elsewhere the changing attitudes of psychoanalysts to religion (Black, 2006).

The Practice of Religions

It is important to remember that the world's major religions are extremely diverse. They emerge essentially in two streams, the 'Abrahamic', deriving from Semitic sources and including Judaism, Christianity and Islam, and the Indian, including Hinduism and Buddhism. All these religions have absorbed different local ways of thinking: classical Greek thought influenced Christianity and Islam profoundly, though in very different ways, and Buddhism has shown a remarkable capacity to adopt elements from shamanism in Tibet, Daoism in China and Shinto in Japan. Moreover, all these religions contain radically different schools, and mainstream schools in all religions nowadays learn from each other and also from secular science, including psychoanalysis, without necessarily noticing they are doing so. The rise of fundamentalisms, which has been such a wretched feature of religious history in the early twenty-first century, is in part a frightened recoil from these developments, especially unfortunate because it blocks the freedom of responsible religious thinkers to reflect on the nature of religious language and objects. Such reflection is urgently needed if the significance of religion is to be recognised by increasingly rationally educated populations. Like everything else to do with psychological 'depth', responsible religion has become a seriously endangered species.

In order to keep this chapter within bounds, I shall focus my remarks here mainly on the nature of religious 'objects'. Freud described religion as an obses-sional neurosis (Freud, 1927: 43). In his first paper about religion, 'Obsessive actions and religious practices' (Freud, 1907), he spelled out this idea in detail. Like the rituals of obsessive clients, those of religion are based, he said, on the renunciation of certain instinctual impulses; they are followed in minute detail on pain of severe guilt, and the believer, like the obsessive, is ignorant of the true motives of his behaviour. The believer is entitled to resent Freud's implication that the psychoanalyst knows the believer's motives better than the believer himself.

Freud, however, is correctly noticing something about religious practices, namely, that they are often repeated, and with great care. Repetition may be a sign of compulsion, undoubtedly, but it may be deliberate and consciously motivated, for example, if something has to be learned (such as the alphabet) or if a recurring need has to be fulfilled (such as preparing breakfast). Thinking of religious repetitions with such models in mind, we may see them rather differently.

One thing we notice is that *what* is repeated is very often the foundational story of the faith. For example, the Roman Catholic mass repeats the story of the events preceding Jesus's death, together with a ritual in which the participants share symbolically in his body. On another scale, both Jewish and Christian faiths have a strongly defined, repeated annual pattern, for Jews mostly commemorating events from history, and for Christians mostly remembering events from the life of Christ. The effect of these repetitions is, so to speak, to turn different important aspects of the faith towards the light: to ensure that a balance is kept and that one element, say, rejoicing, does not eclipse another element, say, penitence, or grief over loss and suffering. Jeremy Schonfield (1999) has suggested that the sequence of Jewish festivals may represent the sort of psychological development that psychoanalysis recognises.

There are also the small-scale repetitions of the believer's private devotions: prayer, meditation and rituals such as lighting candles; hygienic regulations such as eating kosher food; or the wearing of certain garments such as the hijab. This is the area of religious observance which comes closest to looking like, and perhaps often actually being, obsessional in character, but the fact that a behaviour can be enlisted in the service of neurosis does not mean that is its original nature. Washing one's hands is not always evidence of compulsion.

If we think of deliberate repetition as a technique for learning, for emphasising importance and for fulfilling a recurrent need, we may see that religions, by these careful repetitions, set out to inculcate into the believer a culturally constructed and transmitted 'world'. Believers are reminded repeatedly of the main personalities and events of this world; they are assured of its immense importance and the danger of forgetting this world, or of its fading in importance, is energetically defended against.

This world has a large number of different aspects, and though it contains many memorably simple formulas – 'God is love', 'the Lord is One', 'there is no God but God' – no one formulation in fact encompasses it. In that sense, the notion of a 'world' is not inappropriate.

Modern psychoanalysis allows one to say all this with useful concision. A religion sets out to create and maintain a world of internal objects. These are not the familiar 'internal objects' of the object-relations theorists, which are phantasised figures in interaction with one another or the ego, derived from an internalisation of actual experiences with other people, influenced by projections and going back, ultimately, to the earliest events of babyhood or even to prenatal experience. On the contrary, religious objects are internal objects derived from culture. Though they will inevitably chime or clash in various ways with the internal objects derived from the person's own history, that is not their origin and they are in principle distinguishable from these 'personal objects'. Ana-Maria Rizzuto (1979) has examined some of the complex ways in which personal and religious objects become conflated.

The scrupulous care given to defining these religious objects, the countless repetitions by which they are established and the constant emphasis on their impressive qualities – majesty, power, humility, mercy, etc., – all point to the enormous effort made by religion to set up the religious world in the believer's psyche, and to overcome, as we might say, the believer's resistance. 'I believe, help thou my unbelief', says the Psalmist. The believer has to do a great deal of psychic work to maintain their belief. But they have to do it, because only in this way can the religious objects be kept in being. The battle with doubt in the religionist is precisely comparable to the battle with destructiveness in the depressive: it is to keep from collapse an internal world of good objects.

The Birth of Religious Objects

This account, however, does not go far enough. It would describe equally well the characters in a novel, who also make up a world of 'internal objects', and depend on the reader to keep them alive. If the reader gets distracted and puts the novel aside, they may forget the plot, or forget who's who, and then all the charm and magic of the thing will vanish.

So a greater claim has to be made for religious objects: though they depend on the believer's 'memory', they are not just 'fictions' like the characters in a novel; they have a deeper importance, enabling them to convey the nature of reality more deeply, or in a way more illuminating of value, than literal statement. I have proposed elsewhere (Black, 2011) that religious objects can best be understood as 'resources for consciousness', that is, as offering imaginative standpoints that allow the believer to view the world with other values and from other standpoints than those of his ordinary awareness. The religious claim to 'profundity', for example, may not just be a metaphor but may point to a hierarchy of values, in which 'depth' can be measured somewhat objectively by the increasing range of applicability of the value. A God who notes the fall of every sparrow, or a bodhisattva who works for the liberation of all beings, represents a moral and imaginative resource in the psyche which cannot truthfully be owned by ego – 'I' am certainly not capable of such sustained and non-narcissistic compassion – but which may nevertheless be conceived and related to. This relating is done initially by worshiping or meditating on the religious object, and then perhaps later, if only transiently, by some degree of identification with it. In this way, the believer can come over time to embody, to a greater or lesser extent, the values of his religion.

There are many consequences of conceiving religious objects in this way. But one question that presents itself is: what is the origin of these religious objects? How *can* they be different from the sort of imaginative constructions that a novelist or a dramatist creates? Lonely children often invent an 'imaginary friend' to be their playmate; might not 'God' simply be a sort of imagined companion, providing comparable benefits of reassurance and protection from panic, but without wider significance?

The philosopher Charles Taylor (1989) has argued that the ordinary way in which we live life and the ordinary decisions we make every day are dependent implicitly on our having answers to certain evaluative questions, for example: How do I want the world to be? What sort of person do I want to be? When we say to a child, 'Don't talk like that to Granddad!', we do not necessarily spell out, even to ourselves, the moral vision of the world that lies behind our instruction. Nevertheless, it is made with a 'moral horizon', and it conveys a moral attitude that we believe in and which we intend to guide the child as they grow up.

As Taylor says, we vary greatly in the extent to which we allow ourselves to be conscious of the values implicit in our moral horizons, and still more in the extent to which we feel the need to spell out a 'moral ontology' to support them. But regardless of whether we spell it out, a 'moral horizon' implies a 'moral ontology', cloudy and unconscious as it may be, and even although it conflicts with the sort of materialist scientific outlook we may believe we subscribe to.

Religious objects emerge from a pre-scientific stage of human mental development, when human minds were not dominated by the positivistic vision of a physical world that is almost universal now among educated people. It may be hard nowadays even to recognise what Taylor means by a 'moral horizon', and the notion of a 'moral ontology' will sound to many people like a fairy tale. Nevertheless, we are all influenced by our values, and we are all at times confronted by the question of whether we will endorse that influence – that is, act on our values – or set them aside with a cynical feeling that that is mere sentimentalising. The pre-scientific mind, often disparaged as superstitious, was more open to recognising the power of the moral horizon, and less rigid in rejecting the imaginative ontologies it suggested.

As I believe the moral horizon to be very important, and the brutal willingness to disregard it on grounds of 'realism' to be one of the most disturbing portents for our human future, I want to say that we disparage the pre-scientific mind at our peril. That is not to say we should reject science, which is clearly impossible, but it is to suggest that we should open ourselves to our intuitions of a moral horizon, and take seriously the possibility that they tell us of another sort of 'ontology' than the one so familiar from contemporary physics. If we allow ourselves to do this, we find ourselves in contact with the sort of intuitions that have given birth to religious objects.

The evolution of a religious object, for example, the Jewish or Christian notion of God, takes place transgenerationally and is immensely complicated. The editors of the Bible, for example, concealed earlier and conflicting formulations, because of their desire to present an authoritative statement. (Even so, it has been said that there are at least eight different theologies discoverable in the New Testament.) I shall take a slightly less familiar example, therefore, and look briefly at the evolution of a religious object in the history of Buddhism. In Buddhism, earlier texts have been allowed to survive, so it's easier to make out this evolution. I hope this will give a glimpse of how serious religious reflection can develop an object which may indeed in origin have been somewhat comparable to the child's 'imaginary friend', a response to loss, loneliness, joy, wonder, etc., but in the process of transgenerational development can become something profoundly different in order to accommodate a deepening philosophical understanding. It is the nature of all psychological ('internal') objects that they develop in time through ongoing interaction between experience and subjective processes such as reflection and phantasy.

The Buddhist *Trikaya* Doctrine

The Buddhist *trikaya* (three-body) teaching emerged gradually in the first five centuries following the Buddha's death (c483 BCE). It became a central tenet of Mahayana Buddhism, the Buddhism that spread to China, Tibet and Japan. It states that the Buddha is met with in three radically different 'bodies'.

Buddhism first appeared in an India dominated by Brahmanism, with its complex rituals and its meticulously ordered social system governed by caste. The Buddha ignored cult and caste, and he rejected claims to special status for himself. When the Buddha tells his disciple Ananda not to 'hinder himself' with honouring the Buddha's remains after his death (*Digha Nikaya*, ii: 141), any plan to make a cult of his body is explicitly rebuked. In a French translation, the Buddha sums up his role: 'Le Tathagata [Buddha], o brahmane, se borne à montrer le chemin' (Lamotte, 1958: 713). The Buddha is there only to point out the path.

However, after the death of a great teacher, even his most rational followers are drawn towards mythological ways of thinking. W.H. Auden (1966) wrote after Freud's death:

> To us he is no more a person
> Now but a whole climate of opinion.

(Auden, 1966: 168)

As Buddhism spread, that will have been at least as true of the Buddha.

The Sanskrit word used to describe the Buddha's teaching is *dharma*. This word has a wide span of meanings. It has the general sense of a 'true teaching', but also covers 'moral law', 'the order of the universe', and can stretch to mean 'ultimate reality' or 'ultimately real things' (Conze, 1962: 92ff). One of the formulas most used by practising Buddhists is the so-called Triple Refuge: 'I go for refuge to the Buddha,...to the Dharma,...to the Sangha [Buddhist community]'. Thus, within the natural wobble of meaning of an ordinary word, we can see how the Buddha's *teaching*, which is also the Buddha's *ultimate reality* could further become an 'object', in the psychoanalytic sense, to which the believer can go for *refuge*.

The Buddha was strongly opposed to metaphysical speculation; we are told in the *Kalamasutta* (Holder, 2006) that he welcomed doubt and invited his hearers to test his teaching for themselves by practising meditation and observing their own experience. There is a well-known schedule of metaphysical questions which the Buddha refused to answer. One of these was the question of whether he would continue to exist after death. Of this, he said it was neither true to say Yes nor to say No (nor both Yes and No, nor neither Yes nor No). A modern thinker might paraphrase this reply by saying that language is not suited to answering such questions. But the fact that he did not give a straightforward 'No' to the question preserved the possibility that somehow, even if obscurely, there was some sort of survival.

Brahmanism, the source of what later became Hinduism, offered a picture of time as cyclical. The notion of reincarnation, which Buddhism adopted, is part of that picture. This led to myths developing of other Buddhas in other cycles. The historical Buddha, Gautama Siddhartha, came to be seen as the latest in a series of world saviours, who had come to earth at intervals of 20,000 years; their lives are set out in one sutra in such a strict pattern that it became possible, in the words of the translators, 'without the omission of any detail, to arrange them in parallel columns' (T.W. and E. Rhys-Davids, 1966: 1). This caused a certain change in the perception of Gautama. Even if true that his parents' names were Suddhodana and Maya, his chief attendant Ananda, and his enlightenment gained under an assattha tree, this truth is subtly altered when set in parallel with Vipassin, whose parents were Bandhuma and Bandhumati, whose chief attendant was Asoka, and whose enlightenment was gained under a patali tree. Gautama ceases to be fully historical and becomes hoisted towards mythology.

The wish to honour, and the complex feeling of dependency upon, the originator of a system of thought that has become the foundation of one's way of life should come as no surprise to psychoanalysts. The relics of Freud are honoured in museums, and it is still quite difficult to write a psychoanalytic paper without slipping into the mandarin literary manners of James Strachey's elegantly 'Bloomsbury' translation – without, in other words, identifying with an imagined Freud. In a less scientific age, and in the intellectual monoculture of a monastic routine, the Buddha and his teaching came to seem like reliable and solid 'objects'. We meet a powerful example in a dialogue between the Greek king, Milinda, and the Buddhist sage, Nagasena, which dates from about the start of the Christian era. At one point, Milinda challenged Nagasena to explain how the Buddha could say: 'I lead an Order of monks numbering several hundreds', and at the same time have no thought that 'the Order of monks is dependent on me' (two quotations from the sutras). The underlying question is about the Buddha's no-self teaching: surely, the King is implying, the Buddha believed he had a 'self'. Nagasena replied:

> This, sire, is conventional parlance.... As, sire, the earth is the support of beings who are based on the ground and is their home, yet though these beings are based on it, the great earth has no longings such as: 'These are mine'. Even so, sire, the Tathagata [Buddha] is the support of all beings and is their home, yet though these beings are based on him, the Tathagata has no longings such as: 'These are mine.' Or as a massive great cloud that is raining heavily gives growth to grass, trees, cattle and men and maintains their continuity, and though these beings all subsist by rain, yet the great cloud has no longings such as: 'These are mine'. Even so, sire, the Tathagata generates and maintains skilled mental states for all beings, and though all these beings subsist by the Teacher, yet the Tathagata has no longings such as: 'These are mine'. What is the reason for this? It is due to his having got rid of wrong views of self. (*Milinda's Questions*, 224–5)

These images of the Buddha as like the earth, or like a rain cloud, which supports everything but has no need of support itself, are images of an ultimate 'refuge' or 'containing object' – immense, reliable, benevolent and making no demand in return for its services.

The final form of the *trikaya* doctrine gathered all these incipient tendencies into a single system. It described the Buddha as having three bodies: the *nirmanakaya*, the physical body of the historical Buddha; the *dharmakaya*, the vast unsayable world of ultimate reality; and the *sambhogakaya*, the world of symbolic forms and experiences, including Buddhist sayings, scriptures, statues, etc., by which the Buddha becomes known to his followers. The *trikaya* is not, like the Christian Trinity, a relationship of 'persons', but an intellectual structure that organises a very wide range of experiences into a Buddhist framework.

What governed the evolution of this doctrine, however, was not only thinking (though thinking certainly went into it) but also the emotional and imaginative experience of many generations of monks and nuns. Bion (1967: 92) has spoken of the 'disaster' a baby suffers if it meets an object which denies 'the normal employment of projective identification' – that is, is unable to receive the emotional communication the baby is needing to make. The all-receiving, all-supporting central object of Mahayana Buddhism evolved to become a device which, in principle, allowed all the levels of experience to be received, and every sort of experience to find a place and be understood. In doing so, it altered the possibility of development of deeper and richer, more truly ethical personalities in the cultures Buddhism influenced.

Can Religious Claims Be 'True' in Any Sense?

What I have said so far, though more sympathetic to religion, is not incompatible with Freud's arguments. He does not look deeply into the evolution of religious objects (though at the end of his life he attempted to in *Moses and Monotheism* (Freud, 1939)), but he would agree that they emerge over many generations and from the experience of large numbers of believers. He could still say: but they remain wish-fulfilments, essentially childish and self-comforting stories told by people who do not dare face the truth of 'desolate reality'. The fact that so much time has gone into their making has merely adapted them more successfully for their function of wish-fulfilment.

This brings us to the crunch question for religion in response to the psycho-analytic challenge. Can the intuitive-emotional-thoughtful mental exploration, that a higher religion (at its best) is, take us towards 'truth' in any meaningful sense of the word? Is there an evaluative ontology – an account of reality that can be derived from our values – or do we just have to accept that our values are finally arbitrary or at best socially convenient? Can values be in any sense objective?

This is more a philosophical question than a psychoanalytic one (and there are important philosophers including Charles Taylor, Donald Davidson and Ronald Dworkin who would answer it in the affirmative), but psychoanalysis has a tributary argument which is of interest. Winnicott, in 'The Manic Defence' (1935) and later in 'Dreaming, Fantasying and Living' (1971), grappled with the question of how some internal objects, those of certain dreams, for example, can be of great value in psychic life and development, and others, those of 'fantasying' or daydream, may be worthless. He suggests that fantasy proper is about 'internal reality', daydream an omnipotent manipulation of external reality.

Perhaps it is only in hindsight that we can recognise the distinction Winnicott is drawing. We know our internal objects 'by their fruits'. Winnicott's client, who could let time go by while imagining herself walking on a cloud (Winnicott, 1971: 32), has nothing at the end of the time to show for it, and no associations fertile for analysis. It is comparable to an addiction: its function has been to absent her from a difficult present.

There must in principle be another way, not involving hindsight, of making this distinction; it would involve estimating the connection with 'deep unconscious phantasy'. That is easily said but not so easily done. Bion's story (1981) of a client who appeared to do excellent analytic work, but went home one day and committed a carefully prepared suicide, is a warning of how hard it is for even the most experienced psychoanalyst to recognise what is *really* deeply connected.

The objects of religion are also hard to evaluate by themselves, and have to be judged 'by their fruits'. There is an inevitable circularity here. We may evaluate a religious object as good because it leads to a good outcome, but of course it is we who decide that the outcome is good. We can only at the end of the day entrust ourselves to our own judgment and our own moral horizon. This fact has been used by those sceptical of religion (e.g., Britton, 2003) to argue against investing faith in religious objects; but a profound observation of the psychological development of religious believers (e.g., Meissner, 1984: 138–158) shows that major developments are possible within a lifetime of enduring religious commitment. Meissner writes of these more mature religious individuals:

> The love of God in these souls seems wholly unself-conscious, stripped of the residues of infantile narcissism, and yet capable of integration into a life of activity, responsibility, and generative fulfilment. They often seem capable of profoundly meaningful object relations that are characterized by selfless love and acceptance of others. [An appropriate model for understanding such people] might be found in an enlargement and intensification of the meaning of unremitting object love. It is the quality that Erikson has hinted at in his descriptions of ego integrity and wisdom. (157–8)

If religious objects can enable the development of such qualities then we are bound to think that they are in contact with important efficacious causal forces. This implies further that religious statements can have some sort of relation with effective reality, if not necessarily literal truth.

Many people nowadays wish to believe that ego integrity and wisdom can be reached without involving religion. They point to very admirable people, with excellent values, who have no religion, or who even are hostile to religion. In doing so, however, they may be failing to recall what we know about the transgenerational nature of internal objects (partly from psychoanalytic work with, for example, the descendants of Holocaust survivors, in which we see that such descendants may still be governed by fears and circumstances of which they have never been overtly told, but which have been transmitted within their family by silence and invisible signals). We may agree that these excellent people are not consciously religious, without necessarily assuming that their qualities owe nothing to religion. There are many values, for example, some of the ideals of socialism (concern for the poor, equality), which purport to be non-religious but which are in fact transparently continuous with religious values; and the ideals of psychoanalysis (truth-telling, the enormous importance of 'how we treat our objects') are only a short step from those of Judaism and Christianity, the religious backgrounds from which, within one or two generations, many psychoanalysts come. The question for the future is not whether consciously non-religious people with purely abstract ideals can be excellent human beings – plainly they can – but whether those ideals can survive with their full force over generations, in the absence of religious objects to embody them and to allow children and others to engage with them with affect and imagination. The history of the twentieth century, with its murderous pseudo-scientific ideologies of Nazism, Stalinism, Maoism, etc., its millions of destroyed and wasted lives, and its legacy to the twenty-first century of the short-term values of celebrity and greed, make this issue one of considerable urgency. The question of what gives force and effectiveness to values is far from being of merely academic interest.

Let me end by linking with my starting point. When Freud warmly admired Romain Rolland's excellent qualities, he was seeing something derived from religion, but was unable to recognise that it derived from religion. If science is about understanding how the world is put together, the development of psychology may require us to think much more deeply about the long-term psychological functioning of religions, and in particular their transgenerational role in building the sort of imaginative sympathy that allows some of the most important human values to become motivators. One such value, not by coincidence, has to do with the capacity to care for the long-term, transgenerational future.

References

Auden, W. H. (1966) *Collected Shorter Poems 1927–1957*. (London: Faber).

Bion, W. R. (1967) *Second Thoughts*. (London: Heinemann).

Bion, W. R. (1981) 'Evidence', in *Clinical Seminars and Papers*. (Abingdon: Fleetwood Press). 1987.

Black, D. M. (ed.) (2006) *Psychoanalysis and Religion in the 21st Century*. (London: Routledge).

Black, D. M. (2011) *Why Things Matter: The Place of Values in Science, Psychoanalysis and Religion*. (London: Routledge).

Britton, R. (2003) 'Emancipation from the Superego' in *Sex, Death, and the Superego*. (London: Karnac).

Conze, E. (1962) *Buddhist Thought in India*. (Oxford: Cassirer).

Freud, S. (1907) 'Obsessive Actions and Religious Practices' in *SE.IX*. (London: Hogarth Press).

Freud, S. (1927) 'The Future of an Illusion' in *SE.XXI*. (London: Hogarth Press).

Freud, S. (1930) 'Civilization and its Discontents' in *SE.XXI*. (London: Hogarth Press).

Freud, S. (1936) 'A Disturbance of Memory on the Acropolis' in *SE.XXII*. (London: Hogarth Press).

Freud, S. (1939) 'Moses and Monotheism' in SE.XXIII. (London: Hogarth Press).

Grosskurth, P. (1986) *Melanie Klein*. (London: Hodder and Stoughton).

Holder, J. J. (ed.) (2006) 'Kalamasutta' in *Early Buddhist Discourses*. (Indianapolis: Hackett Publishing Co).

Lamotte, F. (1958) *Histoire du Bouddhisme Indien*. (Paris: Louvain).

'M' (Mahendranath Gupta) (1969) *The Gospel of Sri Ramakrishna*. (Madras: Sri Ramakrishna Math).

Meissner, W. W. (1984) *Psychoanalysis and Religious Experience*. (New Haven: Yale University Press).

Milinda's Questions (1969) Vol I, Horner, I.B. (trans.) (London: Luzac).

Rhys-Davids, T. W. and E. (1966) *Sacred Books of the Buddhists*. Vol III. (London: Pali Text Society).

Rizzuto, A. M. (1979) *The Birth of the Living God*. (Chicago: Univ of Chicago Press).

Schonfield, J. (1999) 'Esther: beyond murder', *European Judaism*, 32, (1), 11–25.

Taylor, C. (1989) *Sources of the Self: The Making of the Modern Identity*. (Cambridge: Cambridge University Press).

Werman E. S. (1977) 'Sigmund Freud and Romain Rolland', *International Review of Psychoanalysis*, 4, 225–42.

Winnicott, D. W. (1935) 'The Manic Defence' in *Through Paediatrics to Psychoanalysis*. (London: Hogarth Press).

Winnicott, D. W. (1971) 'Dreaming, Fantasying and Living' in *Playing and Reality*. (London: Pelican).

15

Time and Rites of Passage

Lesley Murdin

Introduction

One of the differences between the conscious and the unconscious mind is that the unconscious does not recognise temporality and has no past or present, whereas the conscious mind has to grapple with all that the past, present and future bring us. Social contexts help us to deal with the essential loneliness of each individual. A rite of passage is a social event or ceremony to mark the process of transition from one developmental or maturational stage to another. Rites are dramas with both social and individual content. Therapists can help people to negotiate rites of passage bringing together the internal and external dimensions which together form the individual's self-perception. These dramas play out at the points of readiness for change and show us that the process of change itself needs recognition because the individual is vulnerable without familiar defences. Ethnographic research has informed our understanding of the nature of psychic change for women and men who all shape, and are shaped, by their place in society and culture. This chapter will examine the way in which individuals enter a social context and integrate internal time with social time.

Internal Time and Social Time

Rites of passage show the nature of the emphasis that each social, cultural and religious group places on the processes of change and development, in leaving one stage of life or attitude of mind in order to reach the next one. Between these two is no-man's land: the process of transition. The human mind changes its structures through experience as Wilfred Bion ascertains in his influential book on the process of learning through experience (Bion, 1962). He pointed out that experiences such as learning to walk must be stored and available to the unconscious, so that people do not have to think about walking consciously each time they wish to walk (Bion, 1962: 8). In the same way, the social context will also affect the impact of personal and private experience on the mind. Even at the basic level of sharing food, human beings devise and maintain rituals (Jones, 2007). The presence of others in these shared meals and ceremonies will affect the internal structures that the individual can develop.

One of the themes that people bring to therapy is the pattern of communication in their family of origin which often includes the way family meals were managed. Of course there are people whose family of origin never met together to eat, but many remember painful tensions between the parents which showed very clearly along with the part played by brothers and sisters. One person remembered a father who was always late. He would be out in the garden and would be summoned to a meal but would never come in until the meal was cold and everyone else was waiting in growing impatience. The children tried to distract the mother from her growing anger or despair. The father's behaviour was a form of control which the son had internalised, so that he could not bear it if his partner was ever late for any arrangement as he felt it as a humiliating wound. The drama that was enacted each meal time had affected internal structures for the son.

The concept of time needs further examination if we are to understand the importance of rites of passage as both internal and external processes for the human individual. In spite of different ways of conceptualising time, most people are at depth frightened of its passage which brings old age and death. Father Time with his scythe could be as frightening as Atropos, one of the three sisters who were the three Fates or *Moirae*. Atropos carries the shears which cut off the life for each one of us. Rites of passage both make the passage of time universal for us and also help us to bear the inevitably lonely passing of life by making it a shared experience.

Hans Meyerhoff wrote of the social time that we share which has become a commodity to be gained or lost: 'Caught within the formidable pressures of time and the social world, the self is reduced to the status of what it can produce, accomplish and achieve or whatever other terms may be used for this purely instrumental relationship' (Meyerhoff, 1955: 114). Our contemporary view of time as a commodity to hoard or to spend is still being mitigated by more measured views, originating for us with the Greeks.

The Greeks divided time through the ways in which it is perceived. For Aristotle, there was the time at which it was necessary or appropriate to act. He defined this view of time as *kairos*. It was the time at which he would, for example, deliver the proof in a rhetorical exercise. In other words, there is a time at which a particular action is appropriate. For the time which we recognise as measuring out our lives, sometimes seeming circular, sometimes an arrow flying forwards with no possibility of reverse, the Greeks used the word *chronos*. This depicts the time that we measure each day with *chronometers* and that we record in *chronicles*. For the Greeks, Chronos was a god often depicted turning the wheel of the zodiac, making events follow each other in sequence.

Rites of passage involve both these depictions of time. They mark the progression of events for all human beings by which we are born, grow up, find partners, grow old and die. They also mark special points for each of us at which we move from one sphere or period to another. They mark not only linear time for each individual but also cyclical time for the society in which they are embedded.

Rites of passage are therefore implicated both in the changes bringing about the everyday movement of an individual forward through the life span and in the specific events of an individual's life such as the achievement of sexual maturity and relationship.

Functions of Rites of Passage

Rites of passage connect individuals to the society and culture through locating them in the social space and time frame in which they will function as adults. They are events common in structure and function to many groups within specific cultures and religions in which each individual joins a collective process to help in leaving one stage of life behind, giving freedom to move forward into the next stage. In this way, rites also alter the individual's own internal structures. Human development follows fundamental patterns and many rites of passage are similar across societies and cultures. Arnold Van Gennep (1960), a German born ethnologist[1] working in France in the first half of the twentieth century wrote:

> Thus we encounter a wide degree of similarity among ceremonies of birth, childhood, social puberty, betrothal, marriage, pregnancy, fatherhood, initiation into religious societies, and funerals. In this respect, man's life resembles nature from which neither the individual nor the society stands independent. (Gennep, 1960: 9)

Against the background of psychological potential, we can look further at the contribution of the anthropologists and ethnographers. Van Gennep proposed that we could see rites of passage fulfilling three main purposes:

1. separation, in which the former stage is left behind often symbolised by death.
2. change, with the help of an experienced member of the community, the initiate passes through a doorway without familiar assurances.
3. entry to a new phase, incorporation into the new place in a new group.

Van Gennep's recognition that social rituals separate us from the stage of life that has gone before may help to illuminate the way in which rites of passage show us a process of change which is expressed externally but has an internal correlate. For example, the adolescent may be sent out to a job or to university without much preparation, feeling stripped of comfort and safety and perhaps dignity. In Evelyn Waugh's novel *Brideshead Revisited* (Waugh, 1945), Sebastian Flyte wanders round Oxford as an undergraduate carrying his teddy bear showing that he is clinging to the stage of life that he is leaving. The next stage is the change which must come about as young people find a way to survive alone by finding new friends in a new context and by shopping, cooking and doing their washing. They must find courage and resources that they will use as adults. Some fail to do this and drop out. The difficulty of negotiating the rite of passage of leaving home, especially if there were difficulties there, may even contribute to ideas of suicide. In this context, the *kairos* of a moment in time and the *chronos* of early adulthood intersect, and the adolescent must negotiate one of the major transitions of life.

Psychology Meets the Theory of Rites of Passage

Bronislav Malinowski, an American anthropologist, took social anthropology in a new direction in 1961 with the publication of *Argonauts of the Western Pacific*. In this work, he argued that what we call *culture* functions to meet the needs of individuals, rather than the needs of a society as a whole entity. The needs of society will be isomorphic to the needs of its individual members. This of course cannot always be true of all individuals, but as a general principle he transferred the focus of the anthropologist to the individual and therefore to the mind of the individual. Malinowski's view of his own function is not far from that of the psychotherapist working with empathy: he must try to enter the other's view of the world (Malinowski, 1961: 25).

In this way, the anthropologist looks at the space between individuals and the society in which they live. The individual has the task of regulating distances between people and between the individuals and the group as a whole. Individuals are of course taught to participate in their social group from their earliest conscious moments. From a Lacanian point of view, each person learns to be subject to the law of the father (Lacan, 1977: 67) which implies both security and fear. The law is expressed by the social or cultural group which takes charge of rituals, determining form and content, claiming some control over the development of each individual through the major life events of birth, sexual maturity and death. Jacques Lacan raised the development of the father's role to the level of a signifier which each individual takes into their mind. This function of signifier (Lacan, 1977: 67) forms a link to the language of the society and the rites of the social law in which the individual lives, and brings them into a social structure.

Development of the Self

Different cultures have taken different ages and stages of development as critical and important in the process of delineating the self. Gender is a variable element of identity but each individual will be assigned to a gender by their first caregivers and social group which will coalesce and form part of the discovery of his or her sexuality. Rites of passage crystallise the process of differentiation by which externals echo an internal development. In England, up to the nineteenth century, little boys were dressed in the same clothes as girls, generally skirts rather than trousers, probably because they enable easier cleaning of the child. At seven, there was often a ceremony known as *breeching* in which the little boy was put into breeches or trousers and so was welcomed into the male sex even though he was still being cared for by a nurse or a nanny who was almost always female. The little boy in his new clothes might go round the village and show them off, being given presents of money. His family and especially his father would be present at the occasion of his being dressed. As recently as the 1950s, boys were still dressed in short trousers until about the age of puberty. The physical changes of puberty are not on the whole celebrated in Western Europe. Girls are told that the onset of menstruation is *the curse* and boys' breaking voices are rewarded by their no longer being admired as cherubic choir boys. This may show us a hint of the envy of the older for the younger which explains some of the pain that is incorporated in the ritual dramas at each life stage. On the other hand, the presence of others at a ritual emphasises that the whole community is supporting the person who is preparing to pass through a change and confirms that it is an appropriate step for the individual.

The State of Transition

The boy may look forward to becoming a man but not all change is welcome. Sigmund Freud (1923) has given us a theory of the unconscious in the 'Ego and the Id' which helps us to understand the extent and the limits of the way in which rites of passage can help us with transition. Ignacio Matte-Blanco (1988), the Chilean psychoanalyst, began with Freud's description of the unconscious where two major modes of functioning are condensation – in which two or more images combine with intense meaning – and displacement – the process by which emotional energy from one object is transferred to another. Matte-Blanco defined more precisely the different strata in which there is more or less closeness to conscious thought. Starting with the level of conscious thought, he found next below it the second stratum where we begin to find conscious thought making condensations but maintaining some classical logic: 'He is *like* a tiger but no sane person will think he *is* a tiger' (Matte-Blanco, 1988: 52–5). At a third, deeper stratum we find symmetrisation of the class. For example,

'All those who are fierce may be equated with mothers and she will then be dangerous as will any part of her' (Matte-Blanco, 1988: 52–5). As we get deeper into the unconscious, distinctions tend to disappear until we reach the deepest stratum in which there are no longer any divisions and all things tend to become one. In this model, it is clear that as there are no distinctions at this level, there can be no division into past, present and future and there can be no contradictions. Of course, conscious thought seeks to undo this situation and to make sure that distinctions can hold. Rites of passage offer a classical logic in which you enter a new state with a clear understanding that you are doing so. On the other hand, the rite itself is a timeless process which links all individuals, past, present and future to each other enabling them to go through a door into an unknown future.

Freud's ideas leading to the different registers of logic in the different strata of consciousness help us to see how change must be at many levels if it is to work for an individual. We are helped by the 'pressure' which the wishes and desires of the unconscious exert to move through the preconscious into conscious thought. We can see that rites of passage may help the process of making the unconscious conscious by showing each of us how we relate to the social unconscious (Fromm, 1955) revealed there.

Turning to the process by which change happens Carl Jung's studies of alchemy provide an image of transformation in the process of psychotherapy (Jung, 1946). The alchemist heated substances in the crucible so that they could melt and merge, and hopefully produce something new, perhaps even gold. In psychotherapy, most practitioners see that each person is changed by contact with the other during the heating of the therapeutic encounter. What emerges at the end of the process is different for both the people involved. There is danger in such engagements and liminal experiences and the potential transitions involved. Liminality carries with it the risk that the client can follow a misleading magus who will not help him or her to get across the threshold but may lead him or her astray. Jung emphasised that 'the doctor, as a person, participates just as much as the patient' (Jung, 1951: para 239). The psychotherapeutic process is mysterious, and its working is often hidden; but it is generally agreed to be intersubjective although the reasons for change are not always clear to us.

The Process of Change

Concepts of change are central to analytic work, and yet the factors that facilitate change remain elusive. Some elements are clearly external, and others are generated within the individual. Rites of passage generally emphasise the mystery and the hidden nature of the process that moves an individual from one state of mind to another. Victor Turner, an anthropologist in the American school, showed that transition is crucial in human life, and his work illuminates the process. He points out, for example, that young men in the process of initiation rites among the Ndembu people of Zambia are given a specific title of *neophyte* or *initiate* but their own name is not used during the initiation rites (Turner, 1994). This implies that the only identity that they have until they emerge into the new identity as adults is *the one who is in a process of change*. This recognises that they have a specific status in their society. Psychotherapists are well aware that someone in the process of change is in a special psychological state which can overwrite other more enduring aspects of their identity. The person in this state is often filled with anxiety that has no particular object and may lose an overriding sense of purpose. States of anger and bitterness may overwhelm a personality which has been optimistic as the past is made present in the process of understanding events in the consulting room. The therapist knows that this state of unease is temporary and can be resolved.

This view of the provisional nature of transition leads to a better understanding of why it is inherently private, and we understand that people may not wish work colleagues or even friends and relatives to know of their status as client. Turner points out that initiates are often secluded from the rest of the social group, and in tribal cultures, faces may be painted and disguised. The initiate is in a position where they are neither one thing nor the other; neither man nor woman, neither adult nor child. In this they share qualities with the experience of confusion felt by the client in psychotherapy. In Swazi rites in southern Africa, the King who is central is secluded because he is believed to be dangerous to himself and others. During the ceremony he is painted with black paint and is seen as a moon in eclipse. The darkness is washed off only at the end of the ceremony when he becomes light and able to be seen (Turner, 1994: 17).

Turner observed that the initiate does not have an identity or any other possessions during the process of transition. This aspect of their status has led to processes involving clothing young adults during initiation ceremonies. Putting on gowns for graduates and white coats for medical students are modern equivalents of robing. In some Christian churches it has been customary to immerse people completely in water or in a river during the process of baptism. This rite emphasises purification as well as the transforming power of water.

Being in Transition

Victor Turner (1967) wrote a seminal essay at the middle of the last century in which, following Malinowski, he shifted the emphasis of the study of transition to psychological implications. Turner saw the cultural processes accompanying the major stages of human life as expressing the archetypal properties of liminality. He was the first anthropologist to point out that the state of being in transition is important in itself for individuals, groups and whole societies. Whereas Van Gennep (1960) had focussed attention on the content of the stages being left behind and gained, Turner pointed out that being in transition itself is of the utmost importance in human psychological life.

The importance of transition in psychoanalysis is clear and has been the focus of writing on both theory and technique. The British psychoanalyst D.W. Winnicott privileged play and argued that play is neither inside nor outside but inhabits a potential space in both ordinary life and psychotherapy (Winnicott, 1971) He was interested in the cultural location of play and wrote:

> I am thinking of something that is in the common pool of humanity into which individuals and groups of people may contribute and from which we may all draw if we have somewhere to put what we find. (Winnicott, 1971: 116)

He goes on to say that there is always a tension between originality and tradition, but that the potential space between the individual and the environment is where cultural experience is located. This tension dramatises and intensifies the experience of rites of passage at the intersection of the individual's life with the life of his social group. According to Winnicott's view, a potential space for this enactment and for internal development is created for each individual in their early relationship with their significant objects and its continued existence depends on trust and confidence which are enabled through the relationship with the mother figure.

Winnicott is making the point that there is not only an inside and outside but also a place in between, and this might well be the location of our cultural experience. We both make and are made by our rituals and rites. They are neither wholly external nor wholly created by the individual, but they enable us to participate in a shared reality. This view accords with Winnicott's well-known concept of the transitional object (Winnicott, 1971). The baby discovers an object which is not part of him but is not wholly separate either, and this can then form a bridge to relating to the outside world. The transitional object is both found and created by the baby. Rites of passage can have this quality. Ceremonies such as marriage have a clear purpose, a framework and dramatic content, depending on the cultural or religious group, but the individuals who participate may elaborate both external form and meaning. The part to be played on the stage of a rite such as marriage is determined by religion or tradition, but its emotional tone is unique to each individual. Some people speak of terror at the start of the ceremony when they realise that they are promising to be united for life. Others view it as a joyful fulfilment of a long held wish to take up the role of wife or husband with the particular status that the title confers.

The psychoanalyst Christopher Bollas (1987) has developed a theory of change based on the transformational object. Building on Winnicott's paper

'The Capacity for Concern' (Winnicott, 1965), on the function of the 'environment mother' who provides a context in which the infant can grow and develop safely, Bollas writes of 'the intersubjective experience that coheres around the rituals of psychosomatic need: feeding, diapering, soothing, playing and sleeping' (Bollas, 1987: 13). If the mother is able to provide a satisfactory experience for the infant, she

> is experienced as a process of transformation and this feature of early object relating lives on in certain forms of object seeking in adult life where the object is sought for its function as a signifier of transformation. (Bollas, 1987: 14)

He argues that we may go on seeking for the 'person, place, event, ideology that promises to transform the self' (1987: 14). In this view, a socially accepted rite of passage may serve the individual as a transformational object enabling and facilitating development of the self.

Since Bollas suggests that we may continue to seek experiences that will act as transformational, and he mentions the perfect partner or the perfect aesthetic experience, we might also conclude that we participate in rites of passage also as holding environments in which we can shelter while some needed change or development takes place. The social acceptance implied in the ritual provides some echo of the acceptance that we might once have had from a good enough loving mother which we seek to recreate.

A client C came to see a psychotherapist because she was suffering from the after effects of a diagnosis of breast cancer. She had a mastectomy and was declared free of the cancer but was on a low dose of Tamoxifen and would be called back to be checked at regular intervals for 5 years. She was very frightened about how she could hope to live a normal life under the shadow of this disease which could return at some point. She had two partners and was living with one and spending time with the other unknown to the first. She felt that she must choose between them or somehow she would be punished for her treachery by the return of the cancer. She was caught in a state of permanent liminality which seemed to have no way out. She began to focus on marriage. If she could just bring herself to marry the man she was living with, all would be well. Her mother would be pleased with her at last, and she would become a proper grown up woman.

The therapy lasted for several years while they wrestled with her need to transform herself into someone who could live into adulthood whether or not she was able to go through marriage. Perhaps the therapy itself had provided something of this experience because she felt that she had enough safety and reliability and someone who would perform the maternal functions for her in symbolic form.

The mother is the prototype of the transformational object but her role can be found in adult life in other forms of ritual holding, particularly when the whole of the social environment comes together to support the individual as in marriage or a funeral. Robert Kegan (1982) showed that the individual can move forward developmentally when held appropriately by their social context. Kegan studied the social background to psychological change and posited that

> the psycho-social environment or 'holding environment' in Winnicott's terms is the particular form of the world in which the person is at this moment in his or her evolution embedded. Since this is the very context in which and out of which the person grows, I have come to think of it as a culture of embeddedness. (Kegan, 1982: 116)

Kegan develops Winnicott's concept of the importance of the holding environment as a necessary condition for any forward movement from one state of mind to another. This holding environment which was originally the arms and voice of the mother and all that she provided for the new born infant becomes the wider context of the social group in which each of us lives and is held more or less safely.

Rites of Purification

Holding implies something firm and safe which does not give way when tested by the individual. Rites of passage involve social rules and customs that inform the mind of the individual. A British anthropologist Mary Douglas (1966) has written about the process of purification in rituals and rites of passage. She examined the prohibitions against certain foods and animals as unclean, for example, in Middle Eastern religions. Her conclusion is that the reason for designating impurity is that these are animals that do not fit clearly and obviously into any category and therefore share the status of liminality or transition. In rites of passage, neophytes are invisible because they cannot be assigned to one group or the other. They are also polluting as they cannot be understood by being assigned to a known category of social existence. This explains the need to separate those who are in this state from the rest of the social group.

Separation and time for reflection allows for illumination. Young men of the Plains Indian tribes were sent into the wilderness to wait to see whether there would be a significant dream (Turner, 1967: 12) The pressure to do this comes not only from the elders of the social group but also from the initiates themselves. Contemporary adolescents in Western Europe evince a strong desire to be separated out from adults by forming groups of their own which have formal or informal structure but exclude the older members of the community. To escape from the need for such social support they might need to find an appropriate symbol such as the totemic animal which protects and nourishes the individual.

Symbols show unconscious displacements away from the body, and therefore are implicated in repression. Following symbolic chains back to the bodily or infantile source is a task of analytic work. Social rites of passage and the therapeutic process can help to find the appropriate symbols for each person's psychological transition.

The Impact of Social Context on Individual Development

The psychotherapist has to be aware that the infant has a sense of time and space which develops from at least the moment of birth towards wider and wider individual and social horizons. The mental growth of each individual is stimulated by physical changes and echoed by required rites of passage raising questions about how a child is inserted into social time and space. Followers of Melanie Klein (1975a; 1975b) tend to emphasise the internal experience, but Donald Winnicott gave attention also to the external, interpersonal dimension (e.g. Winnicott, 1988: 55). One of the earliest rites of separation and development is the process of weaning. Weaning shows the characteristic identified by Van Gennep (1960) in rites of transition but is essentially dominated by the physical and emotional growth stage of the individual. The child reaches a level of physical maturity sufficient to move into a new phase. They are stripped of an important connection to their mother and may associate this change with the increased presence of their father or of other adults. Sometimes there is a new sibling at this time. The child will have to find psychological support to survive in the more lonely position of moving towards adulthood. Gradually the new place can be enjoyed, probably sitting in a high chair, drinking from a cup and eating with utensils, after a transitional period in which feeds from the breast or bottle are reduced and the cup is introduced. At this point, the child begins to be inserted into the social order. The oedipal stage of development begins at a point at which the child recognises that there are others beyond the self and the mother. The father appears and, as Jacques Lacan (1977) points out, he instigates the process of socialisation through being the representative of the social order as such. In Lacan's view, only by identifying with the father in the Oedipus complex can the subject gain entry into this order. The absence of the father function is therefore an important factor in the aetiology of psychopathological structures (Evans, 1996: 61). His presence is marked in many religious rites through the surrogacy of the priest, who could be male or female, and gives legitimacy and power to the entry to a new status.

According to the anthropologists, the last stage of a rite of passage is the installation of the subject in a new position in society where he or she can function in the way that is appropriate to their new status. Rites of passage help individuals and the society in which they are embedded to manage the narcissistic need for control. Luor Barshack (2001), for example, writes of the rituals surrounding death and dying as being part of the societal need to take some kind of control over this unavoidable aspect of humanity. We know that life will inevitably end in death for all of us, and this is therefore a social and communal truth which we can face together. The rites of funeral and wake can give a sense of empathy which may mitigate the narcissism of our wish to control death. On the other hand, the official religion of each culture is likely to teach that death can be overcome in some way, so the personal acceptance of death that is necessary in bereavement is continually in tension with the social defence against it. The difficulty of obtaining this balance is explored by Dunbar et al. (2011) in their recent examination of the social aspect of mind.

Within this tension each individual will have to seek personal resolution through processes of thinking and choice. Maturity and the options for choice certainly vary in different cultures. Psychotherapy provides an opportunity to begin to think about ways of managing change and loss and also the demands of making a new beginning. The end of a human life and the end of a therapeutic relationship have much in common. They are both times when the essence of life or spirit is in transition. The passage must be made, and the rites help the soul to go to another place. Even for atheists, there is a transition to be negotiated by the living and socially constructed rituals can help to bear the sadness of loss. We are born into time and place, and our daily lives are governed by the way in which time passes for us.

Conclusion

This chapter has examined some of the places where individual development is echoed by social rituals at the points where change is inevitable for each person. Some of the characteristics of social rituals may be helping individuals to change and may be relevant to the process that we develop with our clients in our different forms of therapy. The American psychoanalyst, Richard Almond (1999) specifically points to this. Both at the beginning and the end of therapy, there are rituals that help the individual to recognise that a process is taking place. This structure provides the *holding* that many therapists have found to be an essential element of the transformation for their clients (Casement, 1985: 167). Only a person who feels safely held will be able to face change. Understanding the nature of these rituals may help the client and therapist to work together to harness the energy of the social context in the service of the process of individual growth and development.

Note

1. Anthropology is generally considered to be the study of all humanity and ethnology, the study of culture. Writers are given the title which they took for themselves.

References

Almond, R. (1999) 'The patient's part in analytic process', *Journal of the American Psychoanalytic Association,* 47, 519–41
Barshack, L. (2001) *Death and the Political.* (London: Free Association Press).
Bion, W. R. (1962) *Learning From Experience.* (London: Tavistock Press).
Bollas, C. (1987) *The Shadow of the Object.* (London: Free Association Books).
Casement, P. (1985) *On Learning from the Patient.* (London: Routledge).
Douglas, M. (1966) *Purity and Danger.* (London: Routledge).
Dunbar, R, Gamble, C. and Gowlett, J. (2011) *Social Brain, Distributive Mind.* (Oxford: Oxford University Press).
Evans, D. (1996) *An Introductory Dictionary of Lacanian Analysis.* (London: Routledge).
Freud, S. (1923) *The Ego and the Id, SE.XIX.* (London: Hogarth Press).
Fromm, E. (1955) *The Sane Society.* (New York: Holt).
Gennep, A, Van. (1960) *The Rites of Passage.* Vizedom, M. M. (trans.). (London: Routledge). 2004.
Jones, M. (2007) *Why Humans Share Food.* (Oxford: Oxford University Press).
Jung, C. G. (1946) 'The psychology of the Transference' in *The Practice of Psychotherapy,* CW 16. (London: Routledge and Kegan Paul).
Jung, C. G. (1951) 'Fundamental Questions of Psychotherapy' in *The Practice of Psychotherapy,* CW 16. (London: Routledge and Kegan Paul).
Kegan, R. (1982) *The Evolving Self.* (Cambridge Mass: Harvard University Press).
Klein, M. (1975a) *Envy and Gratitude.* (London: Hogarth Press)..
Klein, M. (1975b) Love, Guilt and Reparation. (New York: The Free Press).
Lacan, J. (1977) 'The subversion of the subject' in Sheridan A. (1977) *Ecrits, A Selection.* (Paris: Seuil).
Malinowski, B. (1961) *Argonauts of the Western Pacific.* (London: Dutton).
Matte-Blanco I. (1988) *Thinking, Feeling, Being.* (London: Routledge).
Meyerhoff, H. (1955) *Time in Literature.* (Berkeley: University of California Press).
Turner, V. (1967) 'Betwixt and Between. The liminal in Rites of Passage' in *The Forest of Symbols.* (Ithaca: Cornell University Press).
Turner, V. (1994) 'Cultural construction', *American Ethnologist,* I. 21, 4
Waugh, E. (1945) *Brideshead Revisited.* (Harmondsworth: Penguin Classics). 2000.
Winnicott, D. W. (1965) 'The Capacity for Concern' in, *Maturational Processes and the Facilitating Environment.* (London: Hogarth).
Winnicott, D. W. (1971) *Playing and Reality.* (Harmondsworth: Pelican Books). 1986
Winnicott, D. W. (1988) *Human Nature.* (London: Free Association Books).

Index